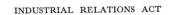

INDUSTRIAL RELATIONS ACT

By the same author:

Essentials of Industrial Law, with D. Keenan
(Pitman Press)

INDUSTRIAL RELATIONS ACT

A Comprehensive Guide

by

CYRIL CRABTREE

LL.B., A.C.I.S., Barrister
Principal Lecturer in Law at the
Mid-Essex Technical College

CHARLES KNIGHT & CO. LTD.
LONDON
1971

Charles Knight & Co. Ltd.
11/12 Bury Street, London EC3A 5AP
Dowgate Works, Douglas Road, Tonbridge, Kent

First published 1971

Printed in Great Britain by
BKT City Print, London
a member of the Brown Knight & Truscott Group

SBN 85314 104 5 (hard cover)
85314 113 4 (soft cover)

CONTENTS

PREFACE

THE Industrial Relations Act received the Royal Assent on 5th August, 1971, and has been declared by many to be one of the most difficult and incomprehensible Acts of Parliament passed in this century. Whilst no doubt this is a wild exaggeration, it must be accepted that difficulties will be experienced, certainly by the layman, in arriving at a complete understanding of it. It is, therefore, proposed in this book, to attempt a simple, though comprehensive explanation of its terms.

Although the Act has still to be interpreted by the Courts, reference has been made in the text to a number of cases decided under the old law, which it is thought may give an indication as to the way in which some of the new provisions will be interpreted in the future. Some of these cases have been summarised in Appendix II and these are indicated in the text by a bold number, e.g. *Rookes* v. *Barnard & others* (1964) (**5**).

In order to make for easier reading, footnotes have been avoided, all references being included in the text.

The book contains in Appendix I an analysis of the procedures for bringing complaints under the Act, showing by whom, and against whom, a complaint may be brought, and indicating what remedies are available.

All references in the book are to the Industrial Relations Act, unless otherwise indicated, and the book is written as though the Act were fully operative. At the time of going to press only the provisions as to the establishment of the Register and the Commission on Industrial Relations were in force, though it is anticipated that by early 1972, the Act will be fully operative.

The following are the proposed operative dates:

December 1971 —Industrial Arbitration Board (the renamed Industrial Court) takes up new role;
—National Industrial Relations Court set up;

Early 1972 —Scope of Industrial Tribunals extended to hear complaints under the Act;

—Introduction of remaining unfair industrial practices;

—Amendments to the Contracts of Employment Act 1963;

—Introduction of provisions on disclosure of information to trade unions and annual statements to employees;

—Registrar investigates registered organisations, both on application and on his own initiative.

More complete details are to be found in the Department of Employment's booklet *Industrial Relations: A Guide to the Industrial Relations Act* 1971.

I am grateful to the Publishers for their help and guidance and to my colleague Hemaka H. Fernando, B.Sc., LL.M., who kindly read through the script and made many helpful suggestions.

C.C.

TABLE OF CASES

TABLE OF STATUTES

Industrial Relations Act, 1971

INTRODUCTION

The Industrial Relations Act, 1971, received the Royal Assent on 5 August, 1971, and the purpose of this book is to analyse and explain this Act, its meaning and its effect and in the course of doing so to clarify some of the areas of controversy which were highlighted during its passage through Parliament.

It has been apparent to successive governments in Great Britain since the end of the Second World War that in spite of, or perhaps because of, full employment, there has been a worsening of industrial relations between employers and employed, whether private or public, and even between employees themselves. The root causes of this phenomenon are difficult if not impossible to isolate, and it would be impertinent of the writer even to attempt the task. Before the war strikes by workers tended to be undertaken only as a very last resort, and when every other avenue of possible settlement had been explored, whereas since the war strikes have been resorted to much more readily. Furthermore, because of the changing nature of industrial organisation the disruptive effect of even a numerically small strike can be extremely serious on the nation's economy. One can take as an example the motor car industry, where many separate firms specialise in the manufacture of one or more of the thousands of parts which go into the construction of a motor vehicle. A stoppage at one of these plants quickly affects the whole car industry immediately the reserve stocks of that particular component have been exhausted, particularly when as is frequently the case some measure of monopoly exists.

Other developed industrial nations appear to have experienced problems similar to our own, and at least two of them, Sweden and the U.S.A., have sought to contain and improve the situation by means of legislation. This legalistic approach did not appear to have very widespread appeal here, and consequently there was an obvious reluctance on the part of government to introduce what might have proved to be unpopular legislation. In the sixties, however, various opinion polls appear to have indicated a changing public attitude to strikes and stoppages in industry, and a more positive desire on the part of the public for legislative control of trade unions and strikers. No doubt influenced by this expression of opinion both of the major political parties began to look more favourably on the legislative approach to the problem.

In April, 1965, the Labour Government then in office set up a Royal Commission on Trade Unions and Employers' Associations, under the Chairmanship of Lord Donovan, a Lord of Appeal in Ordinary. The Donovan Commission, which appears to have concerned itself mainly with the industrial problems in the engineering industry, published its report in June, 1968. This report was followed on 17 January, 1969, by a White Paper on Industrial Relations (Cmnd. 3888) "In Place of Strife, A Policy for Industrial Relations", the main object of which was to give to the Secretary of State a discretionary power to require a 28-day "conciliation pause" in cases where strikes were threatened in circumstances in which adequate discussion had not taken place, or where they were "unconstitutional". And further, where a major official strike was threatened, the Secretary of State was to be given the power to require a union to hold a strike ballot among its members. A new Industrial Board was to be set up with power to impose financial penalties for breaches of orders issued by the Secretary of State, but there was to be no imprisonment for default.

The White Paper was followed by a report by the General Council of the Trade Union Congress, "Programme for Action", published on 19 May, 1969, and placed before a special meeting of the T.U.C. on 5 June, 1969; it contained the following recommendations:

1. To affirm that the movement is unalterably opposed to the proposal that the Government should take powers to impose statutory financial penalties on workpeople or on trade unions in connection either with industrial disputes or with the compulsory registration by trade unions of their rules.

2. To affirm that some of the other proposals made by the Government for changes in the system of industrial relations and in the law relating to trade unions could in principle help to improve industrial relations and to promote trade unions' objectives.

3. To empower the general council to take the further action which they propose for assisting in the improvement of procedures and in the settlement of disputes, and to submit

to the 1969 congress for formal approval appropriate changes in the relevant rules of congress.

They also proposed that the General Council should draw up a list of basic principles which unions would be asked to incorporate in their rules.

The Labour Government in the face of so much hostility and in reliance on future T.U.C. co-operation, finally abandoned its proposals for the legislative reform of industrial relations, continuing to rely on the voluntary nature of trade union control.

In June, 1970, the Labour Government was defeated at the polls by the Conservatives, and the controversy concerning legislative reform started once more. For immediately prior to the publication of the Donovan Report the Conservative Central Office had published (in April, 1968) "Fair Deal at Work", containing the party's policy for industrial reform, and once in power the new government indicated that they were not going to waste any time before their proposals were on the Statute Book.

As a prelude to industrial legislation the new Conservative Government sought the co-operation of the trade unions in discussing with them their proposals for reform. This co-operation did not appear to be readily forthcoming, and when on 5 October, 1970, the government produced "A Consultative Document" which was to serve as a blueprint for their intended legal framework, the T.U.C. made clear that it was implacably opposed to legislative interference, and refused to enter into any discussion with the government.

When the Industrial Relations Act was introduced in the House of Commons as a Bill on 1 December, 1970, by Mr. Robert Carr, Secretary of State for Employment and Productivity, the Labour opposition declared its outright rejection of the Bill, and promised to "fight it all the way". The Bill, however, having been debated before a committee of the whole House, as previously stated, finally received the Royal assent and operates from the date when the Secretary of State makes an order. Different parts of the Act may become operative on different dates (IRA, s. 170).

CHAPTER I

AUTHORITIES

MODERN trade union law, like most of English Law, has its roots in the past, but, perhaps surprisingly, has been based mainly on a statute passed as recently as 1871. The Trade Union Act of that year was regarded by its sponsors as a great charter for the trade union movement, giving as it did legal recognition for the first time to trade unions comprised of working men. The Act in its constituent parts was interpreted from time to time by H.M. Judges, and this led to further legislative addition and amendment, so that exactly one hundred years later a collection of statutes and a substantial body of case law formed the law of trade unions.

It was for the purpose of substantially repealing that law that the present Act was passed to create a framework for harmonious relations between employers and employees. It was thought necessary to begin anew with completely different principles of industrial conduct, and with a new machinery of settling disputes.

In consequence the Trade Union Act, 1871, and much of its subsequent complementary legislative provisions, has been repealed. It therefore becomes necessary to forget the old law and regard the law of trade unions as starting afresh on 6 August, with the Industrial Relations Act, 1971.

NOTE: The Act binds the Crown, see IRA, s. 162.

Framework of Authority

A vitally important feature of this Act is the establishment of a number of bodies with judicial or quasi-judicial functions, which should be thought of as the organisation of authority within which the Act is to work.

The hierarchy of authority established is as follows:
1. THE SECRETARY OF STATE FOR EMPLOYMENT AND PRODUCTIVITY. The Secretary of State is responsible to Parliament for the working

of the Act, which gives him wide powers of administration, conciliation and of negotiation.

2. A NATIONAL INDUSTRIAL RELATIONS COURT. The NIRC is established under IRA,s. 99 comprising H. M. Judges of the High Court and the Court of Appeal, nominated by the Lord Chancellor, in addition to one judge of the Court of Session in Scotland, nominated by the Lord President of that Court, plus any persons appointed by the Sovereign on the recommendation of the Lord Chancellor and the Secretary of State (IRA, s. 99(2)), all of whom must have special knowledge or experience of industrial relations (IRA, s. 99(3)). It is intended that this Court (referred to throughout as the "Industrial Court") shall be both a Court of Appeal on industrial relations matters, and also a court exercising a general supervisory control over industrial relations matters.

IRA,s. 111 provides for transfer of cases from an industrial tribunal to the Industrial Court, and it is expected that cases involving matters of undue complexity will be so transferred, so that a system of precedents will be built up to guide tribunals in the future.

The form of the Court will probably follow a similar pattern to that established by the Restrictive Trade Practices Court.

A person may not be appointed to this Court for a term of less than three years but the Lord Chancellor and the Secretary of State may remove an appointed member at any time on the grounds of incapacity or misbehaviour.

The Industrial Court is a superior Court of record with a central office in London but may sit at any time and in any place in Gt. Britain, and in accordance with directions given by the President of the Court either as a single Court or in two or more divisions concurrently.

Proceedings of the Court are heard by a Judge and not less than two nor more than four appointed members except that with the consent of the parties proceedings may be heard by a Judge and by one appointed member. Their decisions on matters of fact are final, but an appeal lies on a matter of law to the Court of Appeal. (Court of Session in Scotland.)

Normally the Court will sit in public but rules may enable it to sit in private for the purpose of hearing evidence which in the opinion of the Court relates to matters concerning the interests of national security or the disclosure of confidential information.

Any award of compensation made by this Court in proceedings in

England or Wales will have effect for purposes of execution as if it were a judgment for a like amount in the High Court or the appropriate county court (as the case may be) as may be determined in accordance with Industrial Court Rules (IRA Sch. 3).

A person appearing before the Court will be entitled to Legal Aid in the same way that he would if he were appearing before any other Court of similar standing (Hansard 27 May, 1971, Col. 1319).

3. INDUSTRIAL TRIBUNALS. These tribunals already existed before the Act to deal with disputes under the Industrial Training Act, 1964, the Contracts of Employment Act, 1963, the Redundancy Payments Act, 1965, the Docks and Harbours Act, 1966, the Selective Employments Act, 1966, and the Equal Pay Act, 1970, but their powers have been extended by the Industrial Relations Act, 1971 (IRA, s. 100, Sch. 6), to deal with many additional matters under the Act. These tribunals are most important to the system, being concerned as they are with day to day matters (such as unfair dismissal of employees) and complaints under the Act. Their constitution is two members appointed by the minister after consultation with organisations representative of employers or employed persons as he considers appropriate and a legally qualified chairman, a Barrister or Solicitor of seven years' standing. Procedure is informal and ordinary court rules are abandoned. People appearing before them may be represented by a lawyer or by a friend, but in any event the task of the tribunal is to inform itself and come to a satisfactory decision on all the evidence available from whatever source.

A tribunal may require persons to attend and give evidence and produce documents in the same way as in any Court.

Any sums ordered by an industrial tribunal to be paid by way of compensation by a party appearing before it may be recovered by way of execution issued by a County Court.

4. THE INDUSTRIAL ARBITRATION BOARD. Under the Industrial Courts Act, 1919, three methods of dealing with trade disputes are provided.

First, however, there must be a "trade dispute" as defined by the Act, i.e., any dispute or difference between employers and workmen, or between workmen and workmen, connected with the employment, non-employment, terms of employment, or the conditions of labour, of any person. The word "workmen" means any person who has entered into, or works under a contract with an employer, whether the contract be by way of manual labour, clerical work, or otherwise, whether it is expressed or implied, orally or in writing, and whether it is a contract of service or of apprenticeship or a contract personally to execute any work or labour (1919 Act, s. 8). The Act binds the Crown (*ibid*, s. 10), so that Crown servants are included with the exception of persons in the naval, military or air service.

The Industrial Courts Act provides that where there is a trade dispute in existence or apprehended, and a report to this effect is received by the Secretary of State from either of the parties to it, he must take steps with a view to obtaining a settlement of it (*ibid*, s. 11), and to this end he may refer the dispute to—

(a) The Industrial Court (*ibid*, s. 2) or
(b) Arbitration (*ibid*, s. 2), or
(c) A Court of Inquiry (*ibid*, s. 4).

Before reference to the Industrial Court or Arbitration, the Secretary of State must first obtain the consent of the parties, though if other machinery already exists for the settlement of a particular dispute, such machinery must first be used. Reference to a Court of Inquiry is at the discretion of the Secretary of State. (*Ibid*, s. 4.)

Under the Industrial Courts Act, 1919, the Industrial Court was established, and its members include persons appointed by the Secretary of State, some being independent, some representing employers and some representing workmen. One member was to be a woman and all held office for a term fixed by the Secretary of State.

The Court has a president chosen by the Secretary of State from the independent members. This Court is empowered to make rules for itself regulating its procedure, constitution and the right of parties to be represented before it by a barrister or solicitor. The Industrial Court (Procedure) Rules, 1920, provide that the Court may sit in two or more divisions and may be assisted by assessors called by the president, or alternatively consist of a single member. Normally that Court sits in divisions consisting of an independent member (the Chairman), one employer and one employee, and where the members are unable to agree as to their award the matter is decided by the Chairman acting as umpire (*ibid.*, s. 3).

Under the Provisions of the Industrial Relations Act, 1971, this Court will continue in existence, but it is renamed the Industrial Arbitration Board (s. 124), and its powers will remain the same as before except where expressly amended by the new Act. Any references therefore, in any other enactment or statutory instrument passed before the Industrial Relations Act, to the Industrial Court must be construed as a reference to the Industrial Arbitration Board.

This change of nomenclature is bound to lead initially to some confusion in view of the retention of the term Industrial Court for the National Industrial Relations Court.

It is anticipated, however, that the latter will be more commonly referred to as the NIRC.

5. COMMISSION ON INDUSTRIAL RELATIONS. This new body is established under the Act (IRA, s. 120) (and replaces a similar body set up as a Royal Commission by the last Labour Government). It comprises not less than six and not more than 15 members, either full or part-time, appointed by the Secretary of State, who has discretion to alter the number of members by order or by statutory instrument (IRA, s. 120(5)). Its function in the scheme of industrial relations is to consider questions referred to it by the Secretary of State, alone or jointly with any other Minister, relating to industrial relations generally or to industrial relations in any particular industry or in any particular undertaking or part of any undertaking (IRA, s. 121(1)). And further, to consider any question referred to it relating to the following subjects—

(a) the manner in which employers or workers are, or ought to be, organised for the purpose of collective bargaining, including any question as to amalgamation of, or co-operation or other relations between, the bodies in which employers or workers are organised for the purpose of collective bargaining;

(b) procedure agreements (defined on p. 30), or the need for procedure agreements where they do not exist; or any matter for which a procedure agreement can provide;

(c) recognition of bargaining agents and negotiating rights (p. 84, IRA, s. 45) for purposes of collective bargaining;

(d) disclosure of information by employers to their employees or to officials of trade unions or other workers' organisations having negotiating rights;

(e) facilities for training in industrial relations or in collective bargaining, and provisions for enabling persons to take advantage of such facilities without detriment to their acceptance or status as employees or as members of an organisation of workers (IRA, s. 121(2)).

When the Commission has examined any question referred to it, it must make a report to the Secretary of State or Minister initiating the reference (IRA, s. 122). Such report may be made public, or not, as the Secretary of State or Minister considers expedient (IRA, s. 122(3)), and in any event he may exclude from publication any matter in the interest of national security (IRA, s. 122(4)). Furthermore, the Commission must submit an annual report to the Secretary of State including a general review of the development of collective bargaining in the United Kingdom (IRA, s. 123(1), (2)). Copies of such report must be laid before both Houses of Parliament, and published (IRA, s. 123(3)).

Under the provisions of the Wages Councils Act, 1959, the Secretary of State for Employment and Productivity is empowered to create, by order, Wages Councils for particular industries to exercise certain functions, e.g., establishing minimum wage rates, holidays, holiday remuneration, etc., in relation to workers described in the order. When an application is properly made under the Act by bodies representing workers and employers he can make an order entirely on his own initiative, or first refer the matter to a commission of inquiry for consideration. Similarly where an application is made for the abolition or variation of a Wages Council order.

After consideration by the commission of inquiry it will report back to the Secretary of State, making any recommendations it considers justified, who can then act to implement such recommendations.

All the functions hitherto carried out by commissions of inquiry in this respect are now to be exercised by the Commission for Industrial Relations (IRA, Sch. 8).

6. CHIEF REGISTRAR OF TRADE UNIONS AND EMPLOYERS' ASSOCIATIONS. A Chief Registrar is appointed by the Sovereign to hold office during her pleasure (IRA, s. 63(1)). His main tasks are the registration of trade unions and employers' associations, and approving the rules of such bodies (IRA, ss. 68, 72), in addition to carrying out any other duties imposed upon him under the Act.

The Chief Registrar may appoint assistant registrars (IRA, s. 63(2)). He must lay before both Houses of Parliament as soon as practicable after the end of each calendar year a report of his own and his assistants' activities (IRA, s. 64). This return will contain reports concerning statistical material on registered organisations, including financial information and details of the use of the Registrar's powers under the law.

7. CONCILIATION OFFICERS. As stated earlier the single overall objective of this Act is to improve industrial relations, and it has been repeatedly stated at many levels that this cannot be achieved by the use of the legislative process. What really matters is a genuine desire for industrial harmony and a will to understand all the complex issues involved.

This is a philosophical question going beyond the scope of this book, but it was emphasised by the Government many times during the passage of the Act through Parliament that it was hoped, and certainly intended, that conciliation procedures would play a more important part in settling disputes than the provisions of the Act relating to payment of compensation.

IRA, s. 146 requires the Secretary of State to appoint a number of persons to act as conciliation officers, whose function, as the title suggests, is to bring about amicable settlements between parties to disputes, first in relation to disputes arising where a worker seeks to exercise his rights in respect of trade union membership under IRA, s. 5, and secondly where he claims to have been unfairly dismissed from his employment (IRA, s. 22). The conciliation officer has the duty to seek the settlement if requested by either employer or employee involved in the dispute, or even where, though he has not been requested, he considers that his intervention might result in a settlement.

If the employee in question has already been dismissed the conciliation officer must seek to secure his re-engagement, but where that proves to be impossible he must attempt to bring the parties to an agreement on the amount of compensation that should be paid to the employee by the employer.

Claims relating to damages for breaches of contracts of employment, as for breach of any other contract, are made in the ordinary courts, but the Lord Chancellor is empowered under IRA, s. 113 to make an order by statutory instrument to transfer this jurisdiction to the industrial tribunals. (The Secretary of State for Scotland has the same power in relation to Scotland.) If such an order has been made and the industrial tribunals are empowered to hear claims for damages for breaches of contracts of employment the Secretary of State for Employment and Productivity may direct conciliation officers to perform such services as he thinks fit in relation to parties making claims for damages before the tribunal (IRA, s. 146).

Other duties of the conciliation officers include seeking to establish agreement between the parties where an application has been made to the Industrial Court about the non-existence or defectiveness of a procedure agreement (IRA, s. 37), or where an application has been made to the Court for recognition of a sole bargaining agent (IRA, s. 45). Where a member of an organisation of workers or of employers makes a claim to the Registrar that he has been discriminated against by the organisation or one of its officials, or a person claims that he has been refused membership, the Registrar must seek to obtain a settlement by conciliation without it becoming a matter of complaint before an industrial tribunal.

Overriding the particular circumstances in which matters will be referred to conciliation officers there is a general duty on the Court and tribunals to afford the parties the opportunity for conciliation, and indeed to encourage it, so that it is expected conciliation officers will play an increasingly more important role in industrial relations matters.

It must be emphasised that anything communicated to a conciliation officer in connection with the performance of his duties under the Act shall not be admissible in any proceedings before the Industrial Court or any industrial tribunal, unless the person who communicated the information to the officer consents (IRA, s. 146(6)).

CHAPTER 2

GENERAL PRINCIPLES

THE declared objective of this Act is the promotion of good industrial relations in the United Kingdom, a laudable and a necessary objective if the standard of living is to continue rising and the economy expanding. To seek to cure all our industrial ills in one Act of Parliament would indeed be a formidable if not impossible task. This Act will not do this, but it is hoped that an atmosphere will be created within which job security will be taken for granted by every worker as his right (so far as it is humanly possible to guarantee continuous employment) and that where agreements are freely entered into between employers and workers they will be honoured. If disputes do arise there is adequate machinery through which they may be speedily and fairly settled.

The cornerstone of this piece of legislation is to be discovered in Part I of the Act itself which lays down (IRA, s. 1) four general principles for establishing and maintaining good relationships between employers and workers, workers and workers, and between employers and employers;

1. THE PRINCIPLE OF COLLECTIVE BARGAINING FREELY CONDUCTED ON BEHALF OF WORKERS AND EMPLOYERS AND WITH DUE REGARD TO THE GENERAL INTERESTS OF THE COMMUNITY (IRA, s. 1(1)(a)).

In the modern and industrial age the idea of the complete freedom of contract by the individual in his contract of employment has been largely abandoned as something of a myth, in much the same way as in contracts with suppliers of electricity, gas and water, and even of motor cars. The consumer has either to accept the "standard contract" presented by the supplier or to go without the goods.

In the majority of industries wage rates and conditions of work are negotiated between trade unions and employers, or their associations; these become in general the accepted terms of the contracts of employment of the persons affected by them. Whilst generally before this Act these agreements were adhered to, many in fact were ignored or quickly scrapped, resulting in further protracted and often bitter negotiations, still with no guarantee that a further agreement would fare any better. There was no machinery for the legal enforcement of these agreements unless it could be shown that the negotiating bodies, viz., trade unions and employers, were acting as agents of the workers and employers respectively. Furthermore, even if they were acting as agents, not all contracts of service would be amended because there are workers who do not belong to trade unions, and employers who are not members of an association.

The status of these "collective agreements" as they are called, was exemplified in the case *Ford Motor Co. Ltd.,* v. *Amalgamated Union of Engineering and Foundry Workers and Others* (1969) (**1**).

It is intended by the Act to give these agreements a legal recognition and, where *both* parties desire it, a legal enforceability as well (see page 65).

2.   The Principle of Developing and Maintaining Orderly Procedures in Industry for the Peaceful Settlement of Disputes by Negotiation, Conciliation or Arbitration with due regard to the General Interests of the Community (IRA, s. 1(1)(b)).

In the past, disputes which arose, and which in the future will inevitably arise, were settled in a wide variety of ways, from a satisfactorily concluded argument on the factory floor on the one hand, to a Court of Inquiry presided over by a High Court Judge on the other. The Act, as indicated above, has introduced a new system of tribunals, and has introduced also new procedures which will replace or in some cases supplement older ones.

In the past it has appeared that where settlements of disputes have been reached, the interests of the public at large have frequently been ignored, but the Act seeks to protect these wider interests in future settlements.

3.   The Principle of Free Association of Workers in Independent Trade Unions, and of Employers in Employers' Associations, so Organised as to be Representative, Responsible and Effective Bodies for Regulating Relations between Employers and Workers.

This principle of "free association" in independent trade unions was perhaps one of the most controversial parts of the whole Act when it was debated as a Bill in the House of Commons, primarily because the trade unions saw it as the end of the "closed shop" which pertained in many areas of industry.

This "closed shop" principle, which has increased considerably since the end of the second world war, and which was regarded by many as an infringement of individual liberty, works on the simple premise, that every employee in a particular factory or workplace shall belong either to a single named union (in a "one union" shop), or to one of a number of identified unions (in a "multi-union" shop). The reason for the closed shop was to increase solidarity and create a more effective bargaining position for workers in negotiations with their employers.

Where a closed shop was in operation union membership was a prerequisite to obtaining and retaining employment, and could give rise to cases like *Bonsor* v. *Musicians Union* (1955) (**2**). On the other hand it ensured that all persons who were expected to benefit from negotiations, which may lead to a strike, were equally committed, and that if there were any "blacklegs" these could be disciplined by having their union membership withdrawn as a last resort; losing their jobs as a consequence.

As will be seen later (p. 44) the Act seeks a compromise between those who would seek to establish one hundred per cent trade union membership, and those who prefer not to be members, by making provision for "Agency Shops" (to replace the "closed shops"), and allowing for a degree of contracting out on the part of the individual (and in a strictly restricted way of allowing closed shop agreements), viz., "approved closed shop agreement".

4.   THE PRINCIPLE OF FREEDOM AND SECURITY OF WORKERS, PROTECTED BY ADEQUATE SAFEGUARDS AGAINST UNFAIR INDUSTRIAL PRACTICES, WHETHER ON THE PART OF EMPLOYERS OR OTHERS.

One of the most important matters which concerns the worker is the uncertainty of the duration of his employment, and the knowledge that provided he performs his work conscientiously he will "probably retain his job" is not satisfactory. In the past the contract of employment has always been a matter of negotiation between the worker and the employer, frequently including terms agreed with various trade unions, and the right of dismissal has always been with the employer provided he abided by the terms of the contract. The Contracts of Employment Act, 1963, introduced minimum periods of notice to which employees are entitled, and the Redundancy Payments Act, 1965, introduced lump sum payments for those workers dismissed and not replaced, but apart from this there has been little statutory interference generally in the freedom of employment contracts, to guarantee to every worker continuity of employment.

This part of the Act is designed to give job security or compensation, except in those cases where there is a genuine and acceptable reason for terminating workers' contracts, e.g., for redundancy or incompetence. The principle of security of employment, like the other principles in the Act, is based upon fairness, and attempts to balance the interests of all parties in industrial relationships: employers, workers, and the public at large. The specific provisions of the Act designed to achieve this objective will be examined in detail in Chapter 3.

As previously indicated the foregoing general principles are the basis of this Act, and in order that the criteria of fairness can be properly established, it is provided in IRA, s. 2 that within one year of the Act receiving the Royal Assent the Secretary of State must prepare and lay before Parliament a draft Code of Practice which will assist in establishing a proper understanding of the general principles of the Act.

In particular he must bear in mind the need for providing practical guidance with respect to disclosure of information which employers are obliged to make under the Act, and also to the establishment and maintenance of effective means of information and communication between employers and workers. Once this draft is approved by both Houses of Parliament, either in its original form or as amended by Parliament, the Secretary of State must make a statutory instrument specifying the date on which the document is to become effective (IRA, s. 3).

It is clear that the Code of Practice is going to play a vitally important part in the operation of the Act, for this code will contain the detailed rules by which acceptable practices are to be established, and one of the main advantages of a code is that it can be amended from time to time by the Secretary of State should this be found necessary (IRA, s. 2(3)).

If at any time the Secretary of State proposes to revise the whole or part of the draft copy (either as originally approved or subsequently), he must after consultation with the Trade Union

Congress and the Confederation of British Industries prepare a draft, and submit the draft to the Commission for their consideration and advice. (IRA, s. 3.)

Once the code becomes law, it will become the guideline for the conduct of industrial relations as envisaged under the Act, and may be used in the Industrial Court or Industrial Tribunals as a standard of reasonable behaviour. But mere *failure to comply* with the code, *will not* in itself *render any person liable to proceedings* (IRA, s. 4).

CHAPTER 3

RIGHTS OF WORKERS IN RELATION TO EMPLOYERS

Security of Employment

In the past most contracts of employment were entered into on a purely informal basis, their terms were in the discretion of the parties to the agreement, and there was surprisingly little statutory interference. *The Contracts of Employment Act, 1963* (now amended by the Industrial Relations Act, 1971), was the first general measure to circumscribe and formalise these contracts by providing that employers (with certain exceptions) must give to each employee to whom the Act applies certain written particulars with regard to the terms of his employment, and in the event of termination of employment a minimum period of notice.

The Contracts of Employment Act defines an employee (CEA, s. 8(1)) as "an individual who has entered into, or works under, *or where the employment has ceased, worked under* (IRA, Sch. 2), a contract with an employer, whether the contract be for manual labour, clerical work or otherwise, be expressed or implied, oral or in writing, and whether it be of service or apprenticeship", and provides as follows (CEA, s. 4):

1. STATEMENT OF TERMS. Not more than 13 weeks from the commencement of employment the employer must give to each employee (who is to be employed for not less than 21 hours per week) a *written statement* containing the *name* and *identity* of *both parties* to the contract, and the *date* upon which the *employment began* (see CEA, s. 4(10), (11) if employment began five years before 6th July, 1964), and in addition the following particulars—

  (a) The scale of remuneration or the method by which remuneration is to be calculated.
  (b) The intervals at which remuneration is to be paid.
  (c) The terms and conditions relating to hours of work, including times of meal breaks, and overtime.

(d) The terms and conditions relating to—
    (i) entitlement to holidays, including public holidays, and holiday pay (the particulars being sufficient to enable the employee's entitlement, including any entitlement to accrued holiday pay on termination of employment, to be precisely calculated (IRA, s. 20(1), Sch. 2));
    (ii) incapacity for work due to sickness or injury, including any provision relating to sick pay;
    (iii) pension and pension schemes, other than statutory pension schemes, e.g., The Teachers Superannuation Acts.

(If there are no particulars to be entered under categories (a), (b), (c) or (d) this fact must be stated.)

(e) The length of notice to determine the contract which each party must give to the other, or if the contract is for a fixed term the date when the contract expires shall be stated.

(f) *a note*—
    (i) indicating the nature of the employee's rights under s. 5 of the Industrial Relations Act, 1971, in respect of trade union membership and activities (viz., the right to be or not to be a member), and where an agency shop agreement or approved closed shop agreement is in force which applies to him, the effect of that agreement on his rights;
    (ii) specifying by description or otherwise a person to whom the employee can apply for the purpose of settling any grievance he might have relating to his employment, and explaining what steps will then follow that application, or referring to a document which is reasonably accessible which explains those steps. (NOTE: It will be sufficient if the person to whom the employee can apply is referred to as "the shop foreman", "supervisor", etc. This form of reference is preferable to using a personal name as it obviates the necessity to serve further notice in the event of change of such officials (IRA, s. 20(2)).

The employer is obliged to give a written statement as indicated containing the names and identity of both parties to the contract and the date upon which the employment began, but in regard to the particulars in (a) to (f) he may either include them in the statement or refer the employee to some document which the employee has reasonable opportunity of reading in the course of his employment, or which is reasonably accessible to him in some other way (CEA, s. 4(5)).

2. CHANGES IN TERMS. If after the commencement of the employment there is a change in the terms of service the employer shall inform the employee within one month after the change in writing. The writing must contain all the information relating to the change and either be left with the employee or retained by the employer who must ensure that the employee has reasonable opportunities of reading it in the course of his employment or is made reasonably accessible to him in some other way (CEA, s. 4(4)). As in the preceding paragraph the statement may refer the employee to some document containing all or any of the particulars to be given.

NOTE: When the original statement is given to an employee the employer may refer to a document in which all future changes in the terms will be entered, and if the changes are recorded therein within one month after the change has been made, he need not serve a written notice on the employee.

Where there is a change in the name of the employer, but there is no change in his identity (whether of an individual, corporate body or partnership), or there is a change of identity, but the employee's period of employment is unbroken, then this will merely be regarded as a change in the terms and conditions, necessitating a statement to this effect, but where the contract is broken as a consequence, then a new statement has to be served (IRA, Sch. 2, para. 1).

3. EXEMPTIONS FROM REQUIREMENTS.

(i) where the employee leaves the employment within 13 weeks of commencement (CEA, s. 4);

(ii) where an employee leaves the employment, but returns within six months on the same terms and conditions, provided he received a statement on the first occasion;

(iii) where the employee's contract is in writing containing all the particulars referred to above and either a copy has been given to him or he has had a reasonable opportunity of reading it, and a note has been given or has been made reasonably accessible to him, setting out the particulars in note referred to in para. (f) above (IRA, Sch. 2, para. 3);

(iv) persons employed for less than 21 hours per week (CEA, s. 4);

   (v)   registered dock workers, defined by a scheme under the
         Dock Workers (Regulation of Employment) Act, 1946,
         unless engaged in work other than dock work (CEA,
         s. 6(1));
  (vi)   Masters and seamen on sea-going ships of a gross registered
         tonnage of 80 tons or more (CEA, s. 6(2)(a));
 (vii)   the skipper or seamen on a fishing boat required to be
         registered under s. 373 of the Merchant Shipping Act, 1894
         (CEA, s. 6(2)(c));
(viii)   a person working as an independent apprentice recorded
         under s. 108 of the Merchant Shipping Act, 1894 (CEA,
         s. 6(2)(b));
  (ix)   an employee who is the father, mother, husband, wife, son or
         daughter of the employer, though the provision does not
         include a brother or sister of the employer (CEA, s. 6(3));
   (x)   employees engaged in work wholly or mainly outside
         Great Britain, viz., England, Wales and Scotland, unless the
         employee ordinarily works in Great Britain, and the work
         outside Great Britain is for the same employer, thus anyone
         employed in Northern Ireland will be outside Great Britain
         for this purpose (CEA, s. 9(1)).

The Secretary of State has power to vary or extend the list of
exempt occupations (CEA, s. 6(5)).

Where for some reason a person's employment changes in
character and he ceases to be included in the exemptions, his period
of employment will be deemed to have ended and the written
particulars required by CEA, s. 9(4) must be served upon him.

In the case of employees who have been issued with statements
prior to the commencement of these provisions of the IRA the
particulars in paragraphs (d) and (f) (see p. 18) should be regarded
as changes in their terms of service and notice of these changes will
have to be served on the employee within one month of the provisions becoming operative (IRA, Sch. 2, para. 8). NOTE: that if the
existing contract of an employee is in writing and he has not been
served as a consequence with an original statement under the
Contracts of Employment Act within 13 weeks of his taking up
employment, then if the note referred to in paragraph (f) is not
served within one month of the operative date of the section he will
no longer be regarded as an exception; he will therefore have to be
served with a notice as though he were a new employee.

4. MINIMUM PERIODS OF NOTICE. CEA, s. 1 (as amended by IRA, s. 19) specifies the minimum periods of notice to which the employee is entitled in the event of termination of the contract, after the employee has been continuously employed for 13 weeks or more, as follows:

(a) If the period of *continuous employment* is less than two years—1 week.

(b) If the period is two years or more, but less than five years—2 weeks.

(c) If the period is five years, but less than 10 years—4 weeks.

(d) If the period is 10 years but less than 15 years—6 weeks (IRA, s. 19(2)).

(e) If the period is 15 years or over—8 weeks (IRA, s. 19(2)).

In any event, in the absence of a contract to the contrary, an employee who has been in continuous employment for 13 weeks must give at least one week's notice of termination.

Fair and Unfair Dismissal

Whilst it is clear that the foregoing provisions give a measure of job security to an employee, until the Industrial Relations Act there was nothing to prevent an employer from terminating any such contract for whatever reason he thought sufficient, apart from the practical one of losing employees and having to replace them or the possible difficulties of facing industrial action from disgruntled fellow workers.

The Industrial Relations Act extends the security of employees by providing (IRA, s. 22) that every employee (apart from the exceptions listed on p. 27-29) has the right not to be *unfairly dismissed*, and that if he is unfairly dismissed his employer will be guilty of an *unfair industrial practice*. This means that no employee may be dismissed from his job, except for a reason which is *fair* in the circumstances.

Three questions immediately arise, viz.,

(a) who is included in the term employee?

(b) what is meant by dismissal? and

(c) what reasons are fair in the circumstances?

The Act provides answers to all three questions.

1. EMPLOYEE. Employee means an individual who has entered into or works under (or, where the employment has ceased, worked under) a contract of employment (including a contract of apprenticeship) (IRA, s. 167). The extent of this term is not certain, for the expression "worker" is also used in the Act, and as defined it *includes* employee

and therefore is wider in meaning. What can be certain is that in order for there to be an employee there must also be an employer, and in most cases this will not be difficult to establish, because the latter will be paying wages or salaries, stamping national insurance cards and the like, but a question does arise in relation to the Crown. Constitutionally the position of the Crown as an employer has never been certain, and it has always been presumed that employment under the Crown has been at pleasure, so that the relationship could be arbitrarily terminated at any time. Section 162 extends the provisions of the Act relating to employment (otherwise than as a member of the naval, military or air forces of the Crown or any women's services administered by the Defence Council) to the Crown, and specially states (IRA, s. 162(3)(c)) that any reference to dismissal shall be construed as a reference to the termination of Crown employment, Civil servants are therefore included in these provisions in the same way as other employees (IRA, s. 162(3) (a), (b)). (Hansard, House of Lords 10 June, 1971, col. 444).

NOTE: For the purposes of the Industrial Relations Act, neither the expression "employee" nor "worker" includes service as a member of a police force maintained by virtue of any enactment (IRA, s. 167(4)).

2. DISMISSAL. An employee shall be taken as having been dismissed by his employer whether his contract of employment is terminated with or without notice, or where under a fixed term contract that contract expires and is not renewed (but see p. 29).

Dismissal will *not* include the situation where an employee is required to undertake less remunerative work in the same undertaking, e.g., where a weaver is employed on piece work on easily woven materials and is switched to looms in which difficult cloth is being woven resulting in a consequent loss of earnings.

The date of dismissal will of course be the last date of employment when the contract is terminated without notice, but when notice is given, on the date that notice expires. If an employee has been given notice of termination he may decide not to work out that period, and if he does so decide and informs his employer in writing that he is going to leave at an earlier date, the earlier date will be taken as the date of dismissal for the purposes of this Act, and any reason that the employer originally gave for terminating the contract will remain as the reason for the dismissal in any proceedings under the Act (IRA, s. 23).

3. FAIR AND UNFAIR DISMISSAL. The only grounds upon which the dismissal of an employee will be construed as being fair are where:
(a) he is dismissed because of a defect in his capability or qualifications; (b) where his conduct justifies it; (c) where he is redundant; (d) where there is a statutory restriction upon his continued employment; or (e) where there are other adequate reasons justifying dismissal as follows;

(i) *CAPABILITY OR QUALIFICATIONS*

These relate to the employee's *capability* or *qualifications* for performing work of the kind which he was employed by the employer to do, and in this connection "capability" means capability assessed by reference to skill, aptitude, health or any other physical or mental quality, whilst "qualifications" means any degree, diploma or other academic, technical or professional qualifications relevant to the position which is held (IRA, s. 24(2), (7)).

This ground of dismissal should be considered in two parts, firstly in relation to capability and secondly in relation to qualifications.

Where a person has been employed for some time it will normally be clear whether he has the necessary skill and aptitude to perform the functions for which he is employed, and it will be difficult for an employer to establish that the employee is no longer capable, except where it can be shown that there has been a deterioration in skill, which would in many cases be due to ageing or to failing health.

It is likely, therefore, that the question of capability will arise at the outset of employment. For it is clear that a person may undertake employment in circumstances where his capability cannot be assessed accurately before the employment has commenced, and if it is clear after the commencement of the employment that there is lack of capability it will not be unfair of the employer to terminate the agreement under this provision.

In any event, the Act only gives protection to persons who have been continuously employed for at least 104 weeks, so that notice given during this period will not infringe the provisions of the Act.

NOTE: A shorter period may eventually be substituted by order of the Secretary of State after the Act has been in operation for some time.

Even in those cases where a person has been a completely satisfactory employee for a considerable time, his capabilities may deteriorate. Perhaps through illness or because of age he may begin to lose the facility to satisfactorily follow his employment. For example, a steeplejack as he advances in years may suddenly become liable to fits of vertigo, and again it would not be unfair of the employer to dismiss him.

It is probably the second part of the provision, relating to qualifications, which provides some difficulty, for clearly where a person obtains a position of employment by misrepresenting his qualifications there is already a legal remedy to rescind the contract (quite apart from the criminal offence under the Theft Act, 1968). However, two situations would be covered by the provision, viz., (a) where a person obtains employment conditionally upon acquiring certain qualifications within an agreed time, and fails to do so, e.g., a person commences work as an engineer on the understanding that he will obtain a Higher National Certificate within a specified time, or (b) where a person is employed as an apprentice but fails to qualify as a skilled craftsman by the time he reaches 21 years of age.

(ii) *CONDUCT*

What conduct will justify the dismissal of an employee has always been a difficult question and the old problem of justification at common law will undoubtedly still arise.

At common law it was usual to examine reasons for the arbitrary dismissal of an employee under specific headings, viz.,

Incompetence and neglect. Under the provisions of this Act, incompetence would fall within the provisions as to capability, already discussed, whereas neglectful conduct may appropriately be considered either under *capability*, if it were so grave as to amount to incompetence, or under *conduct justifying dismissal*. For a single act of negligent conduct may justify instant dismissal if it causes serious damage to the employer (*Baster* v. *London and County Printing Works* (1899) (**3**), and similarly where the negligence amounts to a series of independent acts which are not in themselves sufficiently grave, but where the cumulative effect may be serious.

Disobedience. Whether or not a servant can be justifiably dismissed for disobeying orders will depend upon the degree of disobedience. Disobedience may be so gross as to show a deliberate flouting of the essential terms of the contract, or so unimportant as to barely affect the performance of the contract at all (*Laws* v. *London Chronicle Ltd.* (1959) (**4**)). Whether an employer is justified in dismissing on this ground will always be a matter of fact in each case.

Disobedience may be so grave as to amount to a repudiation of the contract, as in *Pepper* v. *Webb* [1969] 2 All E.R. 216; a gardener, when asked to put out plants, refused, saying "I couldn't care less about your bloody greenhouse and your sodding garden" was held to have repudiated his contract and instant dismissal was justified.

Misconduct. A servant can be summarily dismissed for misconduct whether inside or outside the service contract, provided the act concerned is sufficiently grave.

This must essentially be a matter of fact in each particular situation, and it may be helpful to bear in mind in this connection the following extract from the judgment of Lord Maugham in *Jupiter Insurance Co. Ltd.* v. *Shroff* [1937] 3 All E.R. 67; "their Lordships would be very loath to assent to the view that a single outbreak of bad temper accompanied, it may be, with regrettable language, is sufficient grounds for dismissal. The lower Court was stating a proposition of mere good sense when it observed that in such cases we must apply the standards of men and not angels and remember that men are apt to show temper when reprimanded".

Whilst it would be unlikely that isolated outbursts of temper would justify dismissal, even a single act of violence or threatening behaviour probably would. In *Tomlinson* v *L.M.S. Railway Co.* [1944] 1 All E.R. 537, the company wished to set up a canteen for the use of their workers, with the canteen managed by a committee of workers. A meeting of the committee was held, outside working hours, and a dispute arose because Tomlinson appointed himself chairman of the meeting, though it was well known that his superior officer usually took the chair. Tomlinson assaulted a fellow-employee and was offensive to his superior. He was consequently summarily dismissed, and claimed damages for wrongful dismissal. It was held in dismissing his appeal that in the circumstances his dismissal was justified.

If misconduct occurs outside the service it may justify dismissal if it interferes with the employer's business or prevents the employee from properly discharging his duties and giving faithful service. (*Pearce* v. *Foster* (1886) 17 Q.B.D. 536).

Immorality. Whether immorality will ever justify dismissal will depend upon whether it makes an employee unfit in the particular circumstances of his employment to do his work, e.g., a teacher, having an illicit affair with a pupil, immoral conduct which adversely affects the reputation or the carrying on of the employer's business.

Drunkenness. The position in relation to drunkenness justifying dismissal was well stated by the Judicial Committee of the Privy Council in *Clouston & Co. Ltd.* v. *Corry* [1906] A.C. 122, as follows:

(a) The matter is a question of fact in each case and also depends upon the degree of drunkenness;

(b) intoxication which is habitual or gross and directly interferes with the business of the employer or with the ability of the servant to render due service, will usually justify dismissal;

(c) an isolated act of drunkenness, e.g., at an office party, which in no way affects the master's business, will not normally justify dismissal.

(iii) *REDUNDANCY*

It is obvious that where a person is redundant it would be unrealistic and unreasonable to expect his employer to continue his employment, and the Act allows for dismissal in these circumstances. What the Act does do, however, is provide a safeguard against any form of discrimination in the event of redundancies and where possible it seeks to prevent redundancy being used as an excuse for terminating the contracts of selected employees unfairly. For it is provided (IRA, s. 24(5)) that where the reason for the dismissal of an employee is redundancy, and it is shown that the circumstances of redundancy applied equally to one or more other employees in the same undertaking who have not been dismissed, *and* the reason why he has been selected is that he had exercised or indicated his intention to exercise his rights to be a member or not be a member of a trade union or participate in trade union activities (as permitted under IRA, s. 5(1)) that such dismissal is unfair. Alternatively that he was selected for dismissal in contravention of a customary agreement or agreed procedure relating to redundancy, e.g., "last in, first out" (unless there was a good reason for departing from such agreement), shall also be considered to be an unfair dismissal.

Redundancy means the same in this Act as in RPA, s. 1(2).

(iv) *STATUTORY RESTRICTION*

This arises where the employee could not continue to work in that position without he or his employer being in contravention of a duty or restriction imposed by or under an enactment. Where the law imposes a restriction upon the employment of persons unless, e.g., they are qualified in a certain way, or are of a minimum age, their appointment would obviously be unlawful at the outset, and the "contract" would not even be valid, therefore there could be no liability for terminating it. This provision, therefore, is concerned with the situation where an appointment is perfectly lawful when made but becomes unlawful subsequently, e.g., a person of 16 is engaged in certain employment, and a new statute provides that no one under the age of 19 shall be employed to do that particular work, or where a female is employed to do certain work, which because of a modification in the Factories Act, she can no longer legally do.

(v) *OTHER MATTERS JUSTIFYING DISMISSAL*

The matters so far outlined as justifying dismissal are not an exhaustive list, for the Act does allow other reasons outside these main categories (IRA, s. 24(1)(b)). The residual matters justifying dismissal must of course be fair, and must be accepted by the industrial tribunals as being fair. It is obviously not possible to list the situations where this provision will prevail. It would, for example include incompatibility, not necessarily between an employer and an employee, but perhaps in a small firm two employees who were at daggers drawn with each other. In a large firm the answer to the problem would be to move either or both of the men to different parts of the undertaking if that were possible, rather than to terminate the employment, whereas in the small firm there would be little alternative but to dismiss one of the men.

It should, however, be noted that the Act provides (IRA, s. 24(6)) that even where it can be shown that the reason for dismissal is covered by the preceding provisions, it may nevertheless be classified as unfair if in the circumstances the employer acted unreasonably in treating it as sufficient reason for dismissing the employee, e.g., where it is clear that the employer was merely using it as an excuse for getting rid of an employee. Each dismissal has therefore to be decided on its own merits in determining whether it is fair or not, and this must be done in accordance with the principles of equity and the merits of the case.

If, therefore, the industrial tribunal was not satisfied that the dismissal was justified in all the circumstances of the case, it would declare the dismissal to be unfair.

Excluded Categories of Employees

As previously indicated (p. 21) the provisions of the Act relating to unfair dismissal do not apply to all employees, and the following are specifically excluded (IRA, s. 27):

(a) in any employment or undertaking where there were less than four employees, including the claimant, at the date of the claimant's dismissal, whether or not they were employed at the same place or in a different place is irrelevant, but provided they have each been employed for at least 13 weeks (except in any case where the reason for dismissal is because a worker exercises his right under IRA, s. 5(1) (i.e., to belong or not to belong to a trade union, see p. 42)).

(b) in any employment where the employer is the husband or wife or a close relative (father, mother, grandfather, grandmother, stepfather, stepmother, son, daughter, grandson, granddaughter, stepson, stepdaughter, brother, sister, half-brother or half-sister (IRA, s. 27(4)) of the employee;

(c) in any employment as a registered dock worker, as defined by any scheme for the time being in force under the Dock Workers (Regulation of Employment) Act, 1946, not being employment by virtue of which the employee is wholly or mainly engaged in work which is not dock work as defined in the scheme;

(d) in any employment as master or as a member of the crew of a fishing vessel, where the employee is not remunerated otherwise than by a share in the profits or gross earnings of the vessel (i.e., not paid except by a share of the catch);

(e) in any employment as a teacher to whom s. 85 of the Education (Scotland) Act, 1962 (dismissal of teachers) applies;

(f) in any employment under a contract which *normally* involves employment for less than 21 hours weekly;

(g) in any employment where under the contract the employee ordinarily works outside Great Britain (this does not include any person employed to work on a ship registered in the U.K. (not being a ship registered at a port outside Great Britain) unless the employment is wholly out of Great Britain or the person is ordinarily resident outside Great Britain);

(h) any employee having completed *less than* 104 *weeks continuous employment* ending with the effective date of dismissal (IRA, s. 28(a));

(i) any employee who before or on the effective date of dismissal had attained the age of 65 if a man, 60 if a woman, or any other age which was the normal retiring age in that particular employment for an employee holding the position which he held (IRA, s. 28(b)).

Whilst the employees in the categories from paragraphs (a) to (i) are excluded from the general provisions relating to dismissal, they will be included of the real or principal reason for their dismissal is that they exercised or indicated an intention of exercising a right under s. 5(1) of the Act, viz., the rights to be or not to be a member of, and to participate in the affairs of, a trade union (IRA, s. 29).

NOTE: The Secretary of State is empowered to add to or vary by Statutory Instrument the provisions relating to excluded cases considered in paragraphs (a) to (i) above (IRA, s. 29(2)) so that he may, for example, reduce the period of 104 weeks at some time in the future. It is interesting to note that the limitation of 104 weeks was for no other reason than to avoid overloading the industrial tribunals in the initial stages, and to restrict applications to those which could be considered as the more deserving (Hansard, House of Lords, 13 May, 1971, col. 1501).

(j) fixed term contracts of two years or more, made *before* the Act, other than contracts of apprenticeship, and the contract has merely not been renewed upon expiry (IRA, s. 30(a)).

(k) fixed term contracts of two years or more whenever made (including apprenticeship contracts), where the contract has merely not been renewed on expiry, provided that before its expiry the *employee* had *agreed in writing* to exclude any claim for unfair dismissal in the event of the contract not being renewed (IRA, s. 30(b)). (It is suggested that it will probably become the practice to include an effective clause in every such contract at the time that it is entered into, as a matter of form.)

(l) Any employee who refuses to join a trade union where an agency shop agreement or approved closed shop agreement is in force, or to pay appropriate contributions where permitted (IRA, s. 6(1), Sch. 1, Pt. IV).

(m) Where it is shown that the dismissal was in order to safeguard national security. (A certificate signed by or on behalf of a Minister of the Crown will be conclusive evidence that the action taken was for the purpose of safeguarding national security) (IRA, s. 159(2)).

Additional Provisions Relating to Dismissal of Employees

From the foregoing it will have been gathered that the Act seeks to establish an acceptable standard in relation to workers' security. But at the same time it is recognised that other standards may in some cases be preferred by workers, and as a consequence provision is made in the Act for an alternative. It is provided (IRA, s. 31) that where as a result of a collective agreement between employers and workers a "procedure agreement" exists, the provisions in such agreement may prevail in place of those provided under the Act. A procedure agreement means "so much of any collective agreement as relates to any of the following matters:

(a) machinery for consultation with regard to the settlement of terms and conditions of employment, and of disputes which arise between an employer or group of employers and one or more workers or organisation of workers, including negotiation and arbitration;

(b) negotiating rights;

(c) facilities for officials of trade unions or other organisation of workers;

(d) procedures relating to *dismissal* and to matters of discipline other than dismissal;

(e) procedures relating to grievances of individual workers (IRA, s. 166)".

Where therefore a procedure agreement does exist an application may be made *jointly* to the Industrial Court by *all the parties* to it to make an order that the part of such agreement relating to dismissal shall be substituted for the rights under IRA, s. 22 discussed above.

The Industrial Court may only make such an order if it is satisfied that every organisation of workers which is a party to the procedure agreement is an independent organisation of workers and may substitute the provisions in the procedure agreement, if:

(a) they provide for procedures to be followed in the event of an employee claiming that he has been unfairly dismissed;

(b) that those procedures are available to all employees within a particular description without discrimination;

(c) the remedies provided in the agreement are as beneficial as those provided in the Act;

(d) the procedures provided for in the agreement include a right to arbitration or adjudication by an independent referee, or by a tribunal or other independent body, in those cases where (because the voting is equal or for any other reason) a decision cannot otherwise be reached; and

(e) the provisions of the procedure agreement indicate with reasonable certainty which employees are to be included (IRA, s. 31(2)).

Once the Industrial Court has substituted the procedure agreement for the provisions in the Act the order will operate so long as the parties desire it, but at any time application may be made by any of the parties to the agreement, or the Secretary of State, to the Industrial Court for the order to be revoked.

NOTE: Even though the collective agreement itself is not in writing, and itself is generally unenforceable, once that part of the agreement relating to dismissal procedures has been approved by the Industrial Court that part will bind the parties.

If the Court is satisfied that it is the desire of *all the parties* to the procedure agreement that it should be revoked, or that the procedure agreement has ceased to fulfil the requirements as listed in (a) to (e), then it must revoke it. Such revocation order may contain any transitional provisions which the Court thinks appropriate, including a stipulation that during the transitional period a dismissed employee may still claim his right under the provisions of the Act (IRA, s. 22) not to be unfairly dismissed (IRA, s. 32(3)).

Remedies for Unfair Dismissal

Having established that an employee has a right not to be unfairly dismissed, the next question is what remedies are available if he is, in fact dismissed, and by whom are those remedies granted.

A complaint may be presented to an industrial tribunal against an employer by a person who claims that he has been unfairly dismissed. The complainant merely has to establish that he has been dismissed, i.e., that the employment has been terminated, *and then the employer must show what the reason (or principal reason), was for the dismissal, and that the dismissal was justified, i.e., not unfair* (IRA, s. 24(1)).

If the tribunal is satisfied that the complaint is well founded, and that it would be reasonable and practicable for the complainant to be re-engaged by his employer, then it can make a recommendation to that effect, stating the terms on which it considers that it would be reasonable for the complainant to be re-engaged. It must be made clear that the tribunal has no power to compel the employer to re-engage the complainant (IRA, s. 106) nor in any event the power to require a worker to return (see IRA, s. 128).

If the tribunal does not make such a recommendation, or makes a recommendation which is not complied with, then it must award compensation to be paid by the employer to the complainant for the unfair dismissal (IRA, s. 106(5)). The amount of compensation is in the discretion of the tribunal, and in assessing the amount payable all factors must be taken into account, including any expenses reasonably incurred by the complainant in consequence of his loss of employment, and also any other benefit he might have obtained, had he kept his employment, e.g., wages and pension benefits. But the amount of compensation will be less where the loss has been aggravated by the complainant himself, e.g., where he has unreasonably refused the offer of re-engagement recommended by the tribunal, or where he has unreasonably failed to mitigate his loss perhaps by failing to seek other employment (IRA, s. 116).

In any event the maximum amount of compensation that can be awarded to the complainant is the equivalent of 104 weeks pay, subject to the limit of £40 per week (£4,160), i.e., the actual weekly amount which the complainant would have earned, subject to the limit of £40 per week for the number of weeks up to 104, that the Tribunal thinks is equitable in the circumstances. These limits may be increased from time to time by the Secretary of State by order approved by Parliament (IRA, s. 118(3)).

NOTE: IRA, s. 161 provides that any agreement purporting to exclude or limit the operation of this Act in relation to contracts of employment shall be void, except in relation to agency shop agreements, or approved closed shop agreements, or where the contract of employment is for a *fixed term of two years* or more and *before the expiry* of the contract the *employee agrees* in *writing*, or where the court has approved a procedure agreement which provides alternative rights, or where the agreement is made subject to a conciliation officer seeking to settle the dispute.

It is important to remember that the proceedings before an industrial tribunal are intended to be informal and not regulated by the rules of evidence and procedure as in a court of law. When a complaint of unfair dismissal is made it will not be necessary for the complainant to *prove* his claim, but rather for the tribunal to investigate and inform itself in the best way it can from all the evidence, which, it is suggested, will best be done by requiring the *employer* to establish that he acted fairly in dismissing the complainant. In other words the burden of proof is upon the employer to show that he acted fairly and not upon the complainant to show that he did not. If an employee complains that he has been unfairly dismissed, he must prove that he has been dismissed (i.e., not left voluntarily). Once he has proved that, it is for the employer to justify the dismissal. The burden of proof is then on the employer to prove that the dismissal was not unfair (IRA, s. 24(1)).

An appeal lies to the Industrial Court from any decision of an Industrial Tribunal (IRA, s. 114(1)). The decisions of the Industrial Court on questions of fact are final, but there is a further right of appeal on matters of law to the Court of Appeal (Court of Session in Scotland) (IRA, Sch. 3, para. 29).

Before leaving the subject of remedies for unfair dismissal, reference must be made to a special category of employees, viz., teachers in voluntary aided schools (Church of England and Roman Catholic schools). The Education Act, 1944, s. 24(2)(a) empowers a local education authority to require the managers or governors of an aided school to dismiss a teacher without the necessity of giving a reason. The managers or governors and not the local education authority are in fact the employers of such teachers. As under the general provisions relating to dismissal the Industrial Relations Act requires a complaint to be made against the "employer", the managers or governors would have a complete defence to a complaint of unfair dismissal in these circumstances under the provision which allows dismissal where continued employment would contravene a duty imposed by statute. Therefore, it is specially provided that in these cases the local education authority shall be treated as though they were the employer for purposes of complaints as to unfair dismissal, and if in fact a dismissal is unfair the local education authority will be expressly liable to pay any compensation awarded (IRA, s. 148).

Unfairly Inducing Dismissal

Under the old law as it was applied to trade unions it was legally possible for workers to strike, or for organisations representing them, e.g., trade unions to threaten to strike or undertake other industrial action, in order to induce employers to dismiss other workers. This was frequently resorted to for the purpose of achieving a "closed shop" where such other workers had refused to join the union, or for getting rid of persons ("blacklegs") who had refused to participate in a strike undertaken by the rest of a group of workers. If the employer acceded to the pressure and dismissed the "offending" workers, after giving the requisite length of notice, the latter had no right of action against the employer, and none against the trade union (Trade Disputes Act, 1906). They might have had a right of action against trade union officials in the latter's private capacity in some limited circumstances (*Rookes* v. *Barnard* (1964) (**5**)) until the Trade Disputes Act, 1965, put an end even to this right of action. It seemed, therefore, that the only right a worker had was not to be dismissed without notice.

Under the Industrial Relations Act an employee is entitled not to be dismissed, even with notice, in circumstances that are unfair, and if he is so dismissed he will be entitled to claim compensation from the employer.

Dismissal in the circumstances outlined above would certainly be unfair for this purpose, for it is provided (IRA, s. 33) that where a worker is dismissed or discriminated against by his employer, the employer may not establish that he acted reasonably merely by showing that he acted under pressure in taking the action he did. So that where an employee is actually dismissed as a result of such an inducement even for a reason falling within IRA, s. 24, e.g., capability, qualifications (pp. 23-27), he will be able to claim that he has been unfairly dismissed, unless the employer can establish a completely independent and legitimate reason for dismissing him.

This might appear to be hard on an employer who feels that he is unable to resist this inducement, but the section does, however, provide that where any *person, trade union* or other *organisation of workers*, or any person acting on behalf of such trade union or organisation, knowingly induces an employer to dismiss an employee, either by—

(a) calling, organising, procuring or financing a strike, or threatening to do so;

(b) organising, procuring or financing any irregular industrial action short of a strike, or threatening to do so;

that such person, etc., shall be guilty of an unfair industrial practice.

This means, therefore, that an employer who is being knowingly induced to dismiss or discriminate against a worker, may bring a complaint in the Industrial Court against the person inducing. And the Court may award compensation where the complainant has suffered loss, or make an order directing the respondent to refrain from continuing the action complained of, or taking the action threatened (IRA, ss. 101 and 105).

NOTE: A worker affected by such inducement will not himself be entitled to bring an action against the trade union, etc. (IRA, s. 105), his right of action is only against his employer.

So that where an employer is being induced, his first steps ought to be to make a claim in the Industrial Court for an order against the party threatening the action. If such an order is granted against any party and such party acts in contravention he will be in contempt of Court.

Alternatively, the employer may dismiss the employee who will then be able to claim compensation from the employer.

IRA, s. 119 provides that where an employer has taken action as a consequence of pressure exercised upon him by another person, and action is being taken against him for an unfair industrial practice (e.g., for dismissing a worker) the employer may require that that person be joined as a third party in the proceedings. And if the industrial tribunal (or the Industrial Court) makes an order for payment of compensation against the employer, and it is satisfied that the third party was responsible, it can require that third party to pay to the employer a part, or all of any sum that he is required to pay by way of compensation. (This is in addition to any amount the party may be required to pay by way of compensation to an employer who has suffered loss, e.g., through lost production or replacing dismissed workers).

NOTE: Where the third party joined with the employer is a trade union official who was acting within the scope of his authority as such, he may not be ordered to contribute, but his union can be ordered to pay. (There is, however, no such restriction in the case of an official who acted on behalf of a (unregistered) workers' organisation) (IRA, s. 119(4)).

Although the action of the person seeking to induce the employer to dismiss or otherwise discriminate against a worker amounts to an unfair industrial practice, the worker does not have a right of action directly against such person (IRA, s. 105(1)) his right of action is limited to one against the employer. Therefore, unless the worker is actually dismissed or discriminated against he has no right of action although threats have been made against the employer to secure his dismissal.

The precise limits of these provisions as to inducing dismissal are difficult to assess as the words in the section (IRA, s. 33) have yet to be interpreted. It is thought that the major difficulties will arise, not in establishing the rights of the worker against the employer, for these seem to be clear (if a worker is dismissed or discriminated against by the employer he can seek his remedy against the employer in an industrial tribunal); but rather in establishing on what ground, and against whom the employer may bring his action.

First, he must establish that some person sought to *induce* him to act in a particular way, and second, that that person in order to make the inducement effective called, organised, procured or financed a *strike*, or *threatened* to do so, or organised, procured or financed any *irregular industrial action short of a strike*, or *threatened* to do so.

Once this has been established the employer now has to place responsibility on some party, and this party may be a person, a trade union, or an organisation of workers.

Organisation of workers is defined as, an organisation (whether permanent or temporary) which either:

(a) consists wholly or mainly of workers of one or more descriptions, and is an organisation whose principal objects include the regulation of relations between workers of that description or those descriptions and employers or organisations of employers, or

(b) is a federation of workers' organisations (IRA, s. 61(1)).

This will therefore include a trade union registered under the provisions of the Act (IRA, s. 61(3)), or a group of workers organised on a permanent though non-registered basis, or even an *ad hoc* group of workers organised on a very temporary basis.

He will, however, have to establish that the person who actually called or threatened, etc., was in fact acting on behalf of the organisation before that organisation can be made liable. If this proves to be difficult or impossible the employer may bring his action directly against the individual who approached him with the inducement in the first place.

In order to establish that any person was in fact acting on behalf of an organisation, it must be shown that such person was actually authorised by that body, for if no such authorisation can be established the organisation will not be responsible. What therefore is the position if a trade union official has actually been forbidden by his union to embark upon such an enterprise, but does so nevertheless?

Secondly, what will amount to "calling", etc., and what will amount to threatening?

It is not possible at this point in time to give an authoritative answer to either of these questions. It is, however, suggested that in the case of the person purporting to act on behalf of an organisation that he will have to have at least the tacit approval of his organisation before such organisation will be liable. Authority to act on another's behalf may arise as a result of direct appointment, or by implication or merely by presumption, these terms are discussed more fully later (p. 160), and it is sufficient to say at this juncture that it is the fact situation which must be the deciding factor. One thing, however, is clear and that is in order to be culpable for having called, organised, procured or financed a strike or other industrial action, the act of doing so must have been unequivocal. The same remark applies to "threatening", but in this case it is much easier to establish, for a statement or even a suggestion can amount to a threat if it can have no other interpretation, and could, of course, include an ill considered remark at the end of a long and fruitless negotiation. In the situation, which we are envisaging the threat must amount to a real attempt to induce, and must in fact succeed, and the casual remark darkly uttered would not be sufficient.

One point meriting comment it is thought, is the slightly different language used in relation to strikes from that relating to irregular industrial action. It appears that a person may be liable for *calling* the former but not the latter, and as the expression *procuring* is used in both cases, it is suggested that calling and procuring have different meanings. Procuring it is thought would include a more serious attempt at producing a situation than merely calling, and the dividing line would be the earnestness and means of the attempt.

Dismissal in connection with a lock-out, strike or irregular industrial action

Where during the course of an industrial dispute one party wishes to bring pressure upon the others a *lock-out* or a *strike* is frequently resorted to by that party in order to precipitate a settlement favourable to himself. There was considerable doubt in the past as to whether or not a lock-out or a strike was a legal termination of the contract of employment, though it was largely academic, for when the dispute was settled the parties resumed their contractual relationship under the new terms. These settlements invariably absolved the parties from liability for any breaches of contract which may have occurred. However, if the other party to a lock-out or strike had wished to regard it as terminating a contract, there appears to have been no legal reason why he should not have done so. It is now provided that where *due* notice has been given by or on behalf of an employee of his intention to take part in a strike, such notice shall not, unless it expressly provides, be construed, either as a notice to terminate the employment or as a repudiation of it (IRA, s. 147).

Lock-out

A lock-out is defined as "action which, in contemplation or furtherance of an industrial dispute, is taken by one or more employers, whether parties to the dispute or not, and which consists of the exclusion of workers from one or more factories, offices or other places of employment, or of the suspension of work in one or more such places, or of the collective, simultaneous or otherwise, connected termination or suspension of employment of a group of workers". (IRA, s. 167).

Lock-outs may not be used as a means of getting rid of unwanted employees, for where a person is dismissed by way of a lock-out, either at the beginning of it or during the course of it, it will amount to an *unfair dismissal* unless the employee is offered re-engagement as from the date of the resumption of work, either upon the same terms upon which he was previously employed, or if in a different position one that is reasonably suitable to him. This offer of re-engagement must be by the original employer, or by a successor of that employer, or by an *associated employer*. If, therefore, the employee is not re-engaged on these terms he will be able to bring a complaint of unfair dismissal (p. 31). The date of resumption of work will be that date upon which other comparable employees, or a majority thereof were offered re-engagement (IRA, s. 25).

It must be emphasised that the mere fact of a lock-out does not from that moment in time give an employee a right to complain of unfair dismissal, he only has such right if, when work is ultimately resumed, he is not offered re-engagement from that date.

What is meant by a *"position reasonably suitable"* to him must always be a matter of fact, and clearly where the employer and the employee agree on the alternative offer there will be no problem. But in those cases where there is a dispute as to the suitability of the alternative employment the employee may complain to the industrial tribunal, and if that tribunal decides that such alternative employment is not reasonably suitable to the employee, he will have been unfairly dismissed for the purposes of the Act. The industrial tribunal therefore becomes the final arbiter as to the suitability or otherwise of the alternative offer.

Secondly, it will be appreciated that at the end of a lock-out there may well be a re-organisation at the place of employment. A replacement of the original employer by an associated employer or by a successor, and an offer by either of these parties to an employee that he may continue to be employed in his original position will satisfy the requirements of the Act. However, associated employers are defined as "any two employers if one is a company of which the other (directly or indirectly) has control, or if both are companies of which a third person (directly or indirectly) has control" (IRA, s. 167(8)), so that the definition will include a great many organisations which have both national and international connections. The question, therefore, may be asked, what is the situation where an associated employer makes an offer to an employee to engage him in a similar position as that in which he was previously employed, but at completely different premises? The simple answer to this would be, if the position is reasonably suitable to him, then it would be sufficient, but if it was at premises miles away from the original place of employment it would probably be unsuitable. Again the industrial tribunal would pronounce on the suitability of the alternative offer, and it is suggested that some guidance as to what may amount to reasonable alternatives could be gained from decisions on suitable alternative employment under the Redundancy Payments Act, 1965.

Strikes and Irregular Industrial Action

A strike is defined as "a stoppage of work by a group of workers, which is concerted by them in contemplation or furtherance of an industrial dispute, whether they are parties to the dispute or not" (IRA, s. 167).

Irregular industrial action short of a strike is defined as—any concerted course of conduct (other than a strike) which is in contemplation or furtherance of an industrial dispute, and which—

(a) is carried on by a group of workers with the intention of preventing, reducing or otherwise interfering with the production of goods or the provision of services, *and*

(b) in the cases of some or all of them, is carried out *in breach of their contracts of employment* (IRA, s. 33(4)).

What the meaning of irregular industrial action is, is not absolutely clear, for in order to come within its terms there has to be a *concerted* course of conduct and a *breach* (or threat of a breach) of a contract of employment other than a strike at the same time. It seems that concerted means no more than "mutually planned or agreed" so that where a single individual were to undertake action independently of his fellows he could not be guilty of irregular industrial action for the purpose of this provision. What amounts to a breach of contract of employment will obviously depend upon the circumstances of each particular case, but the expedient of "working to rule", would *prima facie* not be included. Working to rule is quite specifically adhering rigidly to the terms of the employment, though ironically it frequently has the effect of slowing down production, e.g., railway employees checking for the safety of passengers within the requirements of the "rule book", or persons employed specifically as electricians refusing to undertake work which is clearly more properly undertaken by a joiner. On the other hand, the provision will include "going slow" where such action is not caused by working to rule, but deliberately slowing down a process and taking longer over a job than is normal or can reasonably be expected.

Applying the provisions to specific cases may well be difficult, for there may be no rule book in existence, and here it must be emphasised we are talking about a rule book attached to the contract of employment, as in the railway undertakings, and not rule books of a trade union (though the latter may sometimes be important to establish the terms under which particular contracts of employment are undertaken).

Where, however, a rule book does exist it will contain rules which are adhered to in the normal course of employment, but it may also contain rules which have grown up over a long period, and are not normally used or are somewhat anachronistic and obsolete. It is the strict adherence to the latter that is meant when talking of "working to rule", which is probably a sound argument for management to have a complete reappraisal of some of the existing rules and producing a more realistic work pattern.

One question does remain to be answered, and that is what is the position relating to the "banning of overtime"? The position appears to be that overtime working should be regarded as a purely voluntary undertaking, and where people decide, even by concerted action, not to work it they are not guilty of irregular industrial action. But, in those cases where it is agreed in the contract of employment that overtime will be undertaken as and when the employer reasonably requires it, then to agree to ban overtime in these circumstances, it is suggested, would amount to irregular industrial action. (*Pearson* v. *Jones Ltd.* (1967), 2 All E.R. 1062 (**6**)).

NOTE: Whilst a threat to organise, etc., a strike (even presumably after due notice) or other irregular industrial action falls within these provisions, it will NOT include a threat to work to rule so long as so doing is not in itself a breach of contract.

Where an employee is participating in a strike or other irregular industrial action he may be dismissed for this reason and it will not necessarily amount to unfair dismissal (IRA, s. 26(2)). Where, however, an employee is dismissed because he is participating in a strike or other irregular industrial action, it will amount to unfair dismissal:

(a) where other employees who participated in the same activity were not dismissed for taking part, *or*

(b) where other employees who participated in the same activity were dismissed and they have since been offered re-engagement and he has not

and the real or principal reason that he was selected for dismissal was because he chose to be a member of a trade union, or as a member that he engaged in the activities (p. 43) of the union, or because he chose not to be a member of a trade union (IRA, s. 26(2), (3)).

If this provision were to be taken in isolation there would be no restriction upon an employer who wished to dismiss the workers engaging in a strike or other irregular industrial action, even though his real reason for doing so was because they had exercised their right to be, or not to be, members of a trade union. The restriction only applies where an employer seeks to be selective.

It might be thought that there is an inconsistency in the Act, but IRA, s 5(1), (2) provides that every worker shall have the right to be a member of a trade union and to take part in its activities and that it shall be an *unfair industrial practice* for an employer to prevent or deter a worker from exercising that right. Also IRA, s. 24(4) provides that dismissal is unfair if the reason or principal reason was the exercise of that right or the intention to exercise it.

CHAPTER 4

RIGHTS OF WORKERS IN RELATION TO TRADE UNION MEMBERSHIP

ONE of the more important objects of the Act is to give a worker clearly defined rights, not only as between himself and his employer, but between himself and other workers, and between himself and workers' organisations. These rights are carefully drawn, and a liability is placed upon those who may be responsible for denying or interfering with them. The Act establishes a principle that interference or attempted interference, or denial of those rights is deemed an *unfair industrial practice*.

Fundamental to the concept of workers' rights, as established by the Act, is the voluntary nature of the trade union membership.

IRA, s. 5 provides that as between *himself* and his *employer* every *worker* has the right:

(a) to belong to any trade union* of his choice,

(b) to choose not to belong to any trade union or workers' organisation (except where an agency shop or an approved closed shop agreement is in operation);

(c) if he is a member of a trade union, at any appropriate time (see p. 43), to participate in its activities.

Further it is provided (IRA, s. 7) that any pre-entry closed shop agreements are void, i.e., any agreement made by an employer with a trade union that it will be necessary for any worker to belong to that, or any union, or to be recommended or approved by that union *before* he can take up employment is void, although it may be necessary where an agency shop agreement or an approved closed shop agreement is in operation in a particular undertaking that a person will have to join a trade union subsequent to taking up employment, i.e., a *post entry* closed shop. (For fuller discussion see pp. 53 *et seq.*)

Where any person is refused employment, and he is of the opinion that the reason for the refusal is because a closed shop arrangement

---

*I.e. an organisation of workers *registered* under the Act.

is being operated by the employer he may apply to the Industrial Court to have such agreement declared void.

In order to obviate the possibility of any pressure being brought upon employers to operate a closed shop system, it is provided that it shall be an unfair industrial practice for any person (including a trade union or organisation of workers, or any official of either) to

(a) call, organise, procure or finance a strike or to threaten to do so; or

(b) organise, procure or finance any irregular industrial action short of a strike, or threaten to do so,

for the purpose of inducing an employer to enter into or to comply with a *pre-entry* closed shop agreement, or not to engage workers who have not been recommended or approved for engagement by a trade union or other organisation of workers. (IRA, ss. 33(3), 7(1)).

Right of Worker to belong to Trade Union

As between himself and his employer every worker has the free and absolute right to belong to a trade union, and to take part in its activities, including seeking and accepting appointment as an official, and if elected, to engage in the activities of that office.

This establishes the principle that an employer who refuses to engage, or otherwise discriminates against a worker on the ground that he is a member of a trade union will be guilty of an unfair industrial practice. So that any worker who wishes to belong to a trade union need have no inhibitions about joining, nor in engaging in its activities, though if he does engage in trade union activities, either as a member or as an official, he must do so only during the "appropriate time".

The appropriate time means outside working hours (i.e., outside any time when in accordance with the terms of his contract he is required to work), or during working hours if there is an arrangement with the employer to this effect, or with the latter's consent (IRA, s. 5).

The expression "activities" is not defined by the Act but the word *includes* any activities as, or with a view to becoming, an official of the trade union, the right to seek or accept appointment or election, and if appointed or elected, to hold office as an official (IRA, s. 5(1)(c)). Therefore, according to the ordinary canons of construction the expression will include other activities in addition to these.

"Activities" can be interpreted so widely as to include the collecting of union dues or merely discussing with a colleague over a factory bench the merits of a possible strike, as well as including participation in strikes and other irregular industrial action. Two points must be borne in mind;

(i) Where consent has not been given to participate during working hours in trade union activities, a worker so participating could possibly be dismissed (so long as the dismissal was not unfair under some other provision of the Act). If the expression were to include collecting union dues or the discussion referred to, the worker would be exceeding his rights if he were to engage in that actitivy. It is, however, suggested that these would not be "activities" and that "activities" in this context would only include those matters which might interrupt the smooth running of the employer's business.

(ii) Where consent has been given by the employer, a worker would only infringe his rights to participate in trade union activities if the activities in which he engaged during working hours would by implication be excluded from the general licence, there is, for example, a clear distinction between the activities of seeking union office, and disrupting production by taking industrial action. It is permissible (see p. 41) for an employer to dismiss an employee whilst he is participating in a strike or other irregular industrial action (whether or not called by a trade union) provided that the real reason for the dismissal is for participating in the industrial action and not for exercising his rights as a trade union member.

Right not to Belong to a Trade Union

Every worker has the right not to belong to a trade union or other organisation of workers if he wishes, and if any worker chooses to exercise this right it is an unfair industrial practice for an *employer*, or some other person acting on his behalf, to seek to prevent, deter, dismiss, penalise, refuse to engage or otherwise discriminate against him for exercising that right (IRA, s. 5(2)), including giving or withholding any benefits as an inducement (IRA, s. 5(4)). There is, however, no reason why an employer should not seek to *encourage* a worker to join a trade union which the employer recognises as having negotiating rights in respect of such worker, provided that he does so without any suggestion of reward for compliance or penalty for non-compliance. (IRA, s. 5(3)).

To this general exercise of free choice there are two exceptions, for where there is in operation an *agency shop agreement*, or an *approved closed shop agreement* between an employer and a trade union, a worker may not exercise a complete discretion whether to become a member or not. In these cases the Act makes provision for allowing workers not to belong to a trade union only if they make certain financial contributions.

1. AGENCY SHOP AGREEMENTS (FINANCIAL ARRANGEMENTS)

Where there is an agency shop agreement (see p. 54) in force between an employer and a trade union, a worker may only refuse to be a member of the union subject to the following conditions—

(a) that he agrees to pay to the union *appropriate contributions*, i.e., an amount equivalent to what he would pay according to the rules of the union if he were a member of it (IRA, s. 6(1)), plus where the agency shop agreement so provides an initial payment, which shall not be in excess of any amount that the rules of the union would require him to pay if he were a member of the union. In any event the total payments must not in the aggregate exceed the aggregate amount he would be required to pay if he were a member (IRA, s. 8);

or

(b) where the worker objects on the grounds of *conscience both* to being a member of a trade union *and* also to paying contributions to a trade union in lieu of membership, he may propose to the union that he pay *equivalent contributions*, i.e., an amount agreed between him and a union (IRA, s. 9) to an approved charity. (For meaning of charity see the Income Tax Acts.)

In the event of any dispute relating to the amount of contributions or manner of payment, or whether the conscientious objections are genuine, or which particular charity should receive payments, the dispute may be resolved by an industrial tribunal (IRA, s. 10).

In the event of a worker deciding to pay *appropriate* contributions to the union in place of membership he will not be required to make payment for the first four weeks after taking up a new employment, or for the first three months in the case of an existing worker who becomes subject to an agency shop agreement subsequent to taking up the employment. (NOTE: These periods may be shortened by order of the Secretary of State in the case of any description of workers named in the order (IRA, s. 8(6)).

The periods of four weeks and three months do not apply where the worker agrees to pay *equivalent contributions* to a charity in place of trade union membership, as both the amount payable and the charity have to be agreed between the trade union and the worker (IRA, s. 9).

Where a worker or potential worker exercises his right not to be a member of a trade union, but refuses or fails to pay the appropriate contributions to the union or equivalent contributions to a charity it will *not* be an unfair industrial practice for his employer, or person acting for him, to dismiss him, penalise, refuse to engage or otherwise discriminate against him (IRA, s. 6(2)). It is suggested, that the wording of IRA, s. 6(2) is sufficiently wide as to allow dismissal of an employee by an employer, where the employee has not only refused or failed to pay appropriate contributions or equivalent contributions, but where he has merely fallen into arrears with his payments.

If a worker has agreed to pay appropriate contributions to the trade union with which an agency agreement has been made, and requests his employer to deduct the contributions from his remuneration and pay them on his behalf, then so long as that request remains in force, he shall not be regarded as having refused or failed to pay his contributions if the employer fails to pay on his behalf (IRA, s. 6(3)).

If in fact, a worker does fall into arrears with his union contributions as a member, his union will be entitled to take disciplinary action against him, but failure to pay *appropriate contributions* or *equivalent contributions* is a matter upon which the employer may take action, even to the extent of threatening dismissal. Furthermore, whilst generally speaking it is an unfair industrial practice to induce the dismissal of a worker, it would appear not to be so in this particular case.

2. CLOSED SHOP AGREEMENTS (FINANCIAL ARRANGEMENTS)

Where an approved closed shop agreement (see p. 59) is in force any worker to whom the agreement applies is obliged to be a member of the union (or of one of the unions, if more than one) unless he can claim to be exempted on the grounds of conscience from becoming a member.

If he objects on the grounds of conscience he may propose to the trade union that he should pay appropriate contributions to a charity to be determined by agreement between himself and the trade union.

If the trade union agrees to the proposal, the amount of the contributions, and the charity to which they are to be paid, then the worker shall be "specially exempted" from becoming a member of the union.

The amount of the contributions will be calculated in accordance with the principles of the provisions of the approved shop agreement. If a dispute arises as to the genuineness of his conscientious objections, or the amount, or the charity to which the contributions shall be made, the dispute may be resolved by an industrial tribunal.

If therefore, a worker refuses to become a member of a union in these circumstances, or has refused or failed to pay the appropriate contributions to a charity, it will *not* be an unfair industrial practice for an employer to dismiss or otherwise discriminate against him.

The principles applicable to appropriate contributions considered in para. 1(a) on p. 44, apply equally to appropriate contributions under this heading. (IRA, s. 17, Sch. 1).

Pressure on employer to infringe rights of employees in relation to trade union membership

So far the rights between the *worker* and his *employer* relating to trade union matters have been examined, the position as between the *worker* and *other parties* must now be considered.

It is clearly perfectly lawful for trade union officials and others to seek *peacefully* to *persuade* workers to join, or not to join trade unions and other workers' organisations. It is not, however, permissible for *any person*, including a trade union or other workers' organisation, or any official of either, to call or otherwise assist in arranging a strike or other irregular industrial activity, or threaten to do so, for the purpose of inducing an employer, or person acting on his behalf, to act in such a way that it would deprive a worker of his rights to exercise his free choice in relation to trade union matters (or in order to induce an employer to have a pre-entry closed shop arrangement) (IRA, s. 33).

The object of this provision is clearly to ensure that a worker's interests are not interfered with by third parties through the

employer, and if pressure is put upon an *employer* in this way it will
amount to an unfair industrial practice.

It would appear that whilst the provision is intended to protect
a worker's rights, it is only concerned with the inducement or
attempted inducement of an *employer* by some other person, so that
if a worker chose not to be a member of a trade union, and the
place of employment was not subject to an agency shop agreement,
but in order to induce the employer to dismiss him a trade union
or its officials threatened to call a strike, the provision would apply
and it would be an unfair industrial practice. But if the union or
its officials sought to persuade *the worker himself* to join the union,
and threatened him that they would call out his fellow workers on
strike or persuade them not to talk to him, this would not be an
unfair industrial practice.

The reader might ask the question "does not the Act give a worker
the right to belong or not to belong to a trade union?" and the
answer is yes, but only as between himself and the employer!

Infringement of Rights Relating to Trade Union Membership

In the preceding pages the right of a worker to make a free choice
as to his membership or otherwise, of a trade union, has been
indicated and it is shown that in some circumstances an interference
or attempted interference with that right is an unfair industrial
practice. It is necessary now to examine in more detail where
liability for this particular practice will lie.

IRA, s. 33 provides that it is an unfair industrial practice for
any person (including any *trade union* or *other organisation of workers*) by;

(a) calling, organising, procuring or financing a strike or
     threatening to do so; or

(b) organising, procuring or financing any industrial action short
     of a strike, or threatening to do so;

to seek to induce an employer to discriminate in any way against an
employee who wishes to exercise his free choice in relation to
membership of a trade union.

The expression *any person* is wide enough to include any individual
and clearly where only one single individual is inducing or attempting to induce an employer, identification for the purpose of liability
will not present any difficulty. More difficulty, however, is likely in
relation to trade unions and other organisations of workers, for here,
in a sense, it is legal rather than human persons who are concerned

and as the former can only act through human agents the question of appointment and authority arises.

Liability of Trade Unions

It is provided (IRA, s. 74) that a trade union (i.e., a registered organisation of workers) shall have corporate status, so that identification of a trade union provides no problem. However, for a trade union to be liable it has to act in the way described, and as it can only act through agents, it will be necessary to show that persons ostensibly acting on behalf of a trade union are in fact authorised to do so.

It is suggested that this may be done by examining the list of officials deposited with the registrar and the rules of the union deposited with the registrar. The rules will set out the manner of appointment and extent of authority of individual officials, the acts of whom will be binding upon the union. Even where a person purports to act on behalf of a union, and is not in fact authorised to do so, his activities may be ratified by the union who will then become liable, as though it had originally specifically authorised the act.

Liability of Organisation of Workers

Much more difficulty will be experienced in identifying an organisation of workers, because of the very definition of such bodies which provides that they may be either permanent or *temporary* (IRA, s. 61) and may consist of large or small numbers, provided that the *principal object* of the organisation includes the regulation of relations between themselves and employers. This clearly suggests that, whilst these organisations may include well organised permanent bodies with detailed rules and large funds, they may equally include *ad hoc* bodies with no funds and no real organisation. It will always depend upon the facts in each case who may be defined as the officers of an unregistered workers' organisation. Where it is a well organised and probably permanent association a list of its officials will be readily available, but where it is a purely temporary and *ad hoc* body the status of the persons participating will have to be gathered from the degree of involvement, e.g., acting as spokesman or negotiator.

Remedies Where Pressure is Brought to Infringe Worker's Rights

Where pressure is brought against an employer to induce him to infringe the rights of a worker in such a way that it amounts to, or would amount to, an unfair industrial practice the following remedies are available.

An employer may complain to the Industrial Court that some person is acting or threatening to take industrial action against him in order to induce him to infringe the rights of a worker or workers, and if the Court is satisfied that the complaint is well founded it may make an order directing that the respondent shall refrain from taking or continuing the action he has threatened or taken (IRA, ss. 101(1), (3), 105(1)). The party named in the order may be an individual or a trade union or organisation of workers.

Where a worker has been dismissed or otherwise discriminated against he may make an application to an industrial tribunal for compensation. The tribunal if satisfied that the complaint is well founded will take the action outlined on p. 35, or may order the employer to make compensation to the worker on the following scale:

Where the worker has been *dismissed* he may claim up to 104 weeks wages, up to a maximum of £40 per week, subject to an overall maximum of £4,160 (though the worker must seek to mitigate his loss in any event, i.e., by finding alternative employment if possible). If the worker has not been dismissed but is otherwise discriminated against, e.g., by being put on less remunerative work, he may claim from the employer compensation for lost benefits, expenses, etc. (IRA, ss. 106 and 118).

It will be observed that the worker's right of action is against the employer, and not against the person responsible for the inducement, etc. The employer, however, has a right against the person responsible for where he can show that the action he took was directly attributable to the pressure from that party, he may seek a contribution from him, in an industrial tribunal or the Industrial Court.

Once a tribunal or the Court is satisfied that the third party is responsible for the pressure it may order that party to pay an amount either by way of contribution or by way of a complete indemnity to the employer, to cover any costs and expenses the employer has incurred toward the worker as a consequence of that pressure (IRA, s. 119).

Limits of Liability

Wherever compensation is required to be paid by a trade union under the provisions of the Act, it will always be subject to the following limits (IRA, s. 117);

(a)	trade union with less than 5,000 members ...	£5,000
(b)	trade union with less than 25,000 members but with 5,000 or more	£25,000
(c)	trade union with less than 100,000 members but with 25,000 or more	£50,000
(d)	trade union with 100,000 or more	£100,000

NOTE: These amounts are the maximum amounts which a trade union may be required to pay in any *one case*, but that they are intended only as compensation and *not* as fines or punishment, therefore, the actual amount payable, subject to these limits will be what the complainant can show that he has lost as a result of the activity complained about.

Where any order is made against a trade union (or employers' association) to pay damages or compensation, or for the payment of any costs and expenses, property which belongs to individual members of the union in their private capacity cannot be reached for this purpose. And this rule, also applies even where the order is made against members or officials where the proceedings were brought against them on behalf of themselves *and all* other members of the trade union and employers' association. Furthermore, any funds of a trade union (or employers' association) which under its rules are not to be used for financing strikes, lockouts or other industrial action may not be claimed upon for making compensation (IRA, s. 153).

In relation to an unregistered workers', or employers' organisation, although it does not have corporate status it is provided that any action may be brought against it in the name of the organisation, and any judgment or order directing the organisation to take or refrain from aking any action shall be enforceable, by way of execution, *punishment for contempt* or otherwise, against any property belonging to the organisation as if it were a corporate body. Though, again, funds which by its rules are not to be used for financing strikes, lock-outs or other industrial action may not be claimed upon as in the case of (registered) trade unions nor may any property belonging to any member of the organisation so long as it is not owned jointly or in common with the other members of the organisation (i.e., private property is not available to pay compensation) (IRA, s. 154). In the case of unregistered organisations, however, there are no limits to the amount that such organisations may be required to pay by way of compensation, subject to the rule of course that any amount must be to compensate and not to punish.

Similarly, the case of individuals who are held to be responsible for the pressure and the consequences, there are no limits as to the amount of compensation that they may be required to pay, other than where an individual is acting in his capacity of an official of a (registered) trade union and within the *scope of his authority* on behalf of the union. For he may not be required to make any contribution towards any compensation ordered to be paid by a (registered) trade union (IRA, s. 119(4)). Nor, incidentally, may any person be held personally liable for any unfair industrial practice where he can show that at any time he took the action complained of he was acting within the *scope of his authority* as a (registered) *trade union official* (or official of an employers' association) (IRA, s. 101(4)).

There are no similar restrictions in the case of persons acting on behalf of unregistered organisations of workers.

CHAPTER 5

AGENCY SHOP AGREEMENTS:
APPROVED CLOSED SHOP AGREEMENTS

Since the Trade Union Act, 1871, the single aim of many trade unionists has been the creation of greater solidarity among workers in general, and among workers in particular industries and work-places. Obviously the larger and tighter knit trade union organisation is the more effective it becomes as a bargaining organisation. One of the results of this aim has been the creation of the "closed shop", i.e., where every employee in a particular workplace has to belong to a single union (in a one union shop) or to one of a number of identified unions (in a multi-union shop). It is also clear that where every employee in a particular factory is a member of a single trade union they are in a stronger bargaining position in relation to management than if they are in different unions or in no union at all.

The practical result of the closed shop is that the union or unions negotiate with the employer, reasonably secure in the knowledge that if negotiations fail they can fall back on the ultimate sanction, the withdrawal of labour. For a strike to be effective it is necessary that it should seriously disrupt the production of goods or services, and in the past it was to this end that the discipline procedures of the closed shop unions were aimed; for if members of the union refused to participate in a strike or other industrial action agreed by the executive of the union they could be called to account by the union. The result of this could be a mere reprimand or a fine, or even expulsion from the union. Therefore, as union membership was a pre-requisite to obtaining and retaining employment this meant the loss of employment. Further, where a union held a monopoly position in a factory it could impose control upon work-men, *vis à vis* each other, e.g., to ensure an equitable distribution of overtime working or to restrict output by each individual to an amount reasonably attainable by an average worker.

Many employers in the past have welcomed the closed shop

mainly on the grounds that the conduct and discipline of workmen has been undertaken by a body, in many cases more powerful than the employer himself. Also because it is convenient to know with whom to negotiate when considering terms and conditions of employment, matters of redundancy and so forth. Furthermore the maintenance of standards of competency could be achieved through unions admitting to membership only those persons who have served an approved apprenticeship or period of training.

Unions are not usually based on a single factory or workplace, but are national in character, and whilst many negotiations are conducted at a local level producing agreements which have local or restricted application (e.g., the employees at Ford Motor Co., Ltd., having a different wage structure from Vauxhall employees at Luton) many agreements have a much wider application, e.g., national minimum wages rates for certain tradesmen.

Unions differ very widely in character, and membership of some is possible simply by application and payment of the necessary contributions, whilst other unions restrict membership in various ways. The most common restriction on membership is found in the craft unions, there being a requirement that entry is conditional upon having completed an approved apprenticeship acceptable to the union.

Whether the closed shop principle is thought to be a restriction upon liberty and freedom depends upon the individual's own ideology, but it was thought by the Conservative Government that in the interests of overall industrial harmony some amendment to the principle was necessary and consequently the "agency shop" and the "approved closed shop" were established to take its place.

What is an Agency Shop?

The Act provides (IRA, s. 11(1)) that an "agency shop agreement" means an agreement made between an employer and one or more trade unions (not unregistered workers' organisations) whereby the employer agrees, in respect of workers of one or more descriptions specified in the agreement, that their terms and conditions of employment shall include a condition that every such worker must either—

    (a) be or become a member of that trade union or one of those unions, or

(b) agree to pay appropriate contributions (p. 44) to that trade
union (or one of them) in lieu of membership, or (where
permitted to do so) pay equivalent contributions to a charity.

An agency shop may be one of many different kinds. It may relate
to a part of a factory, it may relate to a factory, it may relate to
several employers, a group of employers, and it can be right across
the board in an industry.

An agency shop may be based entirely upon agreement between
an employer and a trade union or unions, or may come about as
a result of a ballot conducted under the provisions of the Act in
those circumstances where an employer fails to agree with a trade
union to accept an agency shop.

Therefore, if an employer is prepared to make an agreement
with one or more trade unions that all his employees to whom the
agreement is intended to apply shall belong to one of those unions,
then an agency agreement comes into existence.

In effect the initiative is entirely with the employer and trade
union at this point, and no individual worker can complain if he
is required to be subject to the terms of this agreement. Though
where not less than one-fifth of the workers affected by the agreement
wish to have it rescinded they may make application to the Industrial
Court (IRA, s. 14) (p. 57).

Employer Unwilling to agree to an Agency Shop

In the event of an employer being unwilling to make an agency
shop agreement the following procedure must be considered: where
a trade union itself desires an employer to enter into an agency
shop agreement or where a joint negotiating panel (viz., a body
consisting of two or more organisations of workers which with their
authority enters into collective agreements which will bind those
workers) (IRA, s. 44(d)) desires an employer to enter into an agency
shop agreement with one of the trade unions represented on the
panel, and the employer is unwilling to do so, the trade union (or
the joint negotiating panel) can apply to the Industrial Court. The
application must describe the workers to whom it will apply, and
specify the employer and the trade union who are to be parties to
the agreement (IRA, s. 11(2)).

Upon the application being made, the Industrial Court must
first satisfy itself that no similar application was made within the

previous two years (resulting in a non-acceptance by the workers when put to a ballot) relating wholly or in part to the same description of workers (IRA, s. 13(4)), or that during the last two years an agency shop was in existence and on a ballot neither a majority of persons eligible to vote nor two-thirds actually voting, voted for its continuance (IRA, s. 15(3)). If satisfied upon these matters, the Industrial Court must request the Commission for Industrial Relations to take action. Upon receipt of this request the Commission must first consider a possible clash of interests before it can proceed, to entertain the application, because it is possible under the provisions of the Act for an application to be made to the Industrial Court, for the recognition of what is known as a *sole bargaining agent* (i.e., an organisation of workers or joint negotiating panel having exclusive negotiating rights in relation to certain groups of workers (see p. 79)) and if an application has been made to establish a sole bargaining agency, its establishment may make an agency shop agreement ineffective. In other words where there is a sole bargaining agent concerned with workers' conditions of employment, it is clearly incompatible with having a trade union acting independently and negotiating about the same matters.

If there is a question to be settled as to whether there is to be a sole bargaining agency, i.e., if there is a dispute still to be settled, then the Commission cannot proceed with the application for an agency shop. If, however, there is no such dispute the Commission must arrange for a ballot to be taken among the workers to decide whether there is desire for an agency shop agreement or not.

The Commission must first decide which description of workers are to be included, bearing in mind the possibility that other workers represented by that trade union or joint negotiating panel, but not included in the application, should be represented in the ballot. Once the Commission has decided which description of workers should be included in the ballot it must make a report to this effect to the Industrial Court. The next step for the Commission, is to arrange for a secret ballot to be taken among these workers, either by the Commission itself or by some other body under its supervision. Once the ballot has been taken the Commission must report the result to the Industrial Court, and the employer and the trade union (or joint negotiating panel) specified in the application.

The result of the ballot is determined either by a simple majority of the workers entitled to the vote (but if any worker entitled to vote, does not exercise his vote, this will count against the application) or by two-thirds of persons *actually* voting.

If there is a majority either of those eligible to vote or two-thirds actually voting in favour of an agency shop agreement then the employer must enter into an agreement to this effect in respect of those workers, and after the agreement has been made must carry it out so long as it remains in force (IRA, s. 13(1)).

If on the other hand a majority of those eligible or two-thirds actually voting do not vote in favour of an agency shop agreement the Industrial Court must make an order directing that no similar application shall be made in respect of that description of workers and the union and employers named in the application for at least two years from the date that the Industrial Court received the result of the ballot, and further if there is any purported agency shop agreement between those parties during that time, it shall be void.

NOTE: It is an unfair industrial practice for any person (including a trade union or organisation of workers) to take or threaten industrial action, in order to induce an employer not to enter into an agency shop agreement or not to carry out its terms if one is in existence (IRA, s. 13(2)).

Existing Agency Shop Agreements

Even when an agency shop agreement is in force it can be revoked by following a rather similar process to that just discussed. Where *one-fifth* of the workers to whom an agency shop agreement applies desire to end it, an application *in writing* may be made by them to the Industrial Court, provided that if the agreement is one which resulted from a ballot as described above, it has been in force for more than two years (IRA, s. 14).

The Industrial Court must then request the Commission to arrange for a ballot, which will be conducted in the same way, a simple majority of those workers to whom the agreement applies (any vote not cast by a worker entitled to vote, counting against) or two-thirds majority of those actually voting (IRA, s. 15).

When the Commission receives the result of the ballot it must inform the Industrial Court. If there is no majority in favour of rescinding the agreement then it will continue as before, but if a majority vote in favour of rescinding the agreement, the Industrial Court must make an order rescinding the agreement. Whether the application is successful or unsuccessful, no application can be made for at least two years in respect of wholly or in part the same description of workers to reverse the position (IRA, s. 15).

Unfair Industrial Practices in Relation to Agency Shop Applications

It is an unfair industrial practice for any employer to take or threaten to take industrial action in order to knowingly induce a trade union (or joint negotiating panel) or any other person not to make any application to establish an agency shop, or for a ballot to rescind such an agreement. And it is also an unfair industrial practice for any person (including a trade union) to take or threaten to take similar action in order knowingly to induce an employer to enter an agency shop agreement after an application has already been made for a ballot, or to induce an employer not to make such an application (IRA, s. 16).

This limitation on industrial action on the part of any person or trade union does not apply where a ballot has been taken and the voting is in favour of an agency shop agreement, and which the employer has refused to implement. Nor, it would seem for any person or trade union who seeks to induce an employer to enter into an agency shop agreement before any application for a ballot has been made. So that where an employer is being threatened with industrial action unless he makes such an agency shop agreement he ought to make application to the Court for a ballot, after which, the conduct, if continued, of the party threatening, etc., becomes an unfair industrial practice.

Approved Closed Shop Agreements

During the passage of the Industrial Relations Act through Parliament, one of its most controversial aspects was the fact that it outlawed (originally) the closed shop. Objection came not only from the trade unions, but also from industry and other sources as well.

It was suggested that many closed shop agreements already in existence should be allowed to continue in the general interests of industrial harmony, and that in particular, unions like Equity, the Musicians and the Seamen's could only be effective if they were permitted to remain organised on the closed shop principle.

The Government were persuaded by these arguments to modify their original plan to prohibit all closed shops in favour of allowing, subject to severe limitations, some closed shop agreements, to be known as "approved closed shop agreements", into which category the three unions referred to will almost certainly fall.

An approved closed shop agreement is:

> Any agreement made between one or more employers, or an organisation of employers, with one or more trade unions (not unregistered organisation of workers) under which workers of one or more descriptions specified in the agreement shall as a term of their contract of employment, become members of that trade union, or one of those trade unions (unless specifically exempted) Provided that the agreement is made in accordance with proposals approved by an order of the Industrial Court (IRA, s. 17(1)).

In order to establish an approved closed shop agreement, the first requirement is that an employer and a trade union must agree as between each other to have a closed shop. They must then make a joint application (no unilateral application may be made) for approval to the Industrial Court, submitting a draft of their proposed agreement.

The Court may not entertain the application if it either:

(a) is made within two years of a previous application in respect of the same description of workers, or

(b) is made within two years of a ballot being taken in respect of the same description of workers, and they have voted not to accept such an agreement, or have voted to abandon an existing agreement.

If the Court is satisfied that no such prohibition applies, then it must accept the application and refer it to the Commission on Industrial Relations. The Commission must then decide whether the proposed agreement satisfies five criteria (IRA, Sch. 1):

(i) that the closed shop would be necessary to enable the workers to be organised on "the principle of free association of workers in independent trade unions";

(ii) that it is necessary for maintaining reasonable terms and conditions of employment, and reasonable prospects of continuing employment for those workers;

(iii) that it is required for promoting or maintaining stable arrangements for collective bargaining;

(iv) that it is the *only way* to prevent collective agreements relating to those workers from being frustrated;

(v) that these four objectives cannot reasonably be expected to be fulfilled by means of an agency shop agreement.

If when the Commission have considered these matters they arrive at the conclusion that it is not necessary to have a closed shop agreement to achieve *all the first four* objectives *and* that an agency shop agreement would be effective, they must indicate this to the Industrial Court, and proceed no further with the application. On the other hand, if the Commission is satisfied that it is necessary for the workers in question to be comprised in an approved closed shop agreement, they must report this conclusion to the Industrial Court. The Industrial Court must then make an order that they propose to implement the Commission's report, but must give at least one month, but no more than three months, for any of the workers affected by the report to ask for a ballot.

The request for a ballot must be in writing by at least one-fifth of the workers affected by the proposals.

If no request for a ballot is made during the time allowed the Industrial Court must issue a second order implementing this agreement. But if a ballot is requested, then it will be conducted by the Commission, who will state which persons are eligible to vote, either itself or by someone under its supervision. If the voting, which must be in secret, shows either a simple majority of those eligible to vote or two-thirds of those actually voting in favour of the closed shop agreement, the Industrial Court must make an order implementing the agreement. If there is no such majority, or two-thirds actually voting, in favour, the Industrial Court will not approve the proposals, and they will lapse, and as indicated above, no further application may be made for at least two years (IRA, Sch. 1). Any worker eligible to vote, but who does not participate in the ballot, will count against the proposal.

Once a closed shop agreement has been approved by order of the Industrial Court, no further application can be entertained for it to be revoked for at least two years, after which if one-fifth of the workers affected by it apply in writing to the Industrial Court for a ballot to revoke it, the Court must request the Commission to arrange for a ballot to be taken. This ballot will take the same form as the one previously discussed (IRA, Sch. 1).

Even where a closed shop agreement has been approved, persons may be specially exempted from the need to join the union. Where any person is not specially exempted and is a worker to whom the agreement applies then he must become a member, unless he objects on the grounds of conscience from being a member. In this case he can agree with the union that he will pay appropriate contributions to a charity acceptable to himself and the union, the amount of which will be calculated in accordance with principles which must be set out in the approved closed shop agreement.

If a dispute arises as to whether his conscientious objections are genuine, or to which charity the contributions shall be made, or the amount of the contribution, an application may be made to an industrial tribunal to resolve it (IRA, Sch. 1, Pt. IV). In the event of a worker being permitted on grounds of conscience to pay "appropriate contributions" to a charity, he may request his employer to deduct the contributions from his remuneration and pay them on his behalf. Any failure on the part of the employer to collect and pay them will not amount to non-payment by the worker so long as the request remains in force (IRA, s. 17(6)).

Once an approved closed shop has been established the employer will be entitled to dismiss a worker who refuses to join the union other than on grounds of conscience. But, he will not be permitted to make membership of the union a *pre-entry* requirement for the employment of any person, it may only be a *post-entry* requirement. And any person not already a member of the appropriate union who takes up employment will have one month within which to apply for union membership. In the event of an approved closed shop agreement becoming effective *after* a worker becomes employed, such worker will have a period of three months within which to apply for membership (IRA, s. 18(4)). (The Secretary of State may by statutory instrument reduce the periods of one and three months in the case of any approved closed shop agreement (IRA, s. 18(5)).)

The important distinction between an agency shop and an approved closed shop is that in the case of the former a worker has a free choice whether to be a member of a trade union or not as he pleases, provided that he pays appropriate contributions, whereas in the case of an approved closed shop the only ground upon which he can claim not to be a member is that of conscience. Therefore the power of control and discipline is much stronger in the case of the latter than the former, as membership in effect becomes a pre-requisite of retaining employment. For where an approved closed shop agreement exists any worker who is not a member of the appropriate union may be dismissed or otherwise discriminated against by his employer. It becomes imperative, therefore, to establish safeguards to protect the interests of a worker who may lose his membership as a result of being "disciplined" by his union, or who makes application to become a member but whose application is rejected. And it is provided that a worker will only be regarded as a "non-member" if he has been excluded from membership in circumstances where under the rules of the union he had a right of appeal against rejection or expulsion, and his appeal has either been heard and dismissed, or the time for appealing has expired without his having exercised his right (IRA, s. 18(2), (3)).

In other words, where a worker is legitimately excluded from, or is refused membership of, the union he may be discriminated against by his employer. But, where a worker is "unlawfully" excluded from membership he may not be so discriminated against, for whilst in fact he will be a "non-member", he must be treated for the purposes of the approved closed shop provisions as though he were a member.

It is not anticipated that very many closed shop agreements will in fact be approved. The provision allowing for certain closed shop agreements was clearly intended to cater for the very few exceptional cases, such as Equity, the Musicians Union and the National Union of Seamen, already referred to.

Pressure on employers to induce an application for approval of closed shop

Before the Industrial Court will accept an application for an approved closed shop there has to be an agreement between the employer and a trade union to make an application, and it was envisaged by the Government when making provision for approved closed shops that where an agreement could not be reached between an employer and a trade union to make an application, that there may be circumstances where a trade union or organisation of workers will bring pressure upon an employer to seek to persuade him to join in making the application. It is, therefore, provided (IRA, s. 33(3)) that it is an unfair industrial practice for any person (including a trade union or other organisation of workers or an official of either), to

(a) call, organise, procure, or finance a strike or threaten to do so; or

(b) organise, procure, or finance any irregular industrial action short of a strike, or threaten to do so,

for the purpose of knowingly inducing an employer or an employers' association to join in making an application for an approved closed shop agreement.

Review of Ballots (Agency Shop and Approved Closed Shop Agreements)

Where any ballot has been taken either by the Commission or by some body on its behalf for any of the purposes of agency shop or approved closed shop agreements, and it is found by the Industrial Court,

(i) that the report made to the Commission as a result of the ballot was incorrect, or

(ii) that the ballot was so misconducted that it would not be just and equitable to regard it as valid,

the Industrial Court may act as follows,

(a) if it thinks it just and equitable to do so make an order rectifying the error so that the report will operate as amended;

(b) where it would not be just and equitable to rectify a report quash the ballot, and so much of the report as relates to the result of the ballot, and if any order has already been made as a consequence of the report revoke that order. (The effect of this will be the same as if the ballot had never been taken.) (IRA, s. 160.)

CHAPTER 6

COLLECTIVE BARGAINING

THE expression collective bargaining it may be thought requires no definition, for it merely indicates a situation where groups rather than individuals negotiate with each other. This, however, is a general use of the expression and could be applied equally to a group of market traders negotiating the day's price of lamb, or to a group of workers collectively agreeing wage rates with an employer or employers.

It is with collective bargaining between workers and employers with which this legislation is concerned, for whilst workers' contracts of employment are still, in general, matters of individual negotiation, it would clearly be wrong to take the view that they were not influenced by other forces, e.g., wage rates, hours of work, etc., negotiated by the trade unions and workers' organisations, of which they may or may not be members.

It has always been problematical to decide exactly what terms and conditions should be implied into workers' contracts of service, for, apart from the details required to be given to every employee by the Contracts of Employment Act, 1963, their conditions in a great many cases are not specifically stated but merely assumed from the general standards prevailing in the particular occupation in the locality. Whilst it is probable that most of the basic terms of an individual's employment will be discussed whilst he is negotiating to be employed, many will not, and will merely be implied.

The problems of establishing the terms upon which any employment was originally taken, in the context of collective bargaining, is of secondary importance to the subsequent amendment of these contracts. For whilst individual employers may agree with individual employees to a change or revision of their contracts it is more usual in the case of "organised" workers for changes and revision to be negotiated by a trade union or similar organisation, on behalf of their members, with an employer or employers, and imposed upon the workers.

Collective bargaining is undertaken by a wide variety of joint bodies, some who negotiate at a national level, some at a level covering a large industrial organisation and some which negotiate at "plant" level. Examples of the first group are the "Whitley Councils", which were set up by the Government in a number of industries and also for the Civil Service, for settling industrial disputes by negotiation. The Whitley Council for certain employees in local government is the National Joint Council for Local Authorities' Administrative, Professional, Technical and Clerical Services, and comprises 63 members—32 appointed by the employing authorities and 31 by the staff side—and an independent chairman, who is appointed by the Secretary of State for the Environment.

A good example of the second group may be seen if one refers to *Ford Motor Co., Ltd.* v. *Amalgamated Union of Engineering Foundry Workers and Others* (1969) (**1**) where it will be seen that a number of unions, some representing large numbers of Ford workers and some representing relatively small numbers, had what was called a National Joint Negotiating Council. This Joint Negotiating Council was comprised of representatives from these unions and representatives from Ford management. Agreements arrived at by this joint negotiating body were intended to apply to workers in all the Ford works in the United Kingdom.

Finally there are many examples of bodies which operate at plant level, these will include works committees established by agreement with the management and the workers in the factory, and may be very small by comparison.

COLLECTIVE AGREEMENTS

The Act seeks to introduce into collective bargaining a system and an order, and begins by defining a collective agreement as

"Any agreement or arrangement made (in whatever way and whatever form)

    (a) by or on behalf of one or more organisations of workers and one or more employers or organisations of employers, and

    (b) is either an agreement or arrangement prescribing (wholly or in part) the *terms and conditions of employment of workers* of one or more descriptions, or is a *procedure agreement* or both." (IRA, s. 166.)

The parties to a collective agreement are the organisations of workers, and the employers or organisations of employers, and not the members represented by them.

Collective agreements therefore fall into two parts:

(a) *terms and conditions of employment,* i.e., the terms and conditions upon which one or more workers are, or are to be, required to work for their employers, i.e., pay and conditions and

(b) *procedure agreements,* i.e., so much of any collective agreement which relates to any of the following—

   (i)   machinery for consultation with regard to the settlement by negotiation or arbitration of terms and conditions of employment; or other questions arising between an employer or group of employers and one or more workers or organisation of workers;

   (ii) negotiating rights, i.e., rights recognised by an employer or by two or more associated employers to participate, on behalf of all or some of the employees whose terms and conditions of employment could appropriately be the subject of the same negotiations, in negotiations relating to these employees, with a view to the conclusion or modification of one or more collective agreements (IRA, s. 44(b));

   (iii) facilities for officials of trade unions or other organisation of workers;

   (iv) procedures relating to dismissal;

   (v)   procedures relating to matters of discipline other than dismissal;

   (vi) procedures relating to grievance of individual workers (IRA, s. 166).

Collective agreements may come into effect by an agreement or arrangement in writing, orally, custom or practice. It is now provided that where, after the commencement of the Industrial Relations Act, any collective agreement is made *in writing* it shall be conclusively presumed to be legally enforceable if it does not contain a provision stating that the agreement or part of it is not intended to be legally enforceable (IRA, s. 34).

Where, therefore, a legally enforceable agreement is made, a claim for compensation may be made against any party to it who breaks that agreement, or in the case of an organisation if he fails to take reasonable steps to prevent its members breaking the agreement.

If, for example, a legal agreement settles wage rates for a specific period, a union calling a strike for higher pay during that period could be liable to pay compensation, as it could if it made no attempt to stop an unofficial strike for higher pay. Similarly an employer could be liable if he failed to observe the terms of a redundancy agreement.

The other limb of collective agreements is procedure agreements. These make provision for the matters listed above. Under this part of the agreement representatives of workers' organisations and representatives of an employer or employers' organisation will have been given authority to regulate the terms and conditions of employment of one or more descriptions of workers and/or to determine in relation to workers of one or more descriptions any of the matters for which a procedure agreement can provide. This body will be able to act within the scope of the authority that it has been given, and within that area of authority it will be conclusively presumed to have the power to make agreements which are legally binding on the organisation of workers or employers they represent, as though the employers' organisations and workers' organisations had made the agreement themselves.

Where this body makes a decision it does not mean that all its agreements will be legally enforceable, for in order to be legally enforceable these agreements have to comply with one of two criteria, viz.,

(a) where an agreement is made within the scope of the authority of the joint body, and is made *orally*, it must be *intended* by *both* sides to be legally enforceable (IRA, s. 35(3)) or

(b) where any such agreement is *duly recorded in writing*, it will be legally enforceable unless it contains a direction that it shall not be so (IRA, s. 35(4)).

In other words, where any agreement is made orally it must be established by evidence that it was intended to be legally enforceable, whereas an agreement duly recorded in writing will be presumed to be intended to be legally enforceable unless there is a direction to the contrary.

Many of these joint bodies came into existence before the Act, either by agreement or arrangement, e.g., by custom or practice, and these will continue to have authority in the future in the same way as joint bodies established subsequent to the Act.

It must be noted that where under a collective agreement which is legally enforceable a joint body as described is established, the decisions of the joint body will create legal liability for the workers' organisations or employer or employers' organisation if they intend their agreement to be legally binding.

Where a procedure agreement has been made it is probable that the persons representing the workers' organisations will be a local branch official of a union and/or shop steward in the factory, and a representative of the management. Therefore, where decisions are reached it must be borne in mind that if they are *duly recorded in writing* without a clause limiting their enforceability, or where they are made orally, but with the intent that they shall be legally enforceable, then the organisations they represent will be legally bound.

It is important to establish what is meant by "duly recorded in writing on behalf of that body". First it will not include an oral agreement between a shop steward and the factory manager, not even where one or the other makes a written record of it (a fear expressed by trade unionists during the passage of the Act through Parliament). The written record has to be accepted by the body as the appropriate method of recording the conclusion. It would therefore, it is suggested, include, for example, the recorded and approved minutes of a meeting and decision between shop stewards and management representatives, unless there was a minute to the effect that such record should not be binding. So the position is that where any agreement is actually made in writing or recorded in writing with the approval of both parties, it must contain a provision that it is not intended to be legally binding if that is the intention.

A further suggestion is that it will *not* be sufficient to make a blanket provision at the outset of a collective agreement that all decisions arrived at and recorded in writing in the future under a procedure agreement shall not be legally binding. This will have to be done each time a decision is arrived at. But it would be possible to make a blanket provision that no agreement made *orally* would be legally enforceable, and may be a convenient method of resolving the difficulty in the future where one party to an agreement alleges that it was intended that a particular oral agreement should be legally binding.

As shop stewards will, as suggested above, invariably be the representatives of one of the parties to a procedure agreement established by a collective agreement it may be thought to be a good plan to establish at the outset of any collective agreement that only decisions arrived at and duly recorded in writing, and not containing a clause to the contrary, are intended to be legally enforceable, and that oral agreements never are unless *specifically stated* to be so intended. And, as the parties to a collective agreement will be bound by what their representatives decide, within the area of their authority, some standard method should be established for the recording of decisions in writing in order to obviate some of the likely problems created by uncertainty.

Enforceability of collective agreements

What is meant by enforceable must now be explained. First it must again be emphasised that the parties to a collective agreement will be a trade union or organisation of workers on the one hand and an employer or organisation of employers on the other hand, but not the individual workers who are represented by those parties. A collective agreement binds only the parties to it. Where parties are bound by an agreement the question is, in what ways may they break it? In the case of an ordinary contract the answer is simply that they do so if they fail to carry out the terms of the agreement. In the case of a collective agreement however, the answer is somewhat different, for whilst the parties to it are required to honour its terms specifically as in an ordinary contract (and they will be guilty of an unfair industrial practice if they fail to do so) they have an additional burden, for *any party* to a collective agreement will be guilty of an *unfair industrial practice* if he fails to take all steps as are *reasonably practicable* for the purpose:

(a) of preventing persons acting or purporting to act on behalf of that party from taking any action contrary to the undertaking given by that party contained in the collective agreement (or part thereof);

(b) where the party in question is an organisation, of preventing members of that organisation from taking any such action; or

(c) where any action has already been taken as mentioned in (a) or (b), of securing that the action is not continued and further similar action does not recur (IRA, s. 36).

One important point to bear in mind is that when a collective agreement is made in relation to terms and conditions of employment, e.g., a union agrees with an employer that the rates of wages shall go up to £10 per week, that is not at that stage an agreement of employment between the employer and his individual workmen, but if thereafter that agreement is kept and wages are paid at that rate, then a new contract of employment on those terms comes into effect. In other words, no individual employee is bound by terms and conditions until they are imported into his contract of employment. In the case, however, of procedure agreements, these relate to the machinery for negotiation between employers and organisations of workers, and these are not imported into the individual contracts of employment.

Breach of a collective agreement

It is necessary once a legally enforceable agreement has been established that any party to it must not only carry out its terms but must take *reasonably practicable* steps to ensure that, in the case of a trade union or other organisation of workers, the workers it represents, or in the case of employers' association or organisation, its members, do not act in breach of it (IRA, s. 36(2)(b)).

There are two distinct sets of duties on a party to the agreement, viz., (a) a duty to prevent anyone acting, or purporting to act, on its behalf from taking any action contrary to an undertaking given by that party and contained in the collective agreement, and if anyone is in the process of acting in breach of it to seek to prevent it, and (b) in the case of an organisation to ensure that its members do not act contrary to the terms of the agreement.

NOTE: Action taken by a person *other* than the party to the agreement will be regarded as contrary to the undertaking if it had been taken by a party to the agreement it would have been a breach of his undertaking, i.e., doing something that he promised he would not do, or not doing something that he promised he would do (IRA, s. 36(3)).

In the case of (a) there is a clear and positive duty on a trade union or organisation of workers to ensure that its officers and officials honour the terms of a binding collective agreement. This duty is discharged by taking *reasonably practicable* steps, and what is reasonably practicable must always be a question of fact depending upon the circumstances of each particular situation.

An important factor to bear in mind in this connection is the range of authority of trade union officials, with paid officers on the executive at one end and the shop stewards at the other end. It is clear that where a senior paid official of a trade union takes action which amounts to a breach of an agreement, the union will be liable, provided that he is acting within the scope of his authority, unless it took direct and immediate action to prevent the breach. In other words the act of a senior official will generally be the act of the union, but a union might mitigate its liability by the speed of its reaction. It may be necessary in order to curtail the activities of a senior official to resort to the final step of dismissing him. This last step may, however, prove to be difficult for most certainly he will have been elected to office by a voting process of either all the members of the union or their representatives.

In the case of a minor official, e.g., a shop steward taking action in breach of such an agreement, it is suggested that there is an inter-mediate stage before his action binds the union, and that the union will only be liable for his activities when it becomes aware of the activity and fails to take reasonable steps to prevent it. Once a union becomes aware of the "unlawful" activities of a minor official it must issue a clear instruction to that official that he must not pursue that course of action which is against the agreement, and if persuasion fails, it must seek to remove him from office. Again, removing even a minor official from office may be extremely difficult for the normal pattern, in the case of a shop steward, is for him to be elected by members of the local branch of the trade union, and usually he can only be removed from office by the election of a successor. Perhaps a more practical course would be for a senior official of the union to instruct workers in the particular undertaking that the shop steward is acting outside the scope of his authority. Withdrawal of the shop steward's membership may also be resorted to, which can in most cases by done by the union executive for misconduct. This last course would not be an infringement of the member's right to belong to the organisation (discussed later) for his conduct would justify the discrimination.

It must be emphasised that a trade union is not expected to achieve the impossible, but merely to take *reasonably practicable* steps, and when it has done all that can be expected to achieve compliance with the agreement it has discharged its duty.

A similar duty to that imposed on organisations of workers is also imposed on the employer, so that where a foreman or manager of a factory acts or seeks to act in breach of the agreement similar action must be taken by the employer to that of the union, to prevent the breach. Clearly in the case of the employer less difficulty will be experienced in terminating the authority of the offending "official".

The second main point to consider is in relation to (b), i.e., the duty of an organisation to ensure that its members honour the terms of a collective agreement. As already indicated the only part of a collective agreement which directly binds the individual worker is that part which becomes a part of his contract of employment, e.g., wage rates, so that a worker who simply fails to comply with any other parts of a collective agreement has no personal liability. Take as a practical example a procedure agreement which provides for redundancy on the basis of "last in first out". Owing to lack of orders the employer is obliged to invoke its terms, and terminates the employment of one man on that basis. The man happens to be a popular shop steward, and his working colleagues resent his employment being terminated. They feel that another man, who has been employed longer by a few days ought to go first, and make it clear that unless the services of the shop steward are retained and the other person chosen for dismissal they will not work overtime.

Assuming that the refusal to work overtime is not a breach of the individual workers' contracts of employment, and this depends upon the circumstances in each case, the workers will not be liable for refusing to honour the terms of the procedure agreement, but there is a duty upon the organisation to persuade the workers to accept the decision. If the organisation fails to take reasonable steps to persuade the workers to continue working normally the organisation is guilty of an unfair industrial practice.

Perhaps an even more practical example of what is expected of an organisation is to be seen in the following report in a newspaper in May, 1971: "Eighty maintenance men whose unofficial strike stopped all production in the .... car factory were instructed, through shop stewards by a member of the union executive council to return to work." This it is suggested is all that an organisation has to do to comply with the requirement of taking a reasonably practicable step. But it is again emphasised that it will be a question of fact in each particular case.

Again similar duties are imposed upon organisations of employers to ensure that their members comply with agreements collectively made. What are reasonably practicable steps in this case is much more difficult to define and would seem to be limited to persuasion and threat of expulsion from the organisation.

An important point to note is that it is a general rule that where any person induces or threatens to induce a breach of a collective agreement it will be an unfair industrial practice. An exception, however, to that general rule are trade unions and employers' associations, *provided* that *any breach* they *induce* or *threaten to induce* is *restricted to* that part of a collective agreement concerned with *the contract of employment* (IRA, s. 96).

Remedies for breach of a collective agreement

In the event of it being established that any party (trade union, organisation of workers, employer or organisation of employers) *but not individual workers* (IRA, s. 166), to a collective agreement is guilty of an unfair industrial practice, either because that party has broken the agreement or has failed to take reasonable steps to prevent it from being broken, the other party will be entitled to present a complaint against him in the Industrial Court (IRA, s. 36).

If the Industrial Court is satisfied that the complaint is well founded it may grant one or more of the following remedies:

(a) an order declaring the rights of the complainant and the respondent in relation to the act specified in the complaint;

(b) award compensation to the complainant against the respondent in respect of the act complained of;

(c) make an order directing the respondent to refrain from continuing the action complained of, and to refrain from taking any action of a like nature (IRA, s. 101(3)).

No court other than the Industrial Court may entertain (except on appeal) any proceedings brought by a party to a collective agreement against another party to it if the principal purpose of the proceedings is:

(a) to obtain a decision of the court on the construction or effect of the collective agreement, or

(b) to enforce the collective agreement or claim damages for breach of it (IRA, s. 129).

It must be noted that in the event of the Industrial Court making an order directing a respondent to refrain from certain action, and the order is disregarded, an action for contempt could be commenced as a last resort in the High Court against that party.

In addition to its general jurisdiction relating to collective agreements, the Industrial Court has a further jurisdiction. Any party to a collective agreement in writing, not containing a provision that it is not to be legally enforceable (i.e., a binding collective agreement) may apply to the Court for a declaration with respect to any question relating to any provisions of the agreement (IRA, s. 112(1)).

This provision is intended to enable the parties to any such agreements to get what amounts to an authoritative legal ruling on matters upon which no dispute has necessarily arisen, rather than having to wait for relations between the parties to deteriorate to a point of dispute where one of the remedies previously discussed would be sought.

Application to Industrial Court relating to Procedure Agreements

As has been indicated collective agreements are matters to be decided and agreed upon by employers and organisations of workers together, and *prima facie* cannot be imposed upon them by anyone else. However, collective agreements may be divided into two parts, viz., that which relates to pay and conditions of employment, and that which relates to a *procedure agreement*. And whilst it is true that an agreement on pay and conditions can never be imposed by an outside body, this is not strictly true of a procedure agreement.

The Act provides (IRA, ss. 37-43) that a procedure agreement can be imposed in certain circumstances by the Industrial Court. These provisions are intended to be used sparingly to deal with unusually intransigent situations in which the normal processes of industrial relations such as negotiation, conciliation and arbitration, etc., have proved unavailing.

The situations to which they apply are confined to those within a single firm or units of two or more closely associated employers which may consist of a "composite unit" of employers* who share the same procedural arrangements.

*"Composite Unit" means a unit which extends to two or more associated undertakings, and is comprised of the aggregate or part of the aggregate, of those undertakings. (And any reference to "employer" includes a composite unit.)

"Associated undertakings" means undertakings of two or more associated employers.

"Employers" means the employers to whose undertakings the unit extends. (IRA, s. 43(1)).

There must be in existence a problem where the development and maintenance of orderly industrial relations is being seriously impeded, or substantial amounts of working time being repeatedly lost, owing to the absence of agreed procedures or the existence of defective procedures, in the sense of agreements, the terms of which are being disregarded.

Where there is no procedure agreement in existence or where there is an agreement which is defective, an application may be made to the Industrial Court by the Secretary of State, or the employer (or by a composite unit) or by any *trade union* (not an unregistered organisation of workers) recognised by the employer as having negotiating rights in relation to his (or their) undertaking/s (IRA, s. 37).

Where a procedure agreement is in existence however, the only grounds upon which an application can be made are:

(a) that the agreement is unsuitable for settling disputes and grievances promptly and fairly, or

(b) that industrial action (in the form of a strike or lock-out, or other irregular industrial action short of a strike) is being taken in breach of it, i.e., contrary to the intentions expressed in the agreement.

It is suggested that any reference to a procedure agreement in this connection will include oral as well as written agreements but whilst breach of a written and binding agreement may give rise to an action in the Industrial Court for an unfair industrial practice, the only effect a breach of an oral and therefore (generally) non-binding agreement will have, is to restrict the right for a party to make an application to the reasons in (a) and (b). There is of course no such restriction when no agreement exists at all.

Whilst in general applications will be concerned with single firms and perhaps relatively small groups of associated employers, by including the composite unit common procedure agreements may be established over a wider area of industry. A composite unit comprises separate undertakings associated together through a common or overall employer, e.g., British Leyland Motor Company which comprises a large number of otherwise independent companies: Jaguar, Rover, Austin, etc. The reason why a composite unit is specially provided for is that it comprises in law a number of separate employers, i.e., each separate company is an individual employer, but in fact there is really only one employer, i.e., the holding company. Therefore, whilst each component company may have its own procedure agreements and may negotiate independently of the rest it might be thought desirable for the group management to be enabled to negotiate agreements extending to all their factories, thus establishing a common procedure agreement. So for that purpose, it would be treated as a single entity instead of a separate unit, but otherwise each unit will continue to be treated separately.

As the whole object of the Act is to improve industrial relations it is first necessary before the Secretary of State can make an application to the Industrial Court for him to consult the parties involved and try to bring about an amicable settlement of their differences. For this purpose he will use the services of his department and conciliators, and where appropriate, offer voluntary reference to the Commission on Industrial Relations (IRA, s. 37(3)).

Before an employer or trade union may make an application to the Court they must first consult the Secretary of State in order to give him the opportunity to mediate, and again for this purpose he may utilise the same resources as before including a voluntary reference to the Commission (IRA, s. 37(4)).

Only when it is satisfied that the Secretary of State has attempted to bring the parties together will the Industrial Court accept the application. If it then appears to the Court that there are reasonable grounds for believing that the undertaking to which the application relates suffers from one or both of the defects referred to as grounds for the application, and because of that defect—

    (a) the development or maintenance of orderly industrial relations in that undertaking has been *seriously* impeded, or

    (b) there have been substantial and repeated losses of working time in the undertaking,

the Court must refer the matter to the Commission (IRA, s. 37(5)), indicating any suggested remedy as to new or revised provisions that it thinks will improve the situation for the future (IRA, s. 40).

It is of course clear that what will amount to serious impedance and substantial and repeated losses of working time will always be matters of fact to be decided in the light of each set of circumstances, but it will obviously not include a minor dispute nor the odd short stoppage or two.

Action by the Commission on Receipt of Application

When the Commission receives the reference from the Industrial

Court it must of course consider it, and if it appears to the Commission that the undertaking (or that part of the undertaking) to which the application relates does suffer from the defect alleged it can take two courses of action. First, if it appears to the Commission that in order to remedy the defect there have to be new provisions or a revision of the existing provisions, but that they ought to be applied to a larger area of employment than the particular undertaking represents, it may, after consultation with the employer and any trade union likely to be affected, formulate proposals setting out the larger area to which it thinks the new or revised provisions should apply. Once the Commission has formulated those proposals it must send them to the Industrial Court, and at the same time seek to bring them to the attention of any person who in the opinion of the Commission would be affected by them by giving notice or publishing them in an appropriate manner.

From the time that these proposals have been published any person who claims to be affected has *two weeks* in which he may apply to the Industrial Court to consider the proposals, and the Industrial Court may either extend the scope of the reference in accordance with the proposals of the Commission or alternatively direct the Commission that the original reference remains unchanged, i.e., that the Commission should consider the reference in its original form.

If within two weeks, however, no such application is made to the Industrial Court, it must confirm the proposals from the Commission and extend the scope of the reference in accordance with them (IRA, s. 38).

Second, if the Commission does not think that the reference ought to be extended in the first place, or has received back its proposals from the Industrial Court in the modified form, as discussed above, it must, if it considers that new or revised provisions should be applied, decide what parties are to be the parties to any further proceedings on that reference.

These parties will be, parties to any existing procedure agreement which applies to the undertaking (or to the larger area to which the Commission has extended the reference) and any employers, employers' associations or trade unions, who would be appropriate parties to any new or revised provisions decided by the Commission.

Having decided these matters, the Commission must now promote and assist discussions between these parties with a view to obtaining a settlement on the new or revised proposals. So that when they are all agreed the proposals will be capable of having legal effect.

If during these discussions the Commission can be satisfied that the purposes for which the reference was originally made will be adequately fulfilled without continuing the proceedings, it must report to the Industrial Court, and the Court may then withdraw the reference upon the application of any of the parties to it (IRA, s. 39).

If the reference has not been withdrawn in this way, the Commission must at the end of these discussions make a report setting out such new or revised provisions, including any provisions upon which the parties have agreed, plus any additional one of its own, which would be capable of having effect as a legally enforceable contract.

This report must then be sent to the Industrial Court, and to each of the parties to the reference (IRA, s. 40).

At this stage this report does not bind the parties affected by it (unless they agree that it should be so) and they need not consider it further, but at any time within the six months following that report, *any* of the parties to it can apply to the Industrial Court for an order implementing the provisions of it, and unless the Court thinks it necessary, for the purpose of securing acceptance of the recommendations in the report, it must make an order defining the undertaking to which it will apply, and also the parties upon whom it will be binding; and directing that on and after a date specified in the order, and so long as it remains in force that its provisions shall have effect as a legally enforceable contract *as if a contract consisting of those provisions had been made between the parties* (IRA, s. 41).

This means, therefore, that the provisions relating to unfair industrial practices in relation to procedure agreements discussed on pp. 66-74 will apply.

In other words, once an order has been made in these terms it will be just as effective in relation to the parties concerned as though they had made the procedure agreement voluntarily and in writing in the first place. In effect, the Secretary of State and an employer or a trade union have a means whereby they can obtain a procedure agreement however reluctant the other party to the agreement might be.

Limitation on making further application to the Industrial Court

Where a report as discussed above has been submitted by the

Commission to the Industrial Court, whether or not any order was actually made by the Industrial Court, no further application can be made under these provisions for at least two years after the report was submitted to the Industrial Court, if it relates substantially to the same undertaking, unless the Court feels that there is a special reason before that time for an application to be made. But in those cases where an order is actually made in the circumstances just considered, all the parties can together make a joint application to the Industrial Court to revoke or vary the order, and the Court must revoke or vary the order. Further, even if only one of the parties applies to have the order revoked and the Court is satisfied the order is no longer necessary for the purpose of securing observance of the provisions, the Court must revoke it. Though before doing so it might ask the C.I.R. if it is satisfied that the provisions will in fact be complied with without the order being in operation (IRA, s. 42).

There is no inconsistency in the foregoing, i.e., whilst *no new application* may be made to the court under IRA, s. 37 for a procedure agreement for two years, it is permitted to apply at any time to have an order discharged when the order is made under IRA, s. 41.

SOLE BARGAINING AGENCY

In order to facilitate collective bargaining it is necessary for both workers and employers to appoint, or approve, representatives with authority to negotiate respectively on their behalf, and to make arrangements by which both sides will be bound. The first step in setting up a collective bargaining structure is to establish the various groups, or parties, who are going to negotiate with each other. Naturally these groups will represent either employees or employers and the Act recognises this in defining the respective terms of "organisation of workers" and "organisation of employers".

What arrangements are made between a particular employer (or employers) and their employees is a matter for agreement between them, and of course a wide variety of arrangements exist and work perfectly satisfactorily. An employer may recognise one or more trade unions as having the right to negotiate on behalf of his employees or for some of them, in relation to their terms and conditions of employment, for within a single factory there may be a wide variety of interests to be considered with employees being represented by different organisations, e.g., electricians by the

E.T.U., engineering workers by the A.U.E.W. and the clerical staff by an association formed among themselves.

The important thing is that the employer is able to recognise the individual groupings which can be thought of as separate units for collective bargaining purposes.

If the employer recognises the representatives, whether or not they are trade unions, as having the authority to negotiate and to make collective agreements on behalf of the members of the individual groups and these arrangements are operating satisfactorily, there is of course no problem. If, however, a dispute does arise as to who should be recognised as having the right to negotiate on behalf of the various workers in a factory or group of undertakings, or an employer refuses to recognise the representatives of his employees, the dispute has to be resolved in accordance with the provisions of the Act.

The provisions of the Act are concerned with establishing clearly identifiable groups with whom management can negotiate. Many of these groups are already identifiable because of long-standing arrangements, e.g., workers, both skilled and semi-skilled who undertake a number of different functions may be represented by a single trade union or different trade unions in an undertaking. Many workers have no representation at all at present and are not easily identifiable for the purposes of collective bargaining. The provisions of the Act therefore are first of all to establish a clearly identifiable group of workers on whose behalf negotiations may take place, and secondly to establish who shall represent the group of workers once identified.

The Act introduces a new term, "the *bargaining unit*" for the purpose of identifying groups of workers. A bargaining unit means "any employees or descriptions of employees of *one employer* or of two or more *associated employers* in relation to whom collective bargaining in relation to such matters is (or could appropriately be) carried on by an organisation of workers (or by a joint negotiating panel), but *not* if already dealt with under more extensive arrangements." (IRA, s. 44(a)).

"More extensive arrangements" means arrangements for collective bargaining in respect of matters common to different groups of employees, whether of the same employer or not (IRA, s. 44(f)).

In other words a bargaining unit is a group of workers who enjoy a sufficiently close similarity to each other so that they can be regarded as an identifiable group, e.g., because they have a similarity of trade or occupation, and upon whose behalf negotiations may be rationally carried on.

The overriding principles of a bargaining unit are:

(a) That they are all employed by either a single employer, or by an association of employers, so that there is a separate group of workers on the one hand, and a single employer or a single group of employers on the other hand. It is possible, therefore, that the bargaining unit may be restricted to a single factory or undertaking, or may be spread over a number of separate factories or undertakings, provided that in the latter case the employers belong to the same association for the purposes of negotiation. From this it will be seen that there may be a number of separate bargaining units recognised in a single factory.

(b) The second requirement is that the group must not already be provided for in relation to collective bargaining under a more extensive arrangement which includes themselves and other workers.

This provision as to more extensive bargaining arrangements is to obviate the possibility of "fragmentation" in collective bargaining organisation. This fear was expressed by trade unionists when the Act was being debated, for the Act as originally drafted did not include this proviso. This would have meant that small groups of workers, particularly if they played a vital role in an industrial process, could have utilised their separate identity to become a bargaining unit and to negotiate their terms and conditions of employment separately from the other workers of the same employer, possibly to the disadvantage of the latter and to trade union solidarity.

To illustrate the position an example may be taken of a car factory employing 40,000 workers, who are represented by 30 different trade unions, each union including in its membership one or more categories of employee. The unions may negotiate with the management collectively representing all the workers, or may in fact negotiate separately, representing only the workers who are members of that particular union.

Assuming that all the unions negotiate separately and that one union represents all the workers engaged in trimming, painting and final testing of finished motor cars, that group could claim to be regarded as a bargaining unit, but if the unions adopted the more extensive arrangement in that they negotiated collectively, then none of them could claim to be separate bargaining units.

Similarly if the workers engaged in the painting shop were to seek to be recognised as a bargaining unit they would fail whether their union negotiated as a single entity or collectively with the other unions.

If, however, the clerical staff, for example, were not represented in matters of negotiation, they could identify themselves as a separate workers' organisation and claim to be recognised as a bargaining unit.

The provision as to more extensive arrangements also envisages a situation where the collective bargaining set-up covers more than one employer at the same time. For example, there may be a confederation of employers in a particular industry who negotiate collectively with representatives of organisations of workers in their respective employments, so that any individual employees who wish to become a bargaining unit and separate from the rest could not be so recognised if their bargaining arrangements were catered for in the larger pattern.

It is suggested that where an agency shop is in existence, and certainly where there is an approved closed shop, the risk of "fragmentation" is extremely unlikely, for in most cases employees in such undertakings will fall within the provisions of more extensive arrangements.

The more "national" the arrangements are for bargaining, e.g., a confederation of employers with one or more unions (acting collectively), the more unlikely it will be for smaller groups to be recognised as bargaining units (provided always that the interests of the members can be adequately protected by the more extensive arrangements).

Even where it can be established that a group of workers may be classified as a bargaining unit within the definition, it will still be necessary to establish who will be recognised as having the right to represent the group in negotiation. This right to represent the bargaining unit is defined by the Act as "negotiating rights", and this means rights recognised by an employer or by two or more associated employers to negotiate on behalf of all or some of the employees comprised in a bargaining unit, in relation to making or modifying collective agreements (IRA, s. 44(b)).

These negotiating rights might be possessed by individuals,

elected by the workers on a local basis within an undertaking, or may be possessed by a trade union or other organisation of workers on a much wider, perhaps even on a national basis. It is necessary for there to be one spokesman, so to speak, acting on behalf of a bargaining unit, and the Act provides for a "sole bargaining agent"; which means the organisation of workers or joint negotiating panel having exclusive negotiating rights in relation to a particular bargaining unit or units (IRA, s. 44(c)).

The expression joint negotiating panel means a body of representatives of two or more workers' organisations which is established for the purpose of collective bargaining, and is authorised to make arrangements on behalf of the members of those organisations (IRA, s. 44(d)).

In other words there are a number of persons or organisations who individually represent a single bargaining unit or units who together form a panel, the panel acting as single negotiating body in the interests of all the members of the separate organisations. In very many cases, possibly the majority, joint negotiating panels will be comprised only of trade unions, and where this is so these particular joint negotiating panels are referred to as joint negotiating panels of trade unions (IRA, s. 44(e)).

It may be noted; firstly that a single trade union may be the sole bargaining agent for a large number of separate bargaining units under different unconnected employers, and secondly there may be a number of separate bargaining units under the same employer each represented by a different sole bargaining agent.

From what we have said it is clearly possible that the establishment of bargaining units and the recognition of negotiating rights is a matter of agreement between employers and their employees.

Where, however, an agreement cannot be reached between the respective parties first as to who shall be included in a bargaining unit, or who should have the sole bargaining right for a unit, or where arrangements already exist and a group seeks to break away and form a separate negotiating body, i.e., a separate bargaining unit, it may be necessary for an application to be made to the Industrial Court to resolve the problem. Perhaps it will be appreciated that where matters of dispute arise as to whether a group is a bargaining unit within the definition, or ought to be recognised separately from a more extensive arrangement the final arbiter will be the Industrial Court.

Application for recognition of a Bargaining Unit and a Sole Bargaining Agent

When the question arises as to whether there should be a separate bargaining unit and, if so, whether there should be a sole bargaining agent for that unit, and no agreement can be reached between employers and employees as to their establishment, an application can be made to the Industrial Court for reference to the Commission of the following two questions relating to the employees of one employer or of two or more associated employers;

(a)   whether a specified group of those employees should as a whole, be recognised (or, if already recognised, should continue to be recognised) by the employer or employers as a *bargaining unit;* and

(b)   whether, for any bargaining unit which is or should be so recognised, a sole bargaining agent should be recognised by the employer or employers, and if so what organisation of workers or joint negotiating panel should be the sole bargaining agent for that unit (IRA, s. 45(1)).

The application can be made to the Industrial Court by:

(a)   one or more trade unions, or

(b)   the employer (or associated employers), or

(c)   the employer (or employers) jointly with one or more trade unions, or

(d)   the Secretary of State (IRA, s. 45(2)).

Before this application may be made to the Court, however, notice of intention to make it must be given by the party to the Secretary of State, who must seek to achieve an agreement between the parties by utilising any means that appear to him appropriate, including the reference of any relevant matter to the Commission. The Secretary of State will undoubtedly draw heavily upon the services of the Department of Employment, to assist in conciliation (IRA, s. 45(4)(a)). In any event once notice of intention to apply to the Court has been given to the Secretary of State, the party giving it does not in fact have to wait for the Secretary of State to conciliate, he can go ahead with the application (IRA, s. 45(4)(b)). But see IRA, s. 46(1), (2) and below para. (c).

If the Secretary of State wishes to make an application in his own right with respect to a particular group of employees, he must first consult the employer, or employers, and any organisations of workers, or joint negotiating panel appearing to him to be directly concerned in the matter to which the proposed application would relate (IRA, s. 45(3)).

Applications under these provisions have in effect two objectives; first to establish which particular employees shall form a bargaining unit, and the applicant will of course indicate in the application who they should be; and second to establish who should be the sole bargaining agent for that unit.

It may be necessary for an application to be made under this provision in cases where no bargaining unit has been recognised at all, or where a bargaining unit has been recognised by an employer or employers, and members of the same bargaining unit are represented by different trade unions, and the unions, or the various members, cannot agree as to which one shall represent them in negotiations.

Effectively one or more of the trade unions making the application seeks, or seek, to become the sole bargaining agent for that unit, and the expression sole bargaining agent may describe an individual trade union or a panel of trade unions collectively representing the various members of a bargaining unit.

Action by the Industrial Court on receipt of application

Once the Industrial Court has accepted an application under these provisions it must refer the question to the Commission for a report, if it is satisfied that reference of those questions to the Commission is necessary with a view to promoting a satisfactory and lasting settlement by them (IRA, s. 46); unless:

(a) a substantially similar application has been made in the last two years affecting basically the same parties, and that it would not be justified in shortening that time limit (IRA, s. 46(2));

(b) there has been a ballot within the last two years as to the withdrawal of a sole bargaining agent under IRA, s. 53(5) (p. 89);

(c) the applicant (viz., either employer/s or the organisation of workers) has not endeavoured to settle the dispute by utilising the conciliation facilities available (IRA, s. 46(1), (2)).

Function of the Commission in bargaining agency questions

After the application has been referred to the Commission and it appears to the Commission that the parties have already settled their differences it will inform the Industrial Court, who will then with-draw the matter. If however, the parties have not settled their differences the Commission must proceed to investigate the matters referred to it, and the first thing which may occur to the Commission is that in order to obtain a satisfactory and lasting settlement it will be necessary to widen the scope of the reference, but in any event, it cannot extend the scope beyond the employer named in the original application except to an associated employer (IRA, s. 47(3)).

In the event of extending the scope of the reference the Com-mission must inform the Industrial Court and cause notice of these proposals to be given or published to inform any parties who will be affected by the Commission's proposals to extend the scope (IRA, s. 47(2)).

Once these proposals for widening the scope of investigation have been published, any person who would be affected by them may apply to the Industrial Court within two weeks to consider whether in fact these proposals of the Commission are necessary or expedient. If such application is made to the Industrial Court it has three alternatives, viz.,

(a)   to allow the extension as proposed by the Commission, or

(b)   to allow a more limited extension than the Commission proposes, or

(c)   to direct that the scope remain the same as originally intended by the applicant (IRA, s. 47(4)).

If no such application is made to the Industrial Court within the two weeks allowed then the Commission's proposals to extend the reference must be confirmed (IRA, s. 47(5)).

The Commission must now proceed to investigate the application:

(a)   as extended by itself, or

(b)   as modified by the Industrial Court, or

(c)   as originally submitted.

Clearly the investigation must be concerned with the matters in the application, and in order to complete it the Commission may examine the evidence and inform itself as to the best possible way of resolving the dispute.

When the investigation has been completed the Commission must draw up a report setting out its recommendations for resolving the dispute. Copies of this report must be sent to the Secretary of State, employers affected by the recommendations and to every trade union or organisation of workers appearing to the Commission to be directly concerned in the question specified in the reference.

The report must also be published in such manner as the Commission considers appropriate (IRA, s. 48).

The recommendations of the Commission will be concerned with two things, viz., who will be included in the bargaining unit and who will be the sole bargaining agent.

The Commission may recommend that an organisation of workers (or joint negotiating panel) should be the sole bargaining agent whether such organisation is registered as a trade union or not. The Commission must be satisfied that such recommendation would be in accordance with the general wishes of the employees to be included in the bargaining unit. Also that the acceptance of the recommendation will promote a satisfactory and lasting settlement of the question in reference.

Any recommendations by the Commission may be subject to conditions, and in particular it may require the organisation of workers recommended as sole bargaining agents to make sufficient trained officials available for the purposes of conciliation and bargaining, before such organisation can be finally accepted as sole bargaining agent. Further it may require the organisation to give an undertaking that it will not make an application to become recognised as sole bargaining agent for any other bargaining unit of the same employer (IRA, s. 48(4)-(7)). Additionally where there are "more extensive bargaining arrangements" in existence in relation to the employees comprised in the bargaining unit, the Commission may recommend such bargaining arrangements in place of any other agent, in respect of any matters dealt with under such specified arrangements (IRA, s. 48(8)).

Although the Commission has made a recommendation under these provisions as to which employees will form a bargaining unit, and who will be its sole bargaining agent (unless it is accepted by all the parties concerned) it does not become operative until a ballot has been taken among the employees affected (IRA, s. 49).

Ballot before recommendation can become binding

In order to have a ballot an application must be made by either the employer (or if more than one, any of the employers), or by a trade union (or joint negotiating panel of trade unions) to the

Industrial Court within *six* months from the time when the report of the Commission was submitted to the Industrial Court.

Upon the receipt of the application (provided that it is satisfied that any conditions imposed by the Commission in its recommendations have been complied with) the Court must forward the application to the Commission.

If the Commission is satisfied that sufficient time has elapsed since it published its report, recommending the bargaining unit and its sole bargaining agent, for persons to study the recommendations and its possible effects, then it must arrange for a ballot to be taken

The ballot, which must be secret, will be taken among the persons recommended to comprise the bargaining unit, and will be undertaken either by the Commission itself or by someone acting on its behalf, the result being forwarded to the Industrial Court and to the employer and the trade union (or joint negotiating panel of trade unions) (IRA, s. 49).

The result of the ballot will be decided on the majority *actually voting* (i.e., persons who do not actually vote are in no way counted). If the majority vote in favour of the proposal that the recommendation be made binding, then the Industrial Court must make an order defining the bargaining unit and specifying the employer/s and trade union (or joint negotiating panel of trade unions) which is to be the sole bargaining agent.

The order will become effective at the end of two months from when it was made and will continue in force until the organisation to which it refers ceases to be a trade union (or joint negotiating panel of trade unions), or the recognition as sole bargaining agent is withdrawn in the manner discussed under the next heading (IRA, s. 50).

It should be noted that whilst the Commission may recommend an unregistered organisation of workers (or joint negotiating panel) to be a sole bargaining agent only a trade union (or joint negotiating panel of trade unions) may apply to have the recommendation implemented, and that in any case an order of the Industrial Court after a ballot will specify a trade union (or joint negotiating panel of trade unions) as sole bargaining agent. This means that where the Commission investigates a reference made to it and it decides to recommend an unregistered organisation of workers, such organisation will have to register (and become a trade union) during the six months within which (and before) it can apply for a ballot to become the sole bargaining agent.

Withdrawal of recognition as sole bargaining agent

Once a sole bargaining agent has been recognised by one or more employers, whether by agreement with the employers, or under an order of the Industrial Court, it does not mean that there can be no change in the position, for the Act provides (IRA, s. 51) that the recognition may be withdrawn subject to certain conditions being satisfied.

First it is necessary that an employee who is a member of the particular bargaining unit should make application to the Industrial Court on the ground that the organisation of workers (or joint negotiating panel) does not adequately represent the employees in that unit, or a particular section of it to which the applicant belongs.

Secondly, whilst the application may be made at any time after recognition (in cases of agreement with the employer) at least *one-fifth* of the workers affected must have agreed in writing that the application should be made.

Where the sole bargaining agent has been implemented by order of the Industrial Court, no application can be made for at least two years from the making of that order, and at least *two-fifths* of the employees comprised in that bargaining unit, must agree in writing.

NOTE: The proportion is two-fifths where the sole bargaining agent was established by order of the Court, but one-fifth in other cases.

Upon receipt of the application the Industrial Court must submit it to the Commission for examination and possible settlement without withdrawal of the sole bargaining agency, and for the purpose of arriving at a settlement the Industrial Court must set a time limit. If at the end of that time no settlement has been reached the Industrial Court must ask the Commission to arrange for a ballot to be taken among all the employees contained in the bargaining unit, or among a limited number of the employees at the discretion of the Commission. The Commission may recommend one or more ballots depending upon whether it thinks that because of the nature of different jobs or trades etc., that workers ought to be divided into sections for this purpose.

This ballot when taken must be secret, and will be conducted by the Commission itself or by some other body under its supervision (IRA, s. 52).

The result of the ballot will be decided by a simple majority of persons *actually voting* (IRA, s. 53). Its effect will be either to confirm that the organisation of workers (or joint negotiating panel) shall continue to act as sole bargaining agent for the bargaining unit, or that it will not (or where there is more than one ballot the decision of each group will be determined separately).

Once the result has been ascertained the Commission must notify the Industrial Court, the employer and the organisation of workers (or joint negotiating panel). Where the result of the ballot is that the sole bargaining agency should cease, the Industrial Court must make an order directing the employer that he must no longer recognise that organisation of workers (or joint negotiating panel) as sole bargaining agent for that bargaining unit, for at least two years. The order will become effective and binding upon the employer two months after the date upon which the order was made (IRA, s. 53(4)).

Where the Industrial Court has made an order that the organisation of workers (or joint negotiating panel) should cease to be the sole bargaining agent for a bargaining unit, no application can be made by that organisation of workers (or joint negotiating panel) in respect of the same workers (i.e., the same bargaining unit) to which that order related for a period of at least two years (IRA, s. 53(2)(b)). There is of course no reason why some other trade union or joint negotiating panel who claim to represent the workers should not make an application within that time.

If on the other hand the result of the ballot is that the sole bargaining unit should continue, again no further application may be made for at least two years from the date when the result of the ballot was notified to the Industrial Court (IRA, s. 53(5)).

Unfair industrial practices in connection with questions as to recognition of sole bargaining agent and collective bargaining procedures

The essential purpose of this Act is to maintain and improve industrial harmony, and if applications are to be made to the Industrial Court, it is necessary that whilst those applications are being considered the *status quo* should where possible be maintained until the final disposal of the application. In other words industrial action should not be allowed to influence or distort an impartial and independent enquiry, nor intimidate applicants to the Court. The Industrial Relations Act has therefore provided that in connection with collective bargaining procedures, as in relation to other matters, that certain practices shall be deemed to be unfair. These unfair practices may be considered under two main headings.

1. WHERE APPLICATION FOR RECOGNITION AS SOLE BARGAINING AGENT HAS BEEN MADE TO THE INDUSTRIAL COURT

Once notice has been given to the Secretary of State of the intention to apply for recognition of a bargaining unit and sole bargaining agent it is said to be *pending* until it has been certified by the Secretary of State, either, that an agreement has been reached by the parties involved, or it has become apparent for whatever reason that no agreement is likely to be reached without an application to the Industrial Court (IRA, s. 54(1), (3)).

Where an application has actually been made to the Industrial Court for recognition of a bargaining unit and sole bargaining agent where none exists, or for withdrawal of recognition of sole bargaining agent where one does exist, it is said to be *pending*:

(a) until a decision has been made by the Industrial Court that it cannot (for the reasons given above) refer the matter to the Commission;

(b) where any application has been referred to the Industrial Court but has been withdrawn;

(c) until six months have elapsed from the date that the Commission submitted a report to the Industrial Court on such reference (IRA, s. 54(2)).

At any time during which a question is pending under these provisions it shall be an unfair industrial practice:

(a) for any employer *directly* concerned in a dispute relating to that question to institute, carry on, organise, procure or finance a lock-out in furtherance of that dispute or threaten to do so, or

(b) for any person (including any trade union or other organisation of workers or any official of a trade union or such organisation) to call, organise, procure or finance a strike, or organise, procure or finance any irregular industrial action short of a strike, in furtherance of such a dispute, or threaten to do so (IRA, s. 54(4)). (Apparently whether that person is directly concerned in the dispute or not.)

This means that where no voluntary agreement can be reached between an employer and one or more trade unions as to who shall be included in a bargaining unit, and who shall be the recognised sole bargaining agent, and either an application has been made to the Industrial Court to resolve the matter or that notice of intention to apply to the Industrial Court has been given to the Secretary of State, that a dispute exists. Then for the period of time indicated above the employer must not seek to pre-empt the outcome of the application by influencing the parties making application, or the workers to be affected by a subsequent agreement, by actually locking out workers, or in any other way organising or procuring a lock-out either of his own workers or workers of any other employer, not necessarily involved in the dispute. If he does so, he will be guilty of an unfair industrial practice. Similarly, he will be guilty of an unfair industrial practice if he merely threatens to do any of these things, or if he finances or threatens to finance such action.

Whilst it is not absolutely clear what the expression financing includes, it will obviously include *direct* financial assistance given to other employers to induce them to lock out their workers, and presumably it will include financial assistance given by an association of which he is a member to another employer. It will certainly be the case if he continues to make financial contributions to the association after assistance has been given with his knowledge to an employer who in some way is helping to further his particular dispute.

Even though no application has in fact been made to the Industrial Court by a trade union or other employer, an employer will be guilty of an unfair industrial practice if he seeks by such an action or threatens knowingly to prevent an application from being made either for recognition of a sole bargaining agent or the withdrawal of a sole bargaining agency (IRA, s. 55(8)).

Any other person, including trade unions, etc., is equally guilty of an unfair industrial practice if he resorts to industrial action or threatens to do so in order to influence the situation, either to pre-empt the outcome (IRA, s. 54(4)(b)) or knowingly to induce an employer not to comply with an order if made (IRA, s. 55(7)).

It has already been observed that the expression "any person" includes trade unions and other organisations of workers, including officials of either, and the question is how to distinguish between a trade union and its officials. First it is important to remember that a trade union has corporate status (IRA, s. 74) and can be personally liable, but that it can act only through its human agents, i.e., its officials. The first problem is to divide officials into two categories, viz., those who can bind the trade union, and those who cannot bind the trade union. For the trade union is liable for the action of the former, but not the latter. The problem may not be so acute as it appears for trade unions are all registered and a list of its governing body, responsible officers and officials will be deposited with the registrar, and it will be for the acts of these individuals for which the union will be responsible, but not for those of the others. In other words, in the event of compensation becoming payable because of an unfair industrial practice, the trade union funds will be available for the activities of its registered governors, officers and responsible officials, but not for the rest who will of course bear their own liability as will ordinary persons, unless the trade union ratifies, i.e., adopts the action of its minor officials (IRA, s. 101(4)).

The problem of liability of the organisation of workers may not be so easy to solve, for as they are not registered there is no requirement to submit to the registrar a list of officers, etc., as in the case of a trade union, and there may be no such list available. If the latter be the case, the ordinary rules of common law will have to be applied, i.e., as it has been applied to companies in the past. In this connection various tests have been formulated to decide whether a company should be liable for the activities of its servants ostensibly acting on its behalf, e.g., to consider whether a servant was "important" in the hierarchy, or whether he was entitled to act without referring first to a superior, or whether he could be regarded as part of the brain of the company. If these tests are applied it will always be a matter of conjecture as to the possible liability of an organisation for acts done ostensibly on its behalf. Whilst it appears that under the provisions of the Act an individual, by implication, will always be personally liable when acting on behalf of an unregistered organisation (IRA, s. 101(4)) the organisation will only be liable for acts of an official done within the scope of his authority.

Again the problem must be considered, of what is meant by "financing" a strike, etc. It is clear that direct financial assistance is included as in the case of an employer, and where a trade union or an organisation of workers allots funds directly to support individuals participating in strike activity, or "lends" funds to fellow unions or organisations of workers who are so engaged, there will be no doubt that it is financing as envisaged by the Act. The position of other persons is not so clear. Obviously, in their case too direct assistance is included in the term, but what of the situation where an organisation to which an individual belongs gives financial help, can he be said to be financing, merely because his past subscriptions have been used for this purpose? The answer in this case must be an emphatic, No!, but if current subscriptions are being used to *the knowledge* of the subscriber to give financial assistance then *the answer appears* to be yes. If current subscriptions are being used to give assistance without the knowledge of the subscriber, then it is suggested he cannot be regarded as financing:

2. WHERE AN ORDER OF THE INDUSTRIAL COURT REQUIRES AN EMPLOYER TO RECOGNISE A TRADE UNION OR JOINT NEGOTIATING PANEL OF TRADE UNIONS AS SOLE BARGAINING AGENT

Where an order has been made by the Industrial Court (under IRA, s. 50) that a particular trade union or joint negotiating panel of trade unions is to be the sole bargaining agent for a bargaining unit, it will be an unfair industrial practice so long as that order remains in force for—

(a) An Employer:

(i)   to carry on any collective bargaining with any organisation of workers, other than the one named in the order. (Except that where the sole bargaining agent is a joint negotiating panel of trade unions he may agree with the panel to negotiate with only one of their number) or

(ii) to fail to take any action with a view to carrying on collective bargaining with the sole bargaining agent which might be reasonably expected to be taken by an employer who is ready and willing to carry on such collective bargaining properly (IRA, s. 55(1)).

Here then are two requirements which the employer must comply with if he is not to infringe the provisions of the Act: the first, requires the employer to negotiate only with the approved sole bargaining agent, and no other, except that where the sole bargaining agent is a joint negotiating panel of trade unions, such panel may appoint one of its number to carry on all negotiations with that particular employer if he is prepared to accept it. The second provision requires an employer to act in a responsible and reasonable manner in regard to carrying on collective bargaining, and this would include making arrangements for doing so even during working hours if this was thought to be reasonable in the circumstances. But in any event the employer must show that he has a serious intention of making the collective bargaining provisions work.

What are reasonable steps must be judged in subjective terms, but it is suggested that common sense will be an important element in judging what is, or is not, reasonable. Furthermore, the code of practice will give an indication as to the sort of steps an employer might be expected to take in any given situation.

(b) Any person (including a trade union or other organisation of workers, or officials of either) will also be guilty of an unfair industrial practice if he seeks to induce or attempt to induce an employer not to comply with the requirements as outlined above in paras. (i) and (ii) under employer, by—

    (i) calling, organising, procuring or financing a strike, or threatening to do so, or

    (ii) by organising, procuring or financing any irregular industrial activity or threatening to do so.

It will be seen that *any person* who seeks to upset the structure of collective bargaining as established in any particular case by order of the Industrial Court is in the same position as an employer who seeks to do the same thing, except that in the case of any person, not an employer, there is no duty to act positively in a reasonable way to make the procedure work.

The same points made on p. 37 as to the interpretation of the words calling, etc., apply also here. One further comment however, is that any person is liable merely for *calling* or threatening to *call* a strike even though unsuccessful, but there is no liability for *calling* or threatening to *call* for any industrial activity short of a strike. So that it would appear to call unsuccessfully for irregular industrial action short of a strike, or to threaten to do so would not infringe the provisions of the Act. Though how to distinguish between procuring and calling is somewhat difficult.

It is equally an unfair industrial practice for any person knowingly to induce or attempt to induce (by taking or threatening to take industrial action as described) an employer to recognise as a sole bargaining agent for a bargaining unit any organisation of workers who were unsuccessful in an application to the Industrial Court for its recognition as a sole bargaining agent, for two years from the date that the Commission submitted its report to the Industrial Court recommending its non-recognition (IRA, s. 56(6)).

This does not of course mean that such person cannot use ordinary persuasion to induce an employer to accept such trade union, etc., as a sole bargaining agent, but that he must not use industrial action or threats. The distinction between ordinary persuasion and threats may in some cases be difficult to draw. It is suggested that mere forceful language even if at times immoderate would not amount to threats, unless there was a positive declaration that some industrial action might follow an unsuccessful attempt at persuasion.

Finally, where an order has been in existence requiring an employer to recognise a sole bargaining agent, but a further order of the Industrial Court has withdrawn these sole negotiating rights, then again, it will be an unfair industrial practice for any person to conduct himself as described above in order knowingly to induce or attempt to induce the employer to whom the order relates not to comply with the withdrawal order. In other words to seek to induce an employer to continue to negotiate with the sole bargaining agent whose authority to act as such has been withdrawn (IRA, s. 55(7)).

Review of ballots (Collective Bargaining Arrangements)

Where any ballot has been taken either by the Commission or by some body on its behalf for any of the purposes of collective bargaining arrangements, and it is found by the Industrial Court,

- (i) that the report made to the Commission as a result of the ballot was incorrect, or
- (ii) that the ballot was so misconducted that it would not be just and equitable to regard it as valid,

the Industrial Court may act as follows,

- (a) if it thinks it just and equitable to do so make an order rectifying the error so that the report will operate as amended;
- (b) where it would not be just and equitable to rectify a report to quash the ballot, and so much of the report as relates to the result of the ballot, and if any order has already been made as a consequence of the report revoke that order. (The effect of this will be the same as if the ballot had never been taken.) (IRA, s. 160.)

DUTY OF EMPLOYERS TO DISCLOSE INFORMATION

It has often been the complaint of trade union negotiators and others that there has been a reluctance on the part of employers to give detailed information about their undertakings, in order that rational wage structures and working conditions may be negotiated, and that they have gone to the negotiating table frequently ill-prepared through lack of information which they thought they were entitled to have about the undertaking. The Act seeks so far as it is possible within the context of sound commercial principles to put that matter right, for it imposes two separate duties on an employer to disclose information in relation to his undertaking.

A General Duty of Disclosure

For the purpose of collective bargaining between *employers* and *trade union representatives** (viz., officials of a trade union or any person authorised by or on behalf of a trade union to carry on the collective bargaining in question in relation to workers that the union represents) it shall be the duty of the employer to disclose to those representatives all such information in relation to his under-taking as is in his possession, or in the possession of an associated employer. Provided always that the information is both necessary to ensure that collective bargaining would not to a material extent be impeded without it, and it is information which should in accordance with good industrial relations practice, be disclosed for the purposes of collective bargaining (the information must be in writing or confirmed in writing if the representative so requests) (IRA, s. 56).

The Act does not indicate the sort of information that might be expected to be disclosed, but the code of industrial practice lays down the guide lines as to what might be thought reasonable to disclose. It is clear that there is a certain amount of subjectivity in what is reasonable, and the code merely lays down the minimum standard of disclosure, and where there are certain practices which are normally accepted in a particular industry or undertaking, these will take precedence over the provisions of the code.

It is clear that some safeguards are necessary as to the requirement to disclose information, even though the requirement is to disclose only to a trade union or approved trade union representative, consequently the employer shall *not* be required:

*"Trade union representative" means any trade union official, or other person who is authorised by or on behalf of a trade union to carry on collective bargaining and in both cases represent the worker (or some of the workers) in collective bargaining (IRA, s. 56(5)).

(a) to allow inspection of any documents other than those
     specifically prepared for giving the information referred to
     above nor to make a copy or extract of other documents
     (IRA, s. 56(4)(a));
(b) to involve himself in any expense or work to produce informa-
     tion which it is unreasonable to expect in relation to its value
     in the conduct of collective bargaining (IRA, s. 56(4)(b));
(c) to disclose any information the disclosure of which would be
     against national security (IRA, s. 158(1)(a));
(d) to disclose information which he is prohibited by statute from
     disclosing (IRA, s. 158(1)(b));
(e) to disclose information communicated to him in confidence,
     or as a result of a confidential relationship (IRA, s. 158(1)(c));
(f) to disclose information relating specifically to an individual,
     unless that individual first consents (IRA, s. 158(1)(d));
(g) to disclose any information, the disclosure of which would be
     seriously prejudicial to the interests of the undertaking (for
     reasons other than its effect on collective bargaining) (IRA,
     s. 158(1)(e)), e.g., trade secrets and information which
     would be beneficial to a competitor, in particular details of
     contracts in the process of negotiation;
(h) any information obtained for the purpose of bringing,
     prosecuting or defending any legal proceeding (IRA, s.
     158(1)(f)).

In the event of an employer refusing or failing to disclose to officials
or other representatives of the trade union information which he is
required by the preceding provisions to disclose, a complaint may
be presented to the Industrial Court by the trade union. If the
Court finds that the grounds of complaint are well founded it may,
if it considers it would be just and equitable to do so, make one or
more of the following orders—

(a) an order determining the rights of the trade union and of the
     employer in relation to the matters in the complaint;
(b) an order directing the employer to carry out his duty as
     within his power it is possible for him to do;
(c) an order authorising the presentation of a claim by the trade
     union to the Industrial Arbitration Board.

If the trade union wish to present such a claim to the Industrial
Arbitration Board they must do so in writing (IRA, s. 126).

The Board may make an order requiring as from a date to be specified in the award that the requirement to disclose the information shall be a term of the contract of each individual employee represented by that trade union in that particular collective bargaining arrangement.

The date from which the award is to operate must be specified, and that date can even be that on which the employer first refused to disclose.

Such an award means that if the employer refuses or fails to disclose in the future he is in breach of each individual employee's contract of employment (IRA, s. 127).

Duty of major employers to disclose information

In addition to and quite separate from the duty to disclose information under the preceding heading, there is a specific duty imposed by the Act (IRA, s. 57), on all employers who employ 350l or more persons (not including excepted persons) to issue annua statements in writing, containing information about the undertaking in accordance with regulations made by the Secretary of State, to every employee, excluding the following (IRA, s. 57(9)):

(a) persons who normally work for less than 21 hours weekly;

(b) persons who on the date of issue of the annual statement have not been employed for at least 13 weeks;

(c) any person who on the date of issue of the annual statement is outside Great Britain and who under his contract of employment ordinarily works outside Great Britain.

The Secretary of State may by regulation exempt employers from this requirement where he considers it expedient to do so, such exemption applying:

(a) to employers of a prescribed description;

(b) to matters of a prescribed description;

(c) to employers of a prescribed description in respect of matters of a prescribed description;

(d) to one or more particular employers, in respect of certain matters specified in the regulations (IRA, s. 57(5)).

Further, by order, the Secretary of State can increase or decrease the relevant number of employees, viz., 350 (IRA, s. 57(7)).

For this provision to apply, 350 workers (other than excepted workers) must all be employed together on at least one date in each financial year of the undertaking. And the annual statement must be

issued not later than six months after the end of the financial year
to which it relates (IRA, s. 57(1), (2)).

The giving of this information to employees is intended to give
them a feeling of involvement in the undertaking and to create a
feeling of personal importance, quite apart from the practical value
of keeping the employees informed of the undertaking's viability and
its record of success, or failure, in world markets. Again there must
be safeguards as to what information it shall be necessary to disclose,
and whilst regulations made by the Secretary of State will indicate
what matters are to be included, an employer cannot even by
regulation be required,

    (a) to disclose information, the disclosure of which would be
against national security (IRA, s. 158(1)(a));

    (b) to disclose information which he is prohibited by statute
from disclosing (IRA, s. 158(1)(b));

    (c) to disclose any information communicated to him in con-
fidence, or as a result of a confidential relationship (IRA,
s. 158(1)(c));

    (d) to disclose any information relating specifically to an
individual, unless that individual first consents (IRA, s.
158(1)(d));

    (e) to disclose information, the disclosure of which would be
seriously prejudicial to the interests of the undertaking (for
reasons other than its effects on collective bargaining)
(IRA, s. 158(1)(e)), e.g., trade secrets and information
which could be beneficial to a competitor, in particular
details of contracts in the process of negotiation;

    (f) any information obtained for the purpose of bringing,
prosecuting or defending any legal proceedings (IRA, s.
158(1)(f)).

NOTIFICATION OF PROCEDURE AGREEMENTS

From what has been said it will be clear that in many undertakings
there will be no procedure agreements at all whilst in others there
may be a number of such agreements varying widely in character and
efficacy, but the aim of the Act, is to seek by the process of negotiation, and if that fails by compulsion, the establishment of a rational
and viable system whereby both workers and employers can work
harmoniously together.

To ensure that, whilst procedure agreements may vary widely, there is at least a central authority, the Secretary of State, who has a comprehensive knowledge of the existence and acceptance of these agreements. The Secretary of State may make regulations requiring every employer named in them to give him the following information:

(a) whether he is a party to a procedure agreement, or whether he has agreed with any of his employees to observe the terms of any procedure agreement to which he is not a party;

(b) where he is a party to any procedure agreement to furnish the Secretary of State with a copy of it, if it is in writing, or to give particulars of it if it is not in writing;

(c) where he has agreed with his employees to observe the terms of a procedure agreement although he is not a party to it, he must give to the Secretary of State a copy of it if it is in writing, or if the Secretary of State has already been supplied with a copy from some other source, then it is sufficient if the employer merely identifies it. If the agreement is not in writing the employer must merely supply particulars of it;

(d) the descriptions and numbers of all his employees who fall within the terms of any procedure agreement of which he is required to give notice as above, and the description of any employees who are not included;

(e) any other information which the Secretary of State requires in connection with these procedure agreements.

These regulations may specify a maximum period within which this information is to be supplied, though in no case will it be less that six months from the date when the regulations affecting a particular employer become operative. The regulations may also exempt any employers from these requirements where they are already voluntarily supplying the necessary information under some other arrangement (IRA, s. 58).

Offences in connection with the Notification of Procedure Agreements

Any person who is required to supply the information referred to under the preceding paragraphs but fails to do so within the time limits laid down in the regulations will be guilty of an offence and liable on summary conviction to a maximum fine of £100. Any person who:

(a) in furnishing these particulars, makes any statement which he knows to be false, in a material particular, or recklessly makes a statement which is false in a material particular; or

(b) where he is required to supply a copy of a procedure agreement, and he supplies a copy which to his knowledge is not accurate and complete,

will be guilty of an offence, and liable on a summary conviction to a maximum fine of £400 (IRA, s. 59).

It is to be noted that the Industrial Court has no jurisdiction in matters of criminal offences, as these are matters for the ordinary courts, therefore, any such offences will be tried in the magistrates' courts.

NEGOTIATING MACHINERY
UNDER OTHER ENACTMENTS

It is possible that an order of the Industrial Court relating to the establishment of negotiating machinery may in some cases appear to conflict with the provisions of some other statute (e.g., s. 46 of the Coal Industry Nationalisation Act, 1946, requires the Coal Board to set up machinery for consultation and negotiation and gives discretion to the Coal Board as to which unions are brought into the machinery). The Act, therefore, provides (IRA, s. 60) that in the case of a *corporate body* (viz., a registered company or a company formed by charter or statute), which is required by any other enactment to take steps with a view to the establishment of machinery for the settlement by negotiation of terms and conditions of employment, and if such requirement is inconsistent with an order made by the Industrial Court, the order of the Industrial Court shall prevail.

This provision refers only to corporate bodies because, it is suggested, there are no enactments except the Industrial Relations Act which require persons other than corporate bodies to establish negotiating machinery.

CHAPTER 7

WORKERS' ORGANISATIONS, EMPLOYERS' ORGANISATIONS AND TRADE UNIONS

Formation and Registration

Introduction

HISTORICALLY the term "trade union" embraced all those combinations and associations, whether of employees, or of employers or both together, which were concerned to regulate the terms and conditions of employment of labour or of trading generally. An examination of those cases in which the issue was whether an association could or could not be regarded as a trade union reveals that a trade union was, in general, an association which purported to determine the way in which its members disposed of their goods, capital or labour, and where those objects were present as the *main objects* the association was likely to be a trade union.

If it could be established that the main objects of an association were for the regulation of the terms and conditions of work or imposing restrictive conditions on the conduct of any trade or business of its members it was irrelevant whether it was a *permanent* or *temporary* association; it was nevertheless a trade union.

It is clear from this that the term trade union could be applied equally to combinations of employers, combinations of traders or combinations of workers, but it is with the latter that most people associate the term.

Throughout the latter part of the eighteenth and early part of the nineteenth centuries there was a dislike on the part of the authorities of any combination, and this led to the passing of the first anti-combination laws in 1799 and 1800. These Acts were later repealed and re-enacted in a modified form in the Combination Act, 1825, which itself was subsequently repealed and replaced by various Acts concerned with the regulation of trade unions, of which there is a more detailed account under the section on trade unions.

103

The net result of the later legislation was that considerable immunity from legal process was given to persons, whether employers or employees, who engaged in industrial action such as lock-outs and strikes. It was consequently possible, for even a small group of workers, for example where they had a minor dispute over working conditions, to cause considerable disruption by taking industrial action, knowing they could act with impunity, so long as their behaviour did not become illegal and outside the protection of the trade union law.

It is by no means suggested that small groups of workers always acted irresponsibly, nor in fact that larger organisations, whether of workers or of employers, always acted with restraint. But there was a large body of opinion which favoured a change in the structure of trade union organisation, and the result of this has been the Industrial Relations Act.

What the Act has done is to place workers and employers realistically under two separate headings, viz., "organisations of workers", and "organisations of employers", and to reserve the term trade union to describe organisations of workers which are *registered* under the provisions of the statute. An organisation of employers may also register under these provisions, but will be known as *"an employers' association"*. The combinations of workers and employers together in a single organisation is no longer recognised as an entity for the purposes of this Act.

Whilst organisations of workers and organisations of employers are now two separate sets of entities, what follows in this discussion in general applies equally to both types of organisation and it is not therefore proposed to distinguish unless the context otherwise requires it. In order, however, to understand the similarity of the two organisations it is thought advisable first to define both.

Unregistered Organisations of Employers

An organisation of employers is defined "as an organisation (whether permanent or temporary) which consists wholly or mainly of employers or individual proprietors of one or more descriptions, and is an organisation whose principal objects include the regulation of relations between employers or individual proprietors of that description or those descriptions and workers or workers' organisations". This includes federations of employers' organisations i.e. organisations consisting wholly or mainly of constituent or affiliated organisations of employers, and whose principal object is the regulation of relations between employers and workers, or between its constituent or affiliated organisations (IRA, s. 62(1), (2)).

Unregistered Organisations of Workers

As has been seen a group of workers who associate together for the purpose of regulating their terms and conditions of employment is now known as an organisation of workers, and this is defined as "an organisation (including those on the special register (see p. 123)) whether permanent or temporary, which either:

(a) consists wholly or mainly of workers of one or more descriptions and is an organisation whose principal objects include the regulation of relations between workers of that description, or those descriptions, and employers, or

(b) is a federation of workers' organisations, (IRA, s. 61) i.e. consisting of constituent or affiliated organisations, (including those in the special register) or their representatives, whose principal objects include those in para. (a) or include the regulation of relations between its constituent or affiliated organisations".

This definition, though rather similar in many respects to, but replacing the old law, would clearly include those combinations of workers who were previously recognised as trade unions, but it must once more be emphasised that in order to be recognised as a trade union it is necessary for the organisation of workers to register under the provisions of the Act (IRA, s. 61(3)).

The position, therefore, now is that there are two types of workers' organisations, viz. (a) those which comply with the definition but are not registered, and which are referred to throughout the Act simply as "organisations of workers", or "federations of workers' organisations", and (b) those organisations which comply with the definition and which are registered, and which are referred to as "trade unions" (whether they consist of a single organisation of workers or of a federation of organisations of workers, with or without the inclusion of organisations entered in the special register).

The relative position of these two groups of organisations under the new law is different from the old, for the "privileged" position so far enjoyed by all combinations of workers who could be described as trade unions will now generally be reserved for those combinations which are registered.

Organisations of workers who are not registered as trade unions may be large or small, permanent or temporary, and will continue to exist in the future albeit without the benefits, or restraints, of registration, and continue to exercise a considerable influence upon industry and upon people employed therein. For whilst these organisations no longer enjoy the status of trade unions as in the past, they will carry out similar functions of negotiation and conciliation in relation to terms and conditions of employment. The bargaining power of these organisations will still lie in their organisation and numerical strength, and membership of them will doubtless be considered desirable and even necessary in many cases, to ensure the continued improvement in working conditions, and to insure against discrimination in employment, though to a large extent the Act itself insures against the latter.

Conduct of Organisations of Workers
(other than federations of workers' organisations)

If then membership of these organisations is to be regarded as an advantage and a desirable asset by workers it is essential that there should be some guarantee of the right to membership. In order to protect the membership rights of members or of persons who wish to belong to an organisation, the Act lays down a set of guiding principles by which these organisations must conduct their affairs (IRA, s. 65).

These guiding principles are that:—

   (i) Any person who applies for membership of an organisation of workers (other than a federation of workers' organisations) and who can show that he is a worker of the same description as those for whom the organisation wholly or mainly provides may not be arbitrarily or unreasonably excluded from membership. Provided always that the applicant is appropriately qualified (e.g. by training, apprenticeship, etc.) for employment as a worker of that description (IRA, s. 65(2)).

  (ii) Any member of such an organisation is free to terminate his membership by giving reasonable notice and complying with any reasonable conditions (e.g. paying a termination fee to cover administration costs) (IRA, s. 65(3)).

 (iii) No member of the organisation may be arbitrarily or unreasonably:—

        (a) excluded from being or nominating a candidate for any office in the organisation;

    (b) prevented from participating in any ballot of members in connection with the organisation or its officers; or

    (c) prevented from attending or taking part in any meetings of the organisation; (IRA, s. 65(4), (6)).

(iv) Voting by members in any ballot must be kept secret (IRA, s. 65(5)).

(v) Except in respect of non-payment of any contributions, no disciplinary action may be taken against any member unless he has been given:—

    (a) written notice of the charge and been given a reasonable time to prepare his defence;

    (b) a full and fair hearing;

    (c) a written statement of the findings resulting from the hearing; and

    (d) the time for any appeal (if such is allowed under the rules of the organisation) has elapsed (IRA, s. 65(8)).

(vi) A person's membership may not be terminated unless reasonable notice of the proposal to terminate, and the reason for it, has been given to him (IRA, s. 65(9)).

(vii) No restriction may be placed upon any member by any organisation in respect of his instituting, prosecuting or defending proceedings before any court or tribunal, or giving evidence in any such proceedings (IRA, s. 65(10)).

(viii) No member shall be subjected by or on behalf of the organisation to any unfair or unreasonable disciplinary action, nor shall disciplinary action be taken against a member who refuses or fails,

    (a) to take part in any action, or refusal to act, which would amount under the Act to an unfair industrial practice on his part, or

    (b) to take part in a strike which the organisation, or any other person, has called, organised, procured or financed, where the strike has been called, etc., otherwise than in contemplation or furtherance of an industrial dispute, or

    (c) to take part in such strike where such strike, even though in contemplation or furtherance of an industrial dispute, constitutes an unfair industrial practice on the part of the organisation or that person under any of the provisions of the Act, or

(d) to take part in any irregular industrial action short of a strike which the organisation, or any other person, has organised, procured or financed in the circumstances described in (b) and (c) (IRA, s. 65(7)).

Conduct of Organisations of Employers
(other than federations of employers' organisations)

The guiding principles regulating membership of organisations of workers apply, with appropriate modification, to membership of employers' associations.

These guiding principles therefore are:—

(i) Any person who applies for membership of an organisation of employers (other than a federation of employers' organisations) and who is an employer or individual proprietor of the same description as those for whom the organisation wholly or mainly consists shall not be arbitrarily or unreasonably excluded from membership (IRA, s. 69(1));

(ii) to (vii) as for workers' organisations (see above);

(viii) No member shall be subjected, by or on behalf of the organisation, to any unfair or unreasonable disciplinary action, nor shall disciplinary action be taken against a member who refuses or fails,

(a) to take part in any action, or refusal to act, which would amount under the Act to an unfair industrial practice on his part, or

(b) to institute or participate in a lock-out, which the organisation, or any other person, has organised, procured or financed where the lock-out has been organised, etc., otherwise than in contemplation or furtherance of an industrial dispute, or

(c) to institute or participate in a lock-out where such lock-out, even though in contemplation or furtherance of an industrial dispute, constitutes an unfair industrial practice on the part of the organisation or that person under any of the provisions of the Act (IRA, s. 69(2)).

Complaints Against Organisations of Workers or of Employers

In the event of any organisation of workers (or organisation of employers), or any official or person acting on behalf of such an organisation, doing any act which is inconsistent with the foregoing principles it will amount to an unfair industrial practice for which the party affected may make a complaint to an industrial tribunal (IRA, s. 64).

Any person making such a complaint must state what the action alleged to have been taken (or not taken) by the organisation or person acting on its behalf, was, or what the breach committed by the organisation was (IRA, s. 107).

If the tribunal is satisfied that the complaint is substantiated and that the organisation is guilty of an unfair industrial practice or that what occurred was a breach of its rules, and it thinks it is just and equitable to do so, it may grant either or both of the following remedies;—

(a) an order determining the rights of the complainant in relation to the organisation complained about;

(b) an award of compensation to be paid to the complainant by the organisation (IRA, s. 109).

NOTE: There is no upper limit to the amount of compensation an unregistered organisation of workers (or employers) may be required to pay.

The next task is to establish what will amount in any given set of circumstances to an unfair industrial practice under these provisions. Every organisation of workers still retains the absolute right to determine in its own rules the class of worker it seeks to recruit and, provided that those persons appropriately qualified are included, this provision will not prevent the organisation from rejecting an applicant, provided the grounds for doing so are neither arbitrary nor unreasonable. Organisations whose rules so authorise them can reject applicants on clear and specific grounds—as for example where there is an unsatisfactory record of past membership, or where admission would conflict with a Trades Union Congress Award under the "Bridlington Agreement" principles (i.e. the "no poaching of members" agreement of members of organisations affiliated to the Trades Union Congress). If, therefore, an organisation were to reject an applicant on the ground that it has a joint working agreement with other organisations of workers which precludes it from recruiting workers of the type represented by the applicant—that is to say, members or former members of another such organisation—this refusal would not be arbitrary or unreasonable exclusion.

This right of admission must also include the right of re-admission and the principles affecting these provisions would apply equally. But an organisation would be justified in refusing to re-admit someone who was a trouble maker and the sort of person who would be likely to have a disruptive influence on an organisation, or on any other ground so long as it were not arbitrary or unreasonable.

Whilst every member has a right to terminate his membership at any time, the organisation is free to impose reasonable conditions upon members wishing to terminate their membership, such as the payment of arrears by that particular person and perhaps a reasonable sum to cover administrative expenses. If an organisation refused to accept a termination of membership of an individual on these grounds i.e. that he refused to comply with conditions, it would certainly be acting within the law.

Power of Organisations of Workers or of Employers to Discipline Members

The guiding principles applicable to both workers' and employers' organisations are intended to ensure that arbitrary and unreasonable actions are not taken against members, or would-be members. This does not, however, mean that an organisation may not exercise discipline over its members, but that this power of discipline is limited, particularly in relation to members who refuse or fail to participate in industrial action: this is indicated in the guiding principles set out above, see in respect of organisations of workers para. (viii) and in respect of organisations of employers para. (viii). So that whilst an organisation may not discipline a member who refuses to participate in industrial action in circumstances where an unfair industrial practice would be occasioned, there is nothing to prevent a trade union (or employers' association) from disciplining a member for refusing to participate in a strike (or lock-out) so long as the strike does not amount to an unfair industrial practice. Where, for example, a trade union induces a strike to exert pressure on an employer to recognise a closed shop, this would amount to an unfair industrial practice on the part of the union and a member of the union could not be disciplined for refusing or failing to take part in it, but if the union induces a strike by its members, perhaps because it is considered that wage rates are too low, or working conditions are thought to be intolerable, any member may be disciplined for refusing or failing to take part, so long as the strike is not in the particular circumstances an unfair industrial practice (e.g. where a 60-day "cooling off" order under IRA, s. 139 is in force) and the discipline is not arbitrary or unreasonable, and clearly provided for in the rules of the union.

As it is an unfair industrial practice for any person in contemplation or furtherance of an industrial dispute, knowingly to induce another to break a contract to which that other is a party, *unless the person inducing is a trade union or employers' association* (or person acting within the scope of his authority on behalf of either (IRA, s. 96)), it follows that unregistered organisations of either workers or employers will be severely restricted from disciplining members for refusing to strike.

Organisations of Workers and Employers (eligibility and registration)

The advantages of registration cannot be doubted, for a trade union enjoys considerable advantages, both legal and fiscal, over non-registered organisations. These advantages include immunity, subject to limitations, from legal liability when inducing industrial action, the right to apply for recognition as a sole bargaining agent or to enter into agency shop agreements, the limits on compensation they may be required to pay and other (financial) advantages relating to benevolent activities in which they might engage, in addition to being able to require information from employers about the employer's business.

In order that an organisation of workers may apply for registration as a trade union it must be able to establish that it:—

(a) is an independent organisation of workers, and
(b) has power, without the concurrence of any parent organisation to alter its own rules, and to control the application of its own property and funds and those of its branches and sections.

NOTE: A federation of workers' organisations may also register provided that all its constituent members are either trade unions or organisations for the time being on the special register (IRA, s. 67).

Similarly, an organisation of employers which has the power, without the concurrence of any parent organisation, to alter its own rules and to control the applications of its own property and funds and those of its branches and sections is eligible for registration as an employers' association (IRA, s. 71).

Once the decision to register (as a trade union or an employers' association) has been taken, an application to the Registrar must be made in the form and manner required by him, and must be accompanied by:—

(a) a copy of the rules of the organisation and list of officers;
(b) the names and addresses of the branches (if any) of the organisation;
(c) if the organisation has been in operation for more than a year, a copy of its audited accounts, and a return of its affairs for the previous year.

If the Registrar is satisfied that the organisation is eligible for registration as a trade union (or employers' association), and all the requirements above, and any additional requirements imposed by him, have been complied with, he must on payment of £25, or other such sum as may be prescribed by order, register the organisation as a trade union (or employers' association), and issue a registration certificate (IRA, ss. 68, 72). The certificate must state whether it relates to a workers' organisation or to a federation of the same (IRA, s. 73(1)) or to an employers' organisation or federation of employers' organisations (IRA, s. 73(2)) and must include the name of the organisation, which must not be the same as any other organisation on either the ordinary or special register, or so similar as to be likely to deceive (IRA, s. 73).

On the issue of the certificate of registration the organisation becomes a body corporate, unless it is a body corporate already, having perpetual succession and a common seal. All property held in trust for the organisation vests immediately in the trade union, or employers' association, and any existing liability or obligation against any person in his capacity as trustee will transfer to the organisation, and any legal proceedings pending by or against the trustees may be continued by or against the organisation in its registered name (IRA, s. 74).

NOTE: Under the old law trade unions were not corporate bodies and the property of trade unions was held by trustees, any actions had to be brought against the trustees acting on behalf of the union, or against members of the union on behalf of themselves and all other members (i.e. a representative action). As a consequence of the *Taff Vale* (**9**) judgment and the decision in *Bonsor* v. *Musicians Union* (1955) (**2**) *registered* trade unions were regarded as having sufficient corporate existence to sue or to be sued in their registered name.

It is now provided that where any action is commenced against trustees or members, the court may substitute the trade union (or employers' association) without the necessity for dismissing the action and starting again (IRA, s. 131(3), (4)).

Where the organisation was already a corporate body it will already have a name, but the name by which it will be known as a trade union is the name by which it is registered (IRA, s. 74).

After the certificate of registration has been issued the Registrar must look at the rules of the organisation to see whether or not they conform both to the guiding principles of organisations of workers as required by IRA, s. 65 (and organisations of employers, IRA, s. 69), (see page 106), and also with the requirements of IRA, Sch. 4, subject to the Registrar being able to waive any of the requirements in any particular case where there are special circumstances justifying this. The requirements of IRA, Sch. 4 are:—

1. The rules must comply with Sch. 4 subject to the Registrar's power of exemption.

2. The rules must specify the name of the organisation, the address of its principal office, and the objects for which it is established.

3. Where the organisation has branches this must be indicated along with the manner in which it has power to control the activities of those branches.

4. The rules must make provision:—
   (a) for the election of the governing body and for its re-election at reasonable intervals, and
   (b) for the manner in which members of the governing body can be removed from office.

5. The rules must provide for the election or appointment of officers and for the manner in which they can be removed from office. (Officers include unpaid as well as paid officers.)

6. If the organisation has officials who are not officers (whether they are shop stewards, work-place representatives or other officials) the rules must make provision for their election or appointment and for the manner in which they can be removed from office.

7. The rules must specify the powers and duties of the governing body of the organisation, of each of its officers and of officials who are not officers of the organisation.

8. The rules must make provision as to the manner in which meetings, for transacting any business of the organisation, are to be convened and conducted.

9. The rules must specify the manner in which any rules of the organisation can be made, altered or revoked.

10. The rules must specify any body by which, and any official by whom, instructions may be given to members of the organisation on its behalf for any kind of industrial action, and the circumstances in which any such instruction may be so given.

11. The rules must make provision as to the manner in which, for any purposes of the organisation, elections are to be held or ballots taken, including eligibility for voting in any such election or ballot, the procedure preparatory to any such election or ballot, the procedure for counting and scrutiny of votes and ballot papers and the procedure for the declaration or notification of the result of any such election or ballot.

12. If the organisation is a federation of workers' (or employers') organisations, its rules must specify the circumstances (if any) in which the organisation has power to enter into agreement on behalf of its constituent or affiliated organisations.

13. The rules must specify the circumstances and the manner in which the organisation can be dissolved.

Requirements relating to members of organisations

14. The rules must specify the descriptions of persons who are eligible for membership of the organisation, and the procedure for dealing with applications for membership, including provisions for appeals against decisions of the committee or other body responsible for determining such applications.

15. The rules must specify—
    (a) the contributions payable in respect of membership of that organisation (including any contributions payable in respect of admissions or re-admission), and any amount of any such contributions or the basis on which that amount is to be assessed,
    (b) the procedure and penalties in case of default in payment of contributions.

16. The rules must specify—
    (a) any descriptions of conduct in respect of which disciplinary action (whether by way of suspension, expulsion or otherwise) can be taken by or on behalf of the organisation against any of its members;
    (b) the nature of the disciplinary action which can be so taken in respect of each such description of conduct; and
    (c) the procedure for taking disciplinary action, including provision for appeals against decisions of the committee or other body responsible for taking it.
17. The rules must specify the circumstances in which, and the procedure, other than expulsion by way of disciplinary action, by which membership of the organisation can be terminated.
18. The rules must specify a procedure for inquiring into any complaint of a member of the organisation that action contrary to the rules of the organisation has been taken by the organisation or by an official of the organisation.

Requirements relating to property and finances of organisations
19. The rules must make provision as to the purposes for which, and the manner in which, any property or funds of the organisation are authorised to be applied or invested.
20. If any financial benefits are to be available to members of the organisation out of its property or funds, the rules must make provision as to the amounts of those benefits and the circumstances in which they are to be available to members.
21. The rules must make provision—
    (a) for the keeping of proper accounting records, and for the preparation and auditing of accounts, in accordance with the provisions of the Act, and
    (b) as to the rights of members of the organisation to inspect the accounting records and the register of members.
22. The rules must provide for the distribution of the property and funds of the organisation in the event of its being dissolved.

NOTE: Failure to fulfil any of the requirements set out in the Schedule will not invalidate the rules of the organisation, but the Registrar may require them to be altered to comply with these principles, and he may apply to the Industrial Court in the event of refusal to do so (IRA, ss. 75, 76).

It must be made clear at the outset that the task of the Registrar is to examine the rules and be satisfied that provisions have been made in accordance with the list in IRA, Sch. 4. It is left to the trade unions to write their rules as they wish, provided they cover these matters. In other words, certain things have to be specified in the rules, and other things have to be covered by them. For example if one trade union decides to have one type of appeals procedure in relation to the discipline of its members, and another union decides to have a completely different system there is no reason why they should not do so. But, overriding the absolute discretion of the union in these matters is the requirement that they should comply with the rules of natural justice, which the Registrar, of course, will bear in mind when he examines the rules.

It will be noted that rule 4 is concerned with the *governing body*, rule 5 is concerned with *officers* and rule 6 is concerned with *officials* of the organisation, and some difficulty may be experienced in seeking to distinguish clearly between these terms. It is necessary to be able to distinguish, for rule 7 requires that the duties and powers of all three must be specified.

The term "official" in relation to an organisation of workers (or of employers) is defined as "any person who is an officer of the organisation or who (not being such an officer) is a person elected or appointed in accordance with the rules of the organisation to be a representative of its members, or of some of them, including (in the case of an organisation of workers) any person so elected or appointed who is an employee of the same employer as the members, or one or more of the members, whom he is to represent" (IRA, s. 167). Neither "governor" nor "officer" are defined in the Act, and it becomes necessary therefore, to apply a different criteria to decide who they in fact include. A dictionary definition of the former might be "a ruler, one invested with supreme authority, with power to direct and control". In other words a group of persons in the case of a trade union, who have been elected to decide the policy of the organisation, with or without the concurrence of its members. The body of governors could include persons elected, perhaps even for life, from originally within or without the organisation, and may even from time to time include any other members of the organisation, including its officials.

The expression "officer" could be defined as a person who is given power, appointed to perform a specific duty, or set of duties, in connection with an organisation. Perhaps one who is entrusted to make decisions within the policy of the organisation without the necessity of referring first to superiors.

Whilst trade unionists generally reserve the description "official" to the more senior members (usually paid) of their organisation, the term officer is included in the wider expression of "official" which includes not only persons with a specific appointment, but also all other persons who are elected or appointed in accordance with the rules of the organisation to act on its behalf, including it is suggested shop stewards.

As it is clearly necessary for a number of very specific reasons (e.g. unfair industrial practices in a trade union for calling strikes, etc., under this Act) to know the scope of authority of particular officers and officials, the requirements in the rules dealing with this particular point will be of considerable importance.

Action by the Registrar in relation to the rules of an association

If on examination of the rules of the organisation as submitted, the Registrar is of the opinion that the rules of the organisation are defective, i.e. not satisfactory in accordance with the above principles, he must serve notice on that organisation indicating what changes he thinks should be made in them, specifying a time limit of not less than two months within which these changes must be made. Irrespective of any rule to the contrary in the rules of the organisation, the organisation has the power to call and hold meetings for the purpose of making these changes (IRA, s. 94). If when the rules are resubmitted the Registrar finds that they still do not comply, he may give further time in which the organisation can comply with his requirements, but in any event he must not approve the rules until they are satisfactory in accordance with the principles set out above (IRA, s. 75). It might be pertinent at this point to mention that the Registrar frequently acts in an advisory capacity in connection with how union rules ought to be framed, and it is highly probable that the Registrar will make every endeavour to come to an agreement with an organisation before finally rejecting a set of rules.

If the point is reached where the Registrar has to refuse to approve the rules as submitted, or resubmitted, either he or the organisation may make an application to the Industrial Court. Where the Registrar applies, the Court may make an order allowing the organisation even further time to alter its rules (and resubmitting them to the Registrar) or directing that the registration be cancelled. Where the organisation applies, the Court may allow an extension of time for alteration of the rules and resubmission or, make an order directing the Registrar to approve the rules as submitted (IRA, s. 76).

Cancellation of Registration

Once an organisation of workers (or employers) has been registered it remains a trade union (or employers' association) as long as it remains on the register. But at any time after registration an application may be made by the Registrar to the Industrial Court for cancellation of the registration on the following grounds:—

(a) that it was obtained by fraud or mistake, or

(b) that, by reason of a change in its rules or other change of circumstance (e.g. it has ceased to be independent) it is no longer eligible for registration as a trade union (or employers' association), or

(c) that the organisation has failed to keep records of accounts and membership, make annual returns and reports, or have its accounts properly audited (as required by Part IV of the Act).

If satisfied that the Registrar's complaint is well founded in relation to the first two reasons, the Court must cancel the registration, but in the third case it may either cancel the registration or make an order extending the time within which the organisation can remedy the default (IRA, s. 77). No time is indicated in the Act, but it will obviously depend upon the circumstances; for example, it may in some cases be necessary that there should be a complete overhaul by outside consultants of the affairs of some organisations. It must also be noted that any trade union (or employers' association) or officer who wilfully neglects to perform or to comply with a requirement under para. (c) above, may on conviction in a Magistrates' Court be fined up to £100, or £400 for falsifying any such return (IRA, s. 91).

From the foregoing it is clear that the Registrar cannot exercise his powers arbitrarily, but that the real power of control lies with the Industrial Court. For the Registrar cannot refuse to register an organisation, provided it complies with the requirements as to registration, and he cannot cancel the registration of any organisation without the consent of the Court, subject to the next paragraph.

Defunct Organisations

The Registrar may cancel the registration of a trade union:
(a) at the request of the organisation, or
(b) if he is satisfied that the organisation has ceased to exist.
Notice of cancellation under this provision must be given in the London and Edinburgh Gazettes (IRA, s. 92).

Winding Up

If, at any time, it appears to the Chief Registrar that either a trade union or employers' association is insolvent he may appoint an Inspector to investigate. The latter may examine on oath the officers, members or employees, and if the organisation is found to be insolvent a petition may be presented by the Chief Registrar to the High Court for the organisation to be wound up in accordance with the Companies Act, 1948 (IRA, s. 90).

Where the Registrar presents a petition under this section (or where the registration of an organisation has been cancelled as a trade union or an employers' association) the organisation will be regarded as an unregistered company for the purposes of winding up under the Companies Act, 1948.

Dissolution in any other circumstances, as when the members themselves decide on dissolution in accordance with their rules, will not be possible, except by order of the court under the Companies Act, 1948, until there has been lodged with the Registrar a certificate signed by the secretary or by some other officer of the organisation approved for the purpose by the Registrar, that all the property vested in the organisation has been conveyed or transferred by the organisation to the persons entitled to it (IRA, s. 156).

Changes of Rules and Cancellation

Whenever a trade union (or employers' association) wishes to change its rules it must send a copy of all changes to the Registrar within one month from the date that the change in question occurs. As soon as practicable after registering the change, the Registrar must examine the rules as amended, and if they conflict with the principles already set out on pp. 106-108 he may take precisely the same action as upon the original registration of a trade union, viz., give time for alteration in accordance with his suggestions, and failing a satisfactory agreement apply to the Industrial Court. The Court may either extend the time for alteration, or order the registration to be cancelled, or allow the rules as amended (IRA, s. 91).

Registrar's power to investigate complaints and other matters

As has been pointed out above, the powers of the Registrar in relation to matters of registration are somewhat circumscribed by the Industrial Court, but he is nevertheless given certain authority to receive and to initiate complaints.

Where any member of a trade union or employers' association (other than a federation) or any person whose membership has been terminated without his agreement, or whose application for membership has been refused or prevented, feels that the organisation, or someone acting on its behalf, has been guilty of an unfair industrial practice in unreasonably discriminating against him or that it has acted in breach of its rules (other than in relation to the Political Fund (p. 163), or on a vote to amalgamate with some other union for which provisions are already made) he can complain to the Registrar (IRA, s. 81).

If the Registrar is satisfied that such person was eligible to make such complaint (i.e. that he was a member or entitled to be a member of the organisation) and the action was taken against him, then he must investigate the matter and give notice of his conclusions to the applicant and to the organisation, unless he is of the opinion that the complaint is frivolous or vexatious.

If on carrying out the investigation he is satisfied that the complaint is well founded he must endeavour to get a settlement between the complainant and the organisation. If an adequate procedure exists within the organisation for dealing with this particular kind of complaint the Registrar may refer the matter to that procedure, and if not dealt with satisfactorily by the organisation within a reasonable time not exceeding four weeks he must hear the complaint himself. If, however, there is no procedure in the organisation or no satisfactory conclusion is reached where there is such a procedure, and if no settlement is forthcoming it may then become a matter for an industrial tribunal but no communications made to the Registrar whilst he was attempting to bring about a settlement will be admissible to the industrial tribunal without the consent of the person making it.

Time limit for making complaint to Registrar

Any complaint made to the Registrar under the foregoing provisions must be made within a period of four weeks from the date of the occurrence of the unfair action complained of, or of the complainant becoming aware of the reason for the complaint.

Where the organisation has a procedure for dealing with this type of complaint, and the complaint has been considered in the manner established by the rules of that procedure, the complainant may nevertheless apply to the Registrar within four weeks from the date of any decision made thereunder, whether that decision is favourable to the complainant or not. If it was not practicable for the application to be made before, the Registrar may extend the period within which a complaint may be made to him (IRA s. 82).

Registrar's powers to investigate breaches of rules on his own initiative

In addition to the power to investigate complaints made to him the Registrar may on his own initiative investigate where he suspects serious or persistent breaches of the rules of any organisation (other than breaches of rules relating to the restriction on the application of funds for political purposes, or voting on a resolution approving an amalgamation), and if he is satisfied that a breach has occurred he must give notice of his conclusions to the organisation, and endeavour to obtain an assurance that the breach will cease, or not recur. He must also inform any person who could have complained about that particular matter had he so wished.

In any case where the Registrar cannot gain an assurance that the breach will cease, or not recur, he may give notice to the organisation, that if an assurance is not forthcoming within a period specified by him then he will present a complaint to the Industrial Court (IRA, s. 83). If after such time has elapsed it appears to the Registrar no such assurance has been given, or where an undertaking has been given but has not been fulfilled, he may present to the Industrial Court a complaint against that organisation. On being satisfied that the complaint is well founded the Court may make an order directing the trade union or employers' association to remedy or mitigate the matter complained of and to prevent the matter complained of from recurring (IRA, s. 104).

Provisional Register (Pre-existing trade unions)

The position of trade unions in existence before the passing of the Industrial Relations Act is clarified, for the Act makes provision for the institution by the Registrar of a *provisional register*, and distinguishes between unions which are already registered under the Trade Union Acts, 1871 to 1964, and those which are unregistered. All *registered* unions in existence at the time of the passing of the Act will automatically be entered in the provisional register, as soon as practicable after the passing of the Act (IRA s. 78(2)) but non-registered unions must apply within six months of such time to be placed on the provisional register (IRA s. 78(3)). Therefore all *registered* unions will continue to be classified as trade unions whereas *unregistered* unions will cease to be so classified if no application to register has been made within six months.

Once an organisation is placed on the provisional register the Registrar must, within six months from such entry, consider whether it appears to him to be eligible to be placed on the *permanent register* of trade unions and employers' associations. If he is satisfied that it should then be registered, he must issue a certificate of registration, without any further action on the part of the organisation.

If, however, the Registrar is not satisfied that an organisation on the provisional register, ought to be registered on the permanent register, he must notify such organisation, and cancel the registration, unless the reason for his refusal to register it on the permanent register is because its rules are defective. In this case, if he is satisfied that within six months of his serving the notice of refusal to register, the organisation is taking all necessary steps for the purpose of altering its rules to conform, he must serve a further notice allowing such further period as he thinks necessary to enable it to make these alterations.

Before the end of this extended period the organisation must apply in the ordinary way for registration as outlined earlier (pp. 111, 112). If the application is successful the organisation will be entered on the permanent register and the entry on the provisional register will be cancelled. But if no application to register is made, or where it is made unsuccessfully, the Registrar must cancel the entry in the provisional register. In the case of the unsuccessful application he must allow the period for appealing to the Industrial Court to lapse first.

No fee is payable for entry into the provisional register, nor for entry in the permanent register in the circumstances outlined in the previous paragraph. (IRA, s. 79).

Whilst entry in the provisional register does not constitute registration proper for the purpose of the Act (IRA, s. 80) it does in effect maintain the status quo, so that an organisation may still operate as a trade union within the terms of the Act until it is placed on the permanent register, or the entry is cancelled. The purpose of the provisional register is clearly a transitional arrangement, and no entries will be made in it after six months, from the operative date of this section of the Act (IRA s. 78(3)(b)). (IRA s. 170.)

Special Register (**Not applicable to employers**)

As has been indicated the expression trade union describes an organisation of workers registered under the provisions of the Act, and the term worker includes, for this purpose, any person who works:—

(a) under a contract of employment, or

(b) under any other contract (whether expressed or implied, whether oral or in writing) whereby he undertakes to *perform personally* any work or services for another party to the contract who is not a professional client of his, or

(c) in employment under or for the purposes of a Government Department (other than as a member of the armed forces of the Crown) in so far as it does not fall within paras. (a) or (b), or

(d) is engaged in providing general medical services, pharmaceutical services, general dental services or ophthalmic services in accordance with the National Health Service Act, 1946, the employer in this case being any Executive Council (IRA s. 167(1)).

NOTE: The term worker does not include service as a police officer or special constable, or any member of any constabulary maintained by virtue of any general, local or private Act (IRA, s. 167(4)).

Within the term worker, therefore, are a wide variety of wage and salary earners, including manual, sedentary and professional employees.

Organisations representing professionally qualified people fall into three groups, viz.,

1. Those organisations which are concerned with the regulation of terms and conditions of employment and fulfil the same functions as the trade unions in factories, offices, shops and other places where people work, and include in their membership solicitors employed in legal departments in industry, doctors in hospitals, architects by local authorities and engineers in industry.

These organisations fall within the definition of "organisation of workers" and have the right to register as trade unions.

2. Those organisations such as the Law Society whose members work for clients rather than for employers, or the engineering institutes, whose members in the main work for employers, but who have chosen not to concern themselves with the relationship between employers and workers.

These organisations will not be able to register under the Act, unless of course they change their character to conform to the definition of an organisation of workers.

3. Those organisations which consist mainly of professional workers and which are concerned with the employer/worker relationship, but which started off originally without much concern with industrial relations, and have since become incorporated by Charter or by registration under Companies Acts only because their objects were primarily other than representing the interests of workers; but who, over the course of time, have become involved in collective bargaining on behalf of their members. An example is the Royal College of Nursing, which was granted a Charter many years ago and is known mostly for its work for the advancement of nursing as a profession, though it is also the organisation which represents nurses on the Whitley Council for the National Health Service, the body which regulates relations between nurses as employees and their employer in the National Health Service.

Such bodies are not eligible to register as trade unions so long as they remain chartered or incorporated as companies because their principal objects do not include the regulation of relations between employers and workers.

In order to enable the organisations in this third group to obtain trade union status without the necessity of dissolving themselves and starting all over again, a special register has been established specifically for them. Entry in the special register does not create a privileged group as compared with organisations in the ordinary register, it is a mere matter of administrative convenience.

The organisations in the special register are trade unions for the purpose of the Act, in respect of those parts of their activities with which the Act is concerned. They are not, however, to be referred to as trade unions, but as "organisations entered in the special register".

To qualify for entry into the special register an organisation must first of all be either an independent company or chartered body; secondly, a majority of its members should be workers as described above; thirdly, its activities should include the regulation of relations between workers and employers; fourthly, it should have power to alter its own rules and control the application of its property and funds, and those of its branches and sections if any (IRA, s. 84(2), (3)).

Organisations which call themselves professional bodies may be entered on the special register *only if a majority* of the members are workers, even though in some cases these organisations may include employers as well as workers.

A federation may also be entered in the special register provided it is comprised wholly of trade unions or of organisations entered in the special register, or of representatives of such trade unions or organisations, or a mixture of any of them together. But only if the *activities* of such federation *include* the regulation of relations between workers and employers and the trade unions or organisations in the special register are themselves corporate bodies as referred to above (IRA, s. 84(4)).

Where a federation is comprised wholly or mainly of trade unions and/or organisations and/or representatives of trade unions or organisations on the special register, and its main objects as such a federation include the regulation of relations between workers and employers, it will be entered on the ordinary register, even though individually its constituent members which are entered in the special register do not have the regulation of relations between workers and employers as their main objects.

It is only where the federation has main objects other than that of the regulation of relations between workers and employers, but which includes in its activities such regulation of relations as secondary objects, that it can claim to be entered in the special register. (IRA, s. 84(4).)

The factor, therefore, which distinguishes those organisations which are eligible to be entered in the ordinary register from those eligible to be entered in the special register, is that in the first case the main or *principal* object of the organisation is the regulation of relations between workers and employers, whereas in the second case the *activities* of the organisation *must include* such objects. The distinction between *principal objects* and *activities included* will always be a matter of degree to be decided by the Registrar when application is made to register.

Application to Register on the Special Register

An application to register must be made to the Registrar in the form and manner that he may require, and the application must be accompanied by a copy of the rules of the organisation, a list of its officers and the names and addresses of its branches (if any) (IRA, s.85(2)).

Where an application for entry in the special register is made the Registrar will examine the memorandum and articles of association, charter or letters patent (as the case may be). If he is satisfied in relation to the *actual activities* carried on by the organisation that they include the regulation of relations between workers and employers, regardless of whether or not they are in accordance with the articles, and if he is otherwise satisfied that the organisation is eligible for entry in the special register, he will on payment of £25 enter the organisation on the register and issue a certificate of registration (IRA, s. 85). It must be noted, however, that the rules of the organisation are subject to the same scrutiny and approval by the Registrar as in the case of a trade union applying for entry in the ordinary register. He can, therefore, notify an organisation on the special register in what way its rules are defective, and can ask that organisation to make the necessary changes (IRA, s. 86(2)).

Where the application is made by a federation of workers' organisations and the Registrar is satisfied that it is eligible for entry in the special register he will issue a certificate of registration again on payment of a fee of £25 (IRA, s. 85(5)).

Effect of Entry in the Special Register

Once an organisation has been entered in the special register, although it does not become a trade union, all the provisions of the Act apply as though such an organisation were a trade union, so that any reference in this book to a trade union (other than the definition) should be understood to apply to an organisation entered in the special register, with the following exceptions (IRA, s. 86) :

(a) none of the provisions of the Act relating to entry in the provisional register will apply.

(b) none of the duties laid down in the Act as to the keeping of accounts, register of members and the submission to annual audit will apply,

(c) there is no power in the Chief Registrar to apply for a winding-up order under the provisions of this Act.

The reasons why companies and chartered bodies on the special register do not have to satisfy these requirements is not because they are irrelevant, but because these bodies are already subject to corresponding obligations under the Companies Acts, 1948, etc.

CHAPTER 8

TRADE UNIONS
AND DISPUTES

As WAS observed at the beginning of chapter seven, historically the trade union was disliked by the authorities, and throughout the latter part of the eighteenth and beginning of the nineteenth centuries strict legislative control was exercised to discourage them. Even where there was no legislation directly on the point the common law was used to dissuade combinations of both workers and employers, particularly the former.

The effect of the legislation up to 1825 was that collective bargaining over wages and hours of work was allowed but no provision was made to permit strikes and lock-outs, and indeed the common law of restraint of trade and conspiracy was invoked to prevent them.

I OLD LAW

Control of Trade Unions at Common Law

A *restraint of trade* may be described as the placing of a restriction upon an individual to engage in his trade, business or profession, and certainly includes any restriction upon the liberty of a man to dispose of his labour, or employ labour as he wishes. So that where it could be shown that a union or other combination had this object, it was disapproved of by the common law, and its agreements would not be enforced. Where members of an association in order to further its objects, agreed to submit to its decisions and strike if so directed, then the agreement became illegal as being in restraint of trade, and the members could be prosecuted for conspiracy.

A *conspiracy* is an agreement or combination to do something unlawful, or to do something which is lawful by unlawful means. A conspiracy may be a civil wrong, i.e. a tort, if actual loss or damage results to some person, and would also be a crime even if no damage resulted. Thus in many cases where a trade union tried to further its objects by industrial action, the members were guilty of criminal conspiracy unless they could show that their common course of action was undertaken with a single view to protect the genuine trade interests of the combining parties, and not with a view to injuring others (*Mogul Steamship Co. Ltd.* v. *McGregor, Gow & Co.* (1892)) (**7**).

The combined effect of the common law rules regarding restraint of trade and conspiracy was, that if a combination infringed the former, its agreements could not be enforced amongst its members nor against others, whilst infringement of the latter invoked the criminal law, and the members could be prosecuted. In addition, where actual loss resulted to some person, damages could be recovered.

Changes in the Common Law

A Royal Commission was set up in 1867 to enquire into the workings of trade unions and the result of its report was the Trade Union Act, 1871. This Act was the first of a number of Acts dealing specifically with trade unions, which together provided the statutory framework of trade union law until they were in the main repealed by the Industrial Relations Act, 1971.

The principal objects of these Acts were:—

(a) to encourage trade unions to register in accordance with rules established by the Act of 1871;

(b) to modify the law of criminal conspiracy in relation to trade unions by providing that members should not be criminally liable for conspiracy merely because the objects of the union were in restraint of trade;

(c) to give trade unions immunity from actions for damages for civil conspiracy in trade disputes (Conspiracy and Protection of Property Act, 1875, s. 3; Trade Disputes Act, 1906, s. 1);

(d) to give to persons acting in trade disputes immunity from liability for procuring or threatening to procure breaches of *contracts of employment*, i.e. members of trade unions acting in a trade dispute were free from the liability which ordinarily results where a person procures or threatens to procure a breach of contract. (Trade Disputes Act, 1906, s. 3; Trade Disputes Act, 1965, s. 1);

(e) to provide that no action was to be entertained against a trade union, or against any members or officials of a trade union in respect of any tort alleged to have been committed by or on behalf of the union (Trade Disputes Act, 1906, s. 4).

The Trade Union Act, 1871, defined for the first time a trade union, although the definition was later amended by the Trade Union Act (Amendment) Act, 1876, and the Trade Union Act, 1913. The combined effect of these provisions was to produce the following definition of a trade union:—

any *combination* whether *temporary* or *permanent*, the *principal objects* of which are under its *constitution* "statutory objects". Statutory objects are the *regulation* of the *relations* between *workmen* and *masters* or between *workmen* and *workmen* or between *masters* and *masters*, or the imposing of *restrictive conditions* on the conduct of any *trade* or *business* and also the *provision of benefits to members* whether such combination would or would not, if the Trade Union Act, 1871, had not been passed, have been deemed to have been an unlawful combination by reason of some one or more of its purposes being in restraint of trade.

It will be seen from this definition that so long as the object of the combination was the regulation of the relations between the parties mentioned, or was for the purpose of imposing restrictive conditions on the conduct of any trade or business, then it enjoyed immunity within the law as outlined above.

Furthermore, it made no difference whether the combination was a permanent association like the Transport and General Workers Union, or whether it was an ad hoc arrangement of workmen in a factory combining together over a particular dispute with the employer about a bonus scheme, both enjoyed immunity equally.

Types of Trade Unions under the Old Law

Trade unions under the old law could be classified into three groups, as follows:

1. *Registered Unions*

The Trade Union Act, 1871, s. 6, as amended by the Trade Union (Amendment) Act, 1876, provided that any seven or more members of the trade union could, by subscribing their names to the rules of the union and otherwise complying with the provisions of the Act regarding registration, register the union. One of the results of registration was that the union acquired a legal personality of a limited kind separate and distinct from that of its members. A registered union was entitled to certain income tax advantages, and by far the greatest percentage of unions were in fact registered.

2. *Certified Unions*
Any combination which could satisfy the Registrar that its principal objects were statutory objects could ask for a certificate to the effect that it was a trade union within the meaning of the Trade Union Acts. The granting of such certificate did not confer any of the advantages of registration, but was conclusive evidence that the association was a trade union.

3. *Unregistered Unions*
The law relating to membership, objects, powers, contracts, torts and criminal liability of unregistered unions was in general the same as that applicable to registered and to certified unions, as was the law protecting their funds and the activities of their officials. And it will have been gathered from what has already been said that most unregistered unions were in fact ad hoc bodies of a temporary nature.

Trade Unions and the Criminal Law (Old Position)
Before the passing of the Trade Union Acts there were two possible reasons why a trade union might be considered to be liable for a criminal conspiracy:—
  (a) where the purpose of the union was to bring out its members on strike or to lock out employees; or
  (b) if the purposes of the union were in restraint of trade.

At common law, strikes were not illegal if they did not involve the use of unlawful means. Thus an agreement by workmen to remain away from work unless certain wages were paid was perfectly lawful, but it became unlawful when the agreement was to *persuade* men to leave their employment so as to compel employers to raise wages. The use of other means, e.g. threats to strike to persuade employers to raise wages was also unlawful.

The Conspiracy and Protection of Property Act, 1875, s. 3 (as amended by the Trade Disputes Act, 1906, s. 1) remedied this position by providing that an agreement or combination by two or more persons to do or procure to be done any act in contemplation or furtherance of a trade dispute should not be indictable as a conspiracy, if such act, if committed by one person would not be punishable as a crime. A *trade dispute* was defined as *"any dispute between employers and workmen or between workmen and workmen connected with the employment or non-employment, or the terms of the employment, or with the conditions of labour of any person"*. (Trade Disputes Act, 1906, s. 5(3)).

As indicated above, the common law applied equally to lock-outs and to strikes, and as the Trade Union Acts related to combinations of employers as well as to combinations of employees, the amending legislation applied likewise, giving the same protection to employers for potential criminal conspiracies.

Even after the amending legislation of the Trade Disputes Act, 1906, certain strikes remained illegal by virtue of the Conspiracy and Protection of Property Act, 1875. S. 4 of that Act provided that where a person is employed in certain public undertakings or other organisations, having a duty to provide gas or water to inhabitants at large, he commits an offence if he breaks his contract of service having reasonable grounds to believe that such a breach would deprive the inhabitants wholly or to a great extent of gas and water. This provision was extended to the supply of electricity by the Electricity Supply Act, 1919, s. 31. A similar provision was made by s. 5 of the 1875 Act where a person wilfully and maliciously breaks a contract of service or hiring, knowing or having reasonable cause to believe that the consequences of so doing will be to endanger life, cause serious bodily harm or expose valuable property to destruction or injury. In both cases, the offences were punishable by a fine not exceeding £20 or imprisonment for a term not exceeding three months.

The Conspiracy and Protection of Property Act, 1875, s. 4 has now been repealed by IRA, s. 133, although s. 5 of the 1875 Act (see p. 137) has been retained.

Picketing (Old Position)
The Trade Disputes Act, 1906, s. 2 provided that it should be lawful for one or more persons acting on their own behalf or on behalf of a trade union or of an individual employer or firm in contemplation or furtherance of a trade dispute to attend at or

near where a person lived or worked or carried on a business or happened to be, if they did so merely for the purpose of peacefully obtaining or communicating information or of peacefully persuading any person to work or abstain from working. Whilst this section, along with the rest of the 1906 Act, has been repealed it has been re-enacted in IRA, s. 134 but in a modified form.

It will, therefore, be more convenient to consider picketing in more detail, along with the decided cases, under the new provisions (see p. 139).

Although the provisions of s. 2 of the 1906 Act allowed peaceful picketing they did not allow *unlawful persuasion*, for s. 7 of the Conspiracy and Protection of Property Act, 1875, expressly forbids this form of conduct on pain of a £20 fine or imprisonment not exceeding three months. This provision has NOT been repealed, and will also be considered on p. 140.

Trade Unions and the Civil Law (Old Position)

A trade union could, in the course of its functions, commit certain torts, or civil wrongs (e.g. civil conspiracy) and this raised the question of the liability of the trade union and its officials for such torts. As the Trade Union Act, 1871, protected these bodies against criminal liability only, protection in respect of civil wrongs had to be sought elsewhere. This protection was to be found in the common law and in the Trade Disputes Acts of 1906 and 1965.

COMMON LAW

The common law position was, and still is, as stated by Viscount Cave in *Sorrell* v. *Smith* [1925] A.C. 700, 711 and 712, where he advanced two propositions as representing the effects of earlier decisions:—

(a) That a combination of two or more persons wilfully to injure a man in his trade is unlawful and, if it results in damage to him is actionable.

(b) If the real purpose of the combination is not to injure another but to forward or defend the trade of those who enter into it, then no wrong is committed and no action will lie, although damage to another ensues.

These two principles have remained the basis upon which later judgments were founded, and were applied in *Crofter Hand Woven Harris Tweed Co.* v. *Veitch* (1942) (**8**). (Probably the best example of trade union activity in this connection.) It must be observed, however, that in order to gain the protection of the proposition in para. (b) it was, and is, necessary to show more than a mere legitimate interest. It must be established that the act complained of was intended to *forward* or *defend* the genuine trade interests of the combining parties, so that the important factor in absolving liability for civil conspiracy is the *motive* of the combining parties. It must be noted too that however laudable and legitimate the motive may be, the adoption of *unlawful means* such as intimidation to secure the objective would destroy the defence. The tort of intimidation is committed if A threatens to act unlawfully against B with the intention of causing B to act to the detriment of C. If C suffers loss as a consequence, he (C) will have a right of action against A, regardless of whether B's action in relation to C is lawful or unlawful. (See *Rookes* v. *Barnard* (1964) (**5**)).

THE TRADE DISPUTES ACTS, 1906 AND 1965

Whilst it is clear that within the terms of Viscount Cave's proposition there was, and is, some protection at common law from liability for the tort of conspiracy the effectiveness and extent of this protection has not always been clear, and was in fact brought into doubt by the *Taff Vale* (**9**) decision.

As a result of that decision, however, the Trade Disputes Act, 1906, was passed to extend the law in regard to activities of trade unions and their officials. The effects of that Act in relation to civil liability can be summarised under two headings as follows.

1. *Immunity of Trade Unions.* The Trade Disputes Act, 1906, s. 4(1) provided that a trade union could not be sued in tort, and had two objectives. They were:—

   (a) to prevent a registered trade union from being sued in tort in the capacity of a trade union, i.e. a separate legal entity; and

   (b) to prevent unregistered trade unions being sued similarly by means of a representative action against a member or members of the union.

This section did not prevent trade union officials, however, from being sued as individuals, even though they acted on behalf of a trade union, nor did it extend to protect trade unions from being sued for breaches of contracts. But it must be emphasised that the protection against being sued in tort was total, and was wide enough to protect a trade union from an action in tort even though the tort alleged was in no way connected with a trade dispute.

2. *Immunity of Trade Union Officials.* S. 3 of the 1906 Act provided that any act done by a *person* in *contemplation or furtherance* of a *trade dispute* should not be actionable on the grounds *only* that it induced some other person to *break a contract of employment* or that it interfered with the trade, business, or employment of some other person or with his right to dispose of his capital or his labour as he wished.

A trade union official, therefore, obtained his protection under this section, and not under s. 4(1) of the 1906 Act. The protection afforded to trade union officials was much more restricted than that applicable to trade unions, for it was limited to acts done in contemplation or furtherance of a trade dispute, and applied only to inducing or procuring some other person to break a contract of employment, or interfering with the trade or business of another or with his right to dispose of his capital or labour as he wished, in the limited circumstances of a trade dispute. The protection, therefore, did not extend to inducing persons to break contracts other than employment contracts (*Torquay Hotel Company Ltd.* v. *Cousins* (1969)) (**10**), nor did it extend to acts of intimidation, (*Rookes* v. *Barnard* (1964)) (**5**). The Trade Disputes Act, 1965, however, in effect reversed the results of the decision of *Rookes* v. *Barnard,* by providing that an act done in contemplation or furtherance of a trade dispute should not be actionable *only* on the grounds that it consisted in *threatening* either to break or to procure the breach of a contract of employment. Though, of course, intimidation by threats or other unlawful acts, e.g. physical violence, remained actionable.

II THE RIGHT TO STRIKE

The Right to Strike

So far we have concerned ourselves with the historical restrictions imposed by the law upon persons undertaking industrial action, and we have seen that over the last century many of these restrictions have been removed. It is now necessary to consider the present position on the rights of trade unions, and indeed of individuals, to engage in strikes, lock-outs and other industrial activities.

The right to withdraw his labour is a principle which has been regarded by the British working man as an inalienable right for at least the last one hundred years, and the Industrial Relations Act in general does not interfere with that basic principle. On the contrary it not only confirms the right to strike, but also extends the protection of a person who takes part in such activity. At the same time there is some limit on the complete freedom to embark on industrial action where the national interest is threatened (see chapter 10).

IRA, s. 128 provides that no court may issue an order of specific performance to compel any person to perform a contract of employment, nor issue an injunction to restrain him from committing a breach of such contract. Nor may any court prevent a person from working in accordance with a lawful contract of employment by issuing an injunction, and thus compel him to strike or take part in any irregular industrial activity. In other words the section clearly confirms the age-old principle that a worker may choose to work or not to work at his own discretion.

IRA, s. 147 which was intended to give statutory effect to the decision in *Morgan* v. *Fry* (1969) (**11**), extends the protection of the worker by providing that where *due notice* has been given by or on behalf of an employee of his intention to take part in a strike, such notice shall not, *unless it otherwise expressly provides*, be construed, either as a notice to terminate the employment, or as a repudiation of it. As due notice is at least the length of time that the employee is required to give under the terms of his contract, or any enactment— (e.g. Contract of Employment Act, 1963), to lawfully terminate the contract, this means that the section does not protect a worker who goes on strike without giving the due length of notice, i.e. it does not protect the "wildcat" striker. In the case of a wildcat striker, therefore, the employer may if he wishes regard the withdrawal of labour as a repudiation of the contract, and act accordingly, i.e. regard the contract as at an end and/or sue for damages for breach.

If due notice of intention to strike is not to be interpreted as a notice to terminate the contract of employment, the contract must be regarded as subsisting, and if it is still subsisting it would be a breach of a subsisting contract to fail to carry out its terms, so that the section further provides that so long as there is no term expressed or implied in the contract, excluding or restricting a person's right to participate in a strike (i.e. a no strike clause) and so long as *due notice* has been given of a person's intention to strike, then his action in taking part in the strike shall not be regarded as a breach of contract for the purposes of:—

(a) any proceedings in contract brought against him in respect of that contract, or

(b) any proceedings in tort, whether brought against him or against any other person, or

(c) for breach of contract involving possible injury to persons or property (under the Conspiracy and Protection of Property Act, 1875, s. 5, see below), or

(d) unfair industrial practices under IRA, s. 96 (i.e. inducing breaches of contract in contemplation or furtherance of industrial disputes other than by trade unions or employers' associations).

This means, therefore, that as this particular action of taking part in a strike is not to be regarded as a breach of contract (for the purpose of IRA, s. 96) the inducing or threats to induce another person to take part in a strike *only after due notice has been given* will not amount to an unfair industrial practice.

It must be emphasised, however, that nothing said under the foregoing provisions will in any way exclude or restrict any right which an employer has to dismiss (with or without notice) any employee who takes part in a strike (IRA, s. 96(4)) and it will be remembered from p. 41 that an employee who is dismissed while participating in a strike has not been unfairly dismissed.

Furthermore, where an employee has a term, expressed or implied in his contract which excludes or restricts his right to strike, he will be liable in damages for breach of contract if he strikes in breach of it.

Conspiracy and Protection of Property Act, 1875

As has been indicated, where an employee, or someone on his behalf, gives *due notice* of intention to strike, the act of striking will not amount to a breach of contract for the purposes of s. 5 of the Conspiracy and Protection of Property Act, 1875, which provides that: where any person *wilfully and maliciously* breaks any contract of service or hiring, knowing or having reasonable cause to believe that the *probable consequences* of his doing so will be to *endanger human life*, or cause *serious bodily harm*, or to *expose valuable property*, whether real or personal, to *destruction* or *serious injury*, such person is guilty of an offence, triable before a magistrates' court or on indictment and punishable by fine of up to £20 or up to three months' imprisonment.

If, however, a person undertakes strike action without due notice having been given on his behalf, then he will infringe these provisions, provided that he acts wilfully and maliciously in breaking his contract of employment, in the circumstances described in the section.

In the past, prosecutions for this particular offence have been extremely rare, and it is not anticipated that there is going to be a great increase in the future, but it is now made clear by the Industrial Relations Act that where due notice of intention to strike is given this does not amount to a termination of the contract, thus putting into different categories those strikes where due notice is not given (a position that in the past was not absolutely certain) with the result that less sympathy for "wildcat" strikers who irresponsibly put life, limb and valuable property at serious risk might be expected.

III NEW LAW

Trade Unions and Criminal Law (New Position)

We have seen that under the old law (Trade Disputes Act, 1906, s. 1) any agreement or combination between two or more persons to do or procure to be done any act in *contemplation or furtherance of a trade dispute* did not amount to a criminal conspiracy, provided that such act if committed by one person would not be punishable as a crime. In order, therefore, to gain the protection of this provision it was necessary to show merely that the act contemplated would not be unlawful if committed by one person alone. Without this provision *conspiracies* to strike or undertake industrial action could amount to a criminal offence. The Trade Disputes Act, 1906, has been repealed, but this protection has been replaced by IRA, s. 135, which provides that the purposes of any trade union, organisation of workers, employers' association or organisation of employers, shall not, by reason only that they are in restraint of trade, be unlawful, so as to make any member of the organisation liable to any criminal proceedings. These provisions appear to be somewhat wider than the old law in that the act contemplated need not necessarily be in contemplation of an *industrial dispute* (see page 144), though of course the practical effect will be that the acts normally envisaged are strikes, lock-outs and other irregular industrial actions.

Although the actions of these organisations are no longer criminal as being in restraint of trade, they may still be regarded as being unlawful at common law for civil law purposes, and as a consequence any agreements made by such combinations would not be enforceable.

The section therefore provides that any agreement or trust made by such organisation or association will not be void or voidable merely because the purposes of the organisation or association are in restraint of trade. These provisions extend to agreements made by joint bodies established under a procedure agreement.

Picketing (New Position)

The law relating to picketing as was indicated on p. 132 has been modified rather than repealed, and IRA, s. 134 now provides that it will be lawful for one or more persons in *contemplation* or *furtherance* of an *industrial dispute* to attend at or near:—

   (a)   a place where a person *works* or *carries on business*, or

   (b)   any other place where a person happens to be *not being a place where he lives*, and does so *only* for the purpose of—

      (i)   peacefully obtaining information from him, or

     (ii)   peacefully communicating information to him, or

    (iii)   peacefully persuading him to work or not to work.

The area for peaceful picketing has been restricted somewhat by removing the right to picket a person's residence.

It must be noted that in order to be within these provisions picketing must be peacefully carried on and it ceases to be lawful if the activities of the pickets, for example:—

   (a)   obstruct pedestrians by deliberately standing in their way or using violence,

   (b)   include committing or threatening breaches of the peace (*Piddington* v. *Bates*, (1960) (**12**)),

   (c)   obstruct traffic in the highways (*Tynan* v. *Balmer* (1960) (**13**)),

   (d)   induce breaches of contract, other than contracts of employment e.g. by interfering with the delivery of goods to premises (*Torquay Hotel Company* v. *Cousins*, (1967) (**10**)),

   (e)   include soliciting persons to boycott premises such as shops and hotels.

It is, as previously indicated, also unlawful to picket a persons' residence and it may be difficult in some circumstances to distinguish whether pickets are acting lawfully in picketing a factory or unlawfully in picketing a person's residence, for in many industrial areas factories and houses of both managerial staff and of workers are closely situated. It is suggested that the deciding factor in whether the picketing is lawful or unlawful in this context will be the motive and intention of the pickets, for picketing only remains lawful in the absence of intimidation. Where, therefore, something is being done where persons are in the vicinity of both factory and houses, other than communicating with persons attending or leaving the factory, it is probable that the Court would take the view that it was the residence that was being picketed and not the factory.

In connection with picketing it may be opportune to refer at this point to s. 7 of the Conspiracy and Protection of Property Act, 1875, which provides that every person who, with a view to compelling any other person to abstain from doing, or to do, any act which such person has a legal right to do, or abstain from doing, wrongfully and without legal authority,

(a)   uses violence to, or intimidates such person, or his wife, or his children, or injures his property, or

(b)   persistently follows him about from place to place, or

(c)   hides any tools or clothes or other property owned or used by him, or deprives him or hinders him in the use thereof, or

(d)   watches or besets the house or other place where he resides, or works, or carries on business or happens to be, or the approach to such house or place, or

(e)   follows him with two or more other persons in a disorderly manner in or through any street or road,

is, on conviction, liable to pay a fine not exceeding £20 or to imprisonment not exceeding three months.

NOTE: Now that picketing a person's residence is no longer lawful, it will be an offence under s. 7 of the 1875 Act and punishable accordingly. IRA, s. 134 (2) specifically states that an offence under s. 7 of the 1875 Act, is not committed in the circumstances of *peacefully* picketing described above, nor is picketing a tort, unless it becomes unlawful e.g. picketing a person's residence (IRA, s. 134 (2)).

Trade Unions (Employers' Associations) and the Civil Law (New Position)

In examining the present position of trade unions and other persons in relation to possible liability for participating in industrial disputes, it must be borne in mind that the statutory rules, which gave immunity from liability had developed piecemeal over a period of exactly one hundred years, and could be gathered only by referring to a large number of statutes. The Industrial Relations Act, 1971, sweeps away most of these Acts, but re-enacts in a modified form many of their principles. There have been changes of course in principles, and also in terminology and phraseology; and this can lead to misunderstanding by anyone familiar with the old law. It is therefore urged if the reader is conversant with the old legislative provisions, that he approaches the new provisions with a completely open mind and a preparedness to accept that, at least, some of his knowledge is out of date.

The principles developed by the *common law*, however, as outlined above remain unchanged, though perhaps of little significance in view of the wider provisions of the Industrial Relations Act.

Under the trade union legislation from 1871 to 1965, it was not necessary to distinguish between associations of workers and associations of employers, because under the definition of a trade union, both were equally trade unions. The new law, however, does distinguish between the two groups, but effectively the distinction is one of terminology and what is said about trade unions applies equally to employers and employers' associations. It is therefore, proposed to discuss them together unless the context requires a distinction to be made.

The provisions of the present statute, relating to possible civil liability for taking industrial action will be considered under two separate headings viz., tort, and unfair industrial practices.

1. LIABILITY IN TORT

Tort is a term in the law of England used to describe all those wrongs, not arising out of contract, for which a remedy by compensation or damages is given in a court of law. Where a person has suffered loss or damage because of another's negligence or deliberately harmful conduct and seeks to recover damages, he is said to bring an action in tort. The defendant, if the action is successful in the court, is said to be liable in tort.

As we have seen, in the past, persons damaged by industrial action sought to bring actions in tort and to claim damages against the persons or trade unions responsible. A complete immunity, however, from actions in tort, was given by the Trade Disputes Act, 1906, s. 4 to trade unions, and to a lesser extent to individuals (1906 Act, s. 3). That Act has been repealed by the Industrial Relations Act, but the principles of these two sections have been replaced, and in fact extended by IRA, s. 132, which provides that any act done by a person in *contemplation* or *furtherance* of an *industrial dispute* shall not be actionable *in tort* on the ground only:—

(a) that the act induces another person to break a contract to which that other person is a party, or prevents another person from performing such a contract (IRA, s. 132(1)(a));

(b) that the act amounts to a threat that a contract will be broken (whether he is a party to the contract in question does not matter). Alternatively, that he will induce another person to break any contract to which that other person is a party, or will prevent another party from performing such a contract (IRA, s. 132(1)(b));

(c) that the act amounts to interference with the trade, business or employment of some other person or his right to dispose of his capital or labour as he wills (IRA, s. 132(2));

Further that any agreement or combination by two or more persons to do or procure to be done any act in *contemplation* or *furtherance* of an *industrial dispute* shall not be actionable in tort, if the act in question is one which if done without such agreement or combination, would not be actionable in tort.

The section refers to "an act done by *a person* in contemplation . . ." and does not refer specifically to trade unions. Therefore, it raises the immediate question, has the protection of trade unions been removed? The answer to this question is, that by virtue of IRA, s. 74, trade unions are given the status of corporate bodies, and are therefore, artificial persons recognised by the law in the same way as human persons, with the same rights and duties under the law so far as is practically possible. As a consequence, when the Act refers to *a person*, corporate bodies including trade unions are included. Thus the provisions of IRA, s. 132, unlike the old law (Trade Disputes Act, 1906, ss. 3, 4) which distinguishes between persons generally and trade unions, and provided a more extensive immunity in tort in the case of the latter than in the case of the former, makes no such distinction in this connection. The immunity in tort of both trade unions and other persons applies equally as set out in the section.

It must be emphasised that the protection will also apply to unregistered organisations for s. 19 of the Interpretation Act, 1889, provides; "the expression 'person' shall, unless the contrary intention appears, include any body of persons corporate or incorporate for both that Act and any other Act passed thereafter".

To gain the protection of this provision it is necessary that the act amounting to a tort is done in contemplation or furtherance of an industrial dispute: therefore, if an act done is not in contemplation or furtherance of an industrial dispute, or is something other than a tort, e.g. a breach of contract, then the section does not apply; both trade unions and individuals will be liable in the ordinary way. This is one distinction from the old law where a trade union could not be liable in tort whether it was committed in contemplation or furtherance of a "trade dispute" or not.

An example of this last point is a situation where a trade union employs a driver to drive a van on its behalf, and in the course of the driving somebody is knocked down and injured through the driver's negligence. The general rule is that in these circumstances the employer as well as the employee is liable in damages to the injured person. In the past the trade union as the employer could not have been sued for this tort because of its absolute immunity under the Trade Disputes Act, 1906, but now it will be liable because the act was not done in contemplation or furtherance of an industrial dispute.

What is meant by the expression "*contemplation or furtherance*" may be gathered from the old cases decided under the old statutory provisions where similar words were used (e.g. Trade Disputes Act, 1906) and what is meant by the expression "*industrial dispute*" must be gathered from the present Act where it is defined in IRA, s. 167 (1) (see below).

In connection with the expression "contemplation or furtherance", Lord Loreburn L.C., said in *Conway* v. *Wade* [1909] A.C. 506, "I think they mean that either a dispute is imminent and the act is done in expectation of, and with a view to it, or is already existing, and the act done is in support of one side to it. In either case the act must be genuinely done as described and the dispute must be a real thing imminent or existing." For an application of this view that an act done "in contemplation" of a trade dispute means an act done before the dispute arises, whilst any act done "in furtherance" of a trade dispute means an act done when the dispute has come into existence, see *R.* v. *Tears* [1944], 2 All E.R. 403, at p. 405.

"Industrial Dispute" is it seems a somewhat narrower concept than trade dispute, for it is defined as a dispute between one or more employers or organisation of employers and one or more workers or organisation of workers, where the dispute relates wholly or mainly to any one or more of the following:—

(a) terms and conditions of employment, or the physical conditions in which any workers are required to work;

(b) engagement or non-engagement, or termination or suspension of employment, of one or more workers;

(c) allocation of work as between workers or groups of workers;

(d) a procedure agreement, or any matter to which in accordance with this section a procedure agreement can relate (IRA, s. 167 (1)).

NOTE: In a dispute between a Minister of the Crown and one or more workers, or organisations of workers, the Minister will be regarded as an "employer" for this purpose if the dispute relates to matters which have been referred for consideration by a joint body upon which the Minister has a statutory right to be represented, or to matters which can only take effect subject to the Minister's approval (IRA, s. 167 (5)).

"Trade Dispute" included matters connected with employment or non-employment, or the terms of the employment, or with the conditions of labour, of any person (including employed persons not in the employment of the employer with whom the dispute arose), but also included disputes between workmen and workmen (Trade Disputes Act, 1906, s. 5(3)) whereas "industrial disputes" must be between an employer or organisations of employers and workmen or organisations of workmen.

A dispute between a union and an employer, because the employer would not bring pressure to bear on his employees to join the union was held not to be a trade dispute (*Ryan* v. *Cooke & Quinn* [1938], I.R. 512), similarly a dispute between a union and an employer because he induced his employees by legal means to leave the union (*Sheriff* v. *McMullen* [1952], I.R. 236).

In *Huntley* v. *Thornton* [1957], 1 All E.R. 234, at p. 256, it was indicated that a mere personal quarrel could not amount to a trade dispute.

The lawful dismissal of an employee may, however, be the subject of a trade dispute (*Bird* v. *O'Neil* [1960], A.C. 907 P.C. at p. 924).

The definition in IRA, s. 167, of an "industrial dispute", should be regarded as an exhaustive one and it is suggested that it would not include any kind of dispute which cannot be fitted within its terms. Therefore, whilst disputes as to how and in what conditions cargoes should be loaded into a vessel are clearly within its terms, disputes about the destination of the cargoes, e.g. arms for South Africa, are not.

In the event of a dispute arising, the first question must always be, what is the object of the dispute? I.e. what is the final outcome that is intended. If it is, for example a purely political object, then it does not come within the provisions of the section under discussion, so that a trade union which participated would not obtain its protection.

During the passage of the Act through Parliament a number of "one day strikes" were undertaken by trade unions and their members, in the hope of persuading the Government to abandon it. These strikes, it is suggested, fall outside the provisions of the section, and had the Act then been in force, both the trade unions and their members could have been sued in the ordinary courts in tort by employers who suffered damage as a consequence.

It must be remembered, however, that the decision to bring an action in tort always rests with the party suffering the damage, therefore in this case it would be the employer. Situations could of course arise where persons other than employers are damaged by such "unlawful" actions, e.g. power workers with the *approval of their union* may suddenly take industrial action, causing the supply to a refrigeration company to be cut off, resulting in damage to stocks. If the reason for cutting off the power is a dispute which comes within the terms of this definition they are not liable in tort. If, however, the dispute does not come within its terms, let us say because it has arisen over the refrigeration company's recent large contribution to the Conservative Party funds, then they will be liable in tort. (And so now will the union if it induced the strike.)

Once it has been established that the act complained of was done in contemplation or furtherance of an industrial dispute, it is then necessary to establish that the act was limited to the following:—

(a) *Inducements to break contracts*, i.e. that it induced another person to break a contract to which he was a party, or alternatively prevented another person from performing such a contract. It does not therefore, excuse inducements to a person to do something other than break a contract and which causes damage or loss to some other person, nor the utilisation of unlawful methods of inducement like threatening a person with physical violence or blackmail. The provision is restricted to the inducement to break contracts by "non-unlawful means", for the section specifically states ". . . shall not be actionable on the ground *only*". This means that where whatever is done would in itself be actionable as distinct from the inducement to a person to break a contract, then no protection is given under the section. E.g. A is employed by B, and is approached by a trade union official C who seeks to persuade him not to report for work because there is a dispute in the factory over a bonus scheme. Whether A decides to remain away from work or not C is protected under the section, from an action in tort by B. But if C were to threaten A with physical violence in order to induce him, not only would he be liable in law for the threat itself, but would not be protected by the section either.

It will be recalled that the old law, which contained a similar provision, only extended to inducements to break contracts of employment, whereas the present section contains no such restriction. It would appear therefore, that if in the example above A had been about to deliver fuel oil to B's factory with whom there was an industrial dispute with C's union, persuasion by C not to deliver i.e. to induce the driver to break the contract to deliver oil, would be protected. This appears to reverse part of the law as applied in *Torquay Hotel Co. Ltd.* v. *Cousins* (1969) (**10**). Of course, if C were to threaten to damage the lorry, or scatter nails on the highway, the inducement would no longer be protected for the same reason as in the first example.

(b) *Threatening Breaches of Contract.* This is where the action complained of consisted of *threats* that a contract would be broken or would be prevented from being performed, or that some other person would be induced to break a contract or be prevented from performing it. We are concerned here, therefore, with *threats only*, and not with actual inducements. The threats, however, are of two kinds:—

(i) a threat that a contract will not be performed or will be prevented from being performed (but no suggestion in the threat of anyone being induced not to perform), e.g., where an industrial dispute has arisen between employer B and the X union; the X union representative threatens B that unless he agrees to its demands all deliveries of goods by drivers of the X union, to or from the factory will cease, or that all goods of the firm will be "blacked" at the various ports from which they are to be shipped;

(ii) a threat that some other person will be induced to break a contract to which that other person is a party, or that the threatener will prevent another person from performing such a contract, e.g. where an industrial dispute has arisen between employer B and the X union; the X union representative threatens B that unless he agrees to the union demands his suppliers will be induced (perhaps by threats of industrial action) not to make deliveries, or that he will prevent the suppliers from performing their contracts to deliver goods by approaching their delivery drivers.

(c) *Interference with Trade, etc.,* the repealed Trade Disputes Act, 1906, s. 3, provided *that an act done in contemplation or furtherance of a trade dispute should not be actionable on the ground* **only** *that it induced some other person to break a contract of employment* **or** *that it interfered with the trade, business or employment of some other person, or with the rights of some other person to dispose of his capital or labour as he wills.*

It was thought by trade unionists and others that this section gave complete immunity from actions in tort to trade union officials who threatened employers with industrial action in order to induce them to dismiss non-union members. See *Rookes* v. *Barnard* (1964) **(5)** where trade union officials threatened B an employer that they would call for industrial action to be taken against him unless he terminated the employment of C. In an action by C, whose employment had been terminated as a consequence of the threat, the House of Lords decided that C had a right of action for damages against the officials although the termination of employment by the employer was lawful in the circumstances.

The reason for this decision it appears is because the threats on the part of the officials amounted to *unlawful intimidation*, which was something other than a mere inducement to break a contract, etc. For when s. 3 of the Trade Disputes Act, 1906, was examined by the House of Lords they considered both limbs of the section in detail, and concluded that the *threat* of strike action was actionable despite these provisions, if it resulted in an "interference with the trade, business or employment of some other person, or with a right of some other person to dispose of his capital or labour". This was because the conduct would not then be actionable *only* on the grounds of interference, but *also* on the ground of the intimidation involved in the *threat* of strike action.

As a consequence of *Rookes* v. *Barnard* (**5**) the Trade Disputes Act, 1965 (now repealed), was enacted with the declared object of extending immunity in cases like *Rookes* v. *Barnard* : i.e. even to those situations where intimidation was used. The new provision (IRA, s. 132 (2)) enacts *"for the avoidance of doubt it is declared that an act done by a person in contemplation or furtherance of an industrial dispute is not actionable in tort on the ground ONLY thàt it is an interference with the trade, business or employment of another person, or with the right of another person to dispose of his capital or labour as he wills"*. The similarity of the old and the new provision will be apparent, but whilst the present section substantially re-enacts the old provision it extends the protection to *all contracts* and not merely contracts of employment.

It is suggested that the combined result of the House of Lords decision and the new provision is that so long as any act done is a *mere* interference with the trade, etc., of any person it will not be actionable in tort, but if it is independently actionable as a tort, e.g., on the grounds of intimidation, then it will be actionable as such and no protection is provided under the Act. If, however, the act which it is alleged amounts to intimidation, is a threat that a breach of contract in contemplation or furtherance of an industrial dispute will occur, then no action in tort is possible (IRA, s. 132 (1)(b)).

(d) *Combination and Conspiracy.* It will be recalled (see p. 133) that at common law, where two or more persons agree together to do something which causes loss or damage to another person they may be liable in tort, unless they can show that they had a single view of protecting their genuine trade interests. (*Mogul Steamship Co. Ltd.*, v. *McGregor, Gow & Co. Ltd.* (1892)) (**7**).

What amounts to the protection of genuine trade interests has always presented a problem, for whilst it clearly includes the protection of commercial interests, difficulties have been encountered in establishing the boundaries in relation to trade union activities.

The *Taff Vale* **(8)** decision led directly to the enactment of the Trade Disputes Act, 1906, which gave immunity to trade unions from actions in tort for conspiracy. This Act has been repealed and its provisions in this context substantially re-enacted in IRA, s. 132(3), which provides as follows: "An agreement or combination by two or more persons to do or procure to be done any act in contemplation or furtherance of an industrial dispute shall not be actionable in tort, if the act in question is one which, if done without any such agreement or combination, would not be actionable in tort."

The purpose of these provisions is to give legal protection to agreements made between two or more persons, which would otherwise amount to an actionable conspiracy if it caused loss or damage to a third party. It clearly includes trade unions which are always combinations whose declared object is to bring pressure upon employers in order to improve the conditions of their members.

The provisions are not, however, restricted to trade unions but are much more general in their objective.

NOTE: There is no blanket provision under this subsection (or indeed under the Act) which protects trade unions from action for all torts, as there was under the old law.

In analysing the extent of this provision it must again be borne in mind that it is limited to activities which are in contemplation or furtherance of industrial disputes.

Where two or more persons come together, therefore, to plan a course of action in contemplation or furtherance of an industrial dispute, such agreement will not be actionable even though its purpose is to cause loss or damage to a third party, unless the act which is being planned would be actionable if done by one person acting alone. In other words no act which is unlawful if done by one person, is made lawful when done by two or more persons under this provision. Nor will an act which is lawful if done by one person acting alone become unlawful merely because it is agreed to be done by two or more persons. The position at common law (see p. 128) is that though an act if done by one person would be perfectly lawful, it would become unlawful if agreed to be done by two or more persons, provided that damage or loss could be shown, unless it could be clearly established that the object of the agreement was the single object of protecting the genuine trade interests of the combiners. E.g. in the *Mogul* case **(7)**, a number of traders agreed together to fix prices at an artificially low level in order to squeeze competitors out of the business: this is permissible if the object is to improve their own long-term business prospects, and not solely to cause a competitor economic ruin. But in *Quinn* v. *Leathem* [1901], A.C. 495 L employed assistants who were not trade union members, and refused to dismiss them when asked by Q, a trade union official. L did, however, offer to pay any demand by the union if they would admit the assistants to membership, but this was refused. M who often purchased meat from L was approached by Q, who threatened that unless he ceased purchasing from L he would call a strike of M's employees. M complied with the request and ceased buying from L.

L having suffered economic loss brought an action against Q and other officials of the union on the grounds that they had conspired together in order to injure his business. He recovered damages against the defendants individually.

NOTE: In the *Taff Vale* **(9)** case the plaintiff recovered against the trade union itself.

If, therefore, an employee is in dispute with his employer over wage rates, and agrees with other employees of the same employer, that no one will work overtime until an increase in wages is granted, this will be protected by the provision, because it is in furtherance of an industrial dispute.

2. UNFAIR INDUSTRIAL PRACTICES (Trade Union and Employers' Associations' Immunity from Liability in Industrial Disputes.)

As will appear from what has already been said in the preceding pages a new concept was introduced into the law by the Industrial Relations Act, that of the unfair industrial practice, and it is this that we must in the future consider as being of primary importance when we are considering possible liability for industrial action.

Whilst the Act clearly extends immunity from liability *in tort* to both trade unions and persons generally for acts done in contemplation or furtherance of industrial disputes, this immunity does not necessarily extend to liability for *unfair industrial practices*, for IRA, s. 96(1) provides that it shall be an *unfair industrial practice* for any person in contemplation or furtherance of an industrial dispute, knowingly to induce or threaten to induce another person to break a contract to which that other is a party; *unless* the *person inducing* or *threatening* is a *trade union* or *employers' association* or a person acting within the scope of his authority on *behalf of either.*

It might be suggested that in providing immunity in tort for acts committed in contemplation or furtherance of an industrial dispute, and at the same time creating a liability for an unfair industrial practice for such an act, that what the Act has given with one hand it has taken away with the other. For it may be thought to be of little significance if a person has to pay damages whether he is paying for a tort or for what is called an unfair industrial practice. To some extent, at least, this is true but it should be borne in mind that all complaints relating to unfair industrial practices will be heard by the Industrial Court, whilst actions in tort are dealt with in the ordinary court, and that the requirements of the Act are that conciliation should play an important part in the activities of the former, and that in any event different criteria as to liability which are in line with the Code of Practice on Industrial Relations, will be applied by the Industrial Court.

The clear objective of this section of the Act is to discourage what have become known as "wildcat" or "unofficial" strikes by ensuring that only trade unions and employers' associations, or persons acting with authority on their behalf, are given immunity from liability for unfair industrial practice in *inducing* or *threatening to induce* strikes in contemplation or furtherance of *industrial disputes,* whilst leaving unregistered organisations of workers and individuals liable under the Act for such practices.

It is necessary, therefore, to make a clear distinction under this heading between trade unions and employers' associations on the one hand, and unregistered organisations and individuals on the other hand.

It must again be emphasised that we are, as we did under the heading of tort, only discussing acts done in contemplation or furtherance of an industrial dispute.

The possible interpretation and extent of the term "industrial dispute" has already been examined on p. 144, and what has been said about its application to possible liability in tort applies equally to a possible liability for an unfair industrial practice in this context. The meaning of "inducing" must, however, be considered, for unless there is an inducement to another to break a contract, or threat of it, there is no liability in any event for this particular unfair industrial practice.

The dictionary definition of the verb to induce is "to prevail on, to cause or produce in any way": but it is suggested that in the connection in which we are here using the expression it involves five elements, viz.,

(a) knowledge that a contract exists (or possibly knowledge that a particular course of trading involving the continual making of contracts exists);

(b) there must be an intention (which is perhaps the most important element) for unless it is done deliberately there can be no liability;

(c) there must be an actual breach of the contract which has been induced (except where we are concerned with threats to induce);

(d) the breach must actually be caused by the inducement;

(e) there must be damage before a cause of action arises.

Where therefore, a newspaper or television broadcast gives a report of industrial activities it is very difficult to see how it could even be remotely in danger of incurring liability, for there will be lacking one or more of the elements described. In any event a mere comment even if in colourful and descriptive style would not suffice. The reporting of inflammatory words of a union leader or of an employer in the course of an industrial dispute, because it is thought that people ought to know what is going on, would still lack the elements of inducing. Of course, it would clearly be possible to use a newspaper for the purpose of inducing, where it is brought out not simply as an act of journalism but to persuade people to break their contracts.

This apparently complete immunity intended to apply to trade unions and employers' associations is subject to some qualification for even they may be guilty of an *unfair industrial practice* for taking three types of action viz., (a) for inducing *breaches of binding collective agreements;* (b) taking what is known as *"sympathy action";* (c) for taking *industrial action against "extraneous" parties.*

(i) *Inducing breaches of binding collective agreements.* Where a trade union or employers' association induces or threatens to induce a breach of a collective agreement other than any part of a collective agreement which is incorporated in a contract of employment, it will be guilty of an unfair industrial practice (IRA, ss. 36, 96).

(ii) *Sympathy action.* When an industrial dispute arises, a practice which is often resorted to in an endeavour to ensure a settlement in favour of one of the parties to it, is to seek support from persons who are not immediately involved. In the case of workers' organisations they may obtain support from workers in other organisations in the same factory or in organisations in other factories. This support may be a full strike or merely consist of "blacking" (i.e. refusing to handle) goods or the work of a particular firm which may be engaged in a dispute, or refusing to do work which would otherwise be done by those persons who are engaged in a dispute.

It is now provided that it would be an unfair industrial practice for any person (including a trade union or employers' association) in contemplation or furtherance of an industrial dispute *to take* or *threaten to take* any of the steps listed below, if the purpose for doing so is to support another person who himself is doing something which is in contemplation or furtherance of an industrial dispute *but which is an unfair industrial practice:*

(a) calling, organising, procuring or financing a strike;

(b) organising, procuring or financing any irregular industrial action short of a strike;

(c) instituting, carrying on, organising, procuring or financing a lock-out. (IRA, s. 97).

This is a fairly limited provision, and it is intended to apply where any person, including a trade union or employers' association in contemplation, etc., takes any of the steps specified in paras. (a), (b) or (c) for the purpose of supporting any action already taken by some other party whose action in the circumstances amounts to an unfair industrial practice under the provisions of the Act. Therefore, where any action amounting to an unfair industrial practice is taken by any person, any supporting (or sympathy) action will amount to an unfair industrial practice, even where the supporting action is taken by a trade union or an employers' association. But in the case of a trade union or employers' association there is an important qualification, for if the original action was taken by one or more *officials* or *members* of the trade union or employers' association AND the only reason that the original action was an unfair industrial practice was by virtue of IRA, s. 96 (i.e. a person in contemplation or furtherance of an industrial dispute, knowingly inducing or threatening to induce another person to break a con-

tract) then the trade union or employers' association will not be
guilty of an unfair industrial practice (IRA, s. 97 (3)).

The reason for this exception is that if an official (or member) acts
outside the scope of his authority in inducing other persons to break
their contracts his action could not otherwise be adopted (i.e. made
official) without the trade union or employers' association becoming
liable.

In circumstances therefore, where a dispute suddenly arises
between an employer and a shop steward (or other trade union
member) and the shop steward (or member) calls other employees
out on strike, without first obtaining the authority of the union, the
union will escape liability under this provision if it adopts the
action, (unless the action by the shop steward (or member) is an
unfair industrial practice by virtue of some other part of the Act,
e.g. seeking to establish a closed shop).

A further example is where an *unregistered organisation* of workers
is involved in inducing persons to break employment contracts
because of a dispute with the management over wage rates: this
would amount to an unfair industrial practice, and if a trade union
in order to support that organisation of workers sought to persuade
the employer to settle and took or threatened to take any action
as specified in paras. (a), (b) or (c) above, the union would be
guilty of an unfair industrial practice. If, however, the first party
in the example were a trade union then the action by the second
trade union would *not* be an unfair industrial practice under this
provision because the act by the first trade union would not itself
be an unfair industrial practice.

Whether an individual member of the organisation will be guilty
of an unfair industrial practice under this provision will depend
upon his degree of participation. Where he merely acquiesced in
the industrial action whether by joining the strike or "blacking"
work or goods, he will not be liable, but where he actively calls or
organises or finances, etc., the industrial action then he will be
liable. If therefore, a number of workers acted simultaneously
without being induced then no one would be guilty of an unfair
industrial practice.

In referring to the refusal to do work or handle goods in support
of other unfair industrial action, the assumption is that such refusa
will in itself amount to an irregular industrial practice i.e. that
such refusal will in fact amount to a breach of a contract of employ

ment. If, for example, a joiner refused to do the work of a maintenance engineer who was on strike, then it would not be a breach of
his contract of employment, and consequently would not be an
irregular industrial action. There has to be a refusal by a worker
to do something which he could by reason of his contract of employment be expected to do before it will amount to irregular industrial
action.

(iii) *Industrial action, extraneous parties.* The definition of an industrial dispute clearly establishes that it is a dispute between workers on
the one hand and an employer or employers on the other. We have
seen that where an act is done by a person in contemplation or
furtherance of an industrial dispute knowingly to induce some other
person to break a contract, that it is not actionable as a tort, but that
it is actionable as an unfair industrial practice unless it is done by a
trade union or employers' association. Further, that where such an
act is done even by a trade union or employers' association in
breach of a collective agreement or in support of some other person
committing an unfair industrial practice, then that also becomes an
unfair industrial practice.

The next step is to consider the position in relation to purely
innocent third parties (i.e. extraneous parties) who are deliberately
being prevented from performing their contracts because of an
industrial dispute in which they are in no way concerned.

The Act provides that it shall be an unfair industrial practice
for any person (including a trade union or employers' association)
in contemplation or furtherance of an industrial dispute *to take* or
threaten to take any of the following steps:

(a) calling, organising, procuring or financing a strike;
(b) organising, procuring or financing any irregular industrial
     action short of a strike;
(c) instituting, carrying on, organising, procuring or financing
     a lock-out,

if he knows, or has reasonable grounds for believing, that another
person has entered into a contract, *other than a contract of employment,*
with another party to that dispute *and his principal purpose* (i.e. his
intention) for taking the step is to induce that other person to break
the contract, or to prevent him from performing it, provided that the
other person is not a party to the dispute nor has given any material
support in contemplation or furtherance of it (i.e. an extraneous
party) (IRA, s. 98).

This may be explained in diagrammatic form:—

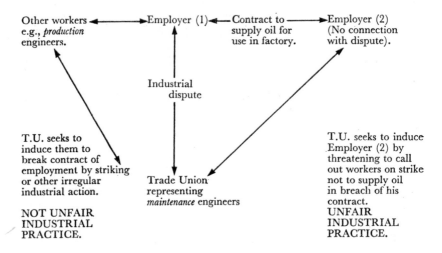

The effect of this section therefore, is to give a right of action in the Industrial Court against a party who induces breaches of contract with parties who are in no way concerned with an industrial dispute. The section only applies where the *intention* is to bring about a breach of a contract other than a contract of employment. And perhaps it is unnecessary to stress that in any event it does not apply to the *peaceful persuading* of suppliers not to deal with an employer involved in an industrial dispute so long as it does not amount to *inducing* a breach of contract. It will not therefore, include a trade union or person acting on its behalf, who persuades workers employed by an extraneous employer to join a strike to show solidarity, so long as the *real intention* is not to bring about a breach of contract between that employer and the employer in the dispute.

For the purposes of this provision a person is still an extraneous partly even though he—

(a) is an associated employer of the employer involved in the industrial dispute, so long as he is not in fact involved himself. But, he will not be involved *merely because of being associated*, perhaps in quite a different field of industry; or

(b) is a member of an organisation of employers of which a party to the dispute is also a member; or

(c) has contributed to a fund which may be available for the relief of losses incurred by a party to the dispute, so long as when his contributions were paid, the fund was established without specific reference to the dispute. If of course, one employer lent a sum of money to another employer who was involved in a dispute, for the purposes of helping him to overcome a difficulty created by the industrial dispute he would be *financing*, and would therefore no longer be an extraneous party. He will become a legitimate target for industrial action; or

(d) supplies goods to, or provides services for, a party to the industrial dispute in pursuance of a contract entered into *before* the industrial dispute began, or is a party to such a contract under which he is or may be required to supply goods to, or provide services for, a party to the industrial dispute (IRA, s. 98(3)).

Summary of Distinction between Liability in Tort and for Unfair Industrial Practice

As will have become apparent from what we have said in the last few pages, the precise relationship between liability in tort and liability for an unfair industrial practice is extremely difficult to establish, and it may assist the reader to have a brief summary of what the position is thought to be:

1. *No industrial dispute in existence.* Any person inducing or threatening to induce a breach of contract will be liable in tort as under the old law, actionable in the ordinary courts.

NOTE: The immunity given by IRA, s. 132 against actions in tort applies only where the action in question is in contemplation or furtherance of an industrial dispute. Therefore it will be a tortious act to induce or threaten a breach of contract not in contemplation or furtherance of an industrial dispute, e.g. in contemplation or furtherance of a "political" strike and it will be actionable in the ordinary courts. There is no alternative action available in the Industrial Court for an unfair industrial practice, for in order to be actionable in this court as an unfair industrial practice the act must have been done in contemplation or furtherance of an industrial dispute.

2. *Industrial dispute in existence.* Where an industrial dispute is actually in existence, which is a matter of both fact and law regard-

less of what the parties wish to call it, *any act* done in contemplation or furtherance of it will not be actionable in tort, but where any person *other than* a trade union or an employers' association (or official thereof acting within his authority), induces or threatens to induce a breach of contract *with a party to that dispute* he will be guilty of an unfair industrial practice actionable in the Industrial Court.

3. *Industrial dispute in existence.* Where any person does any act which is intended, or might reasonably be expected, to induce a breach of contract (other than a contract of employment) between an *extraneous party* and a *party to the dispute*, then it will not be actionable as a tort, but it will be actionable as an unfair industrial practice in the Industrial Court.

4. *Industrial dispute in existence.* Where there is in fact an industrial dispute in existence and any party to that dispute, (including a trade union or employers' association) does any act which induces any breach of contract between *two extraneous parties*, neither of whom has a contract with a party to the dispute, he will be liable in tort, actionable in the ordinary courts, and not guilty of an unfair industrial practice.

It is obvious that there will be circumstances in which a person has difficulty in distinguishing between what amounts to a tort and what amounts to an unfair industrial practice, and there will be occasions when an action is commenced in tort in the ordinary courts and it is then discovered that the matter is really within the jurisdiction of the Industrial Court, or industrial tribunal, as an unfair industrial practice. Alternatively proceedings may be commenced in the Industrial Court or an industrial tribunal for what is thought to be an unfair industrial practice.

In order to avoid the possibility of overlapping jurisdiction, and the encroachment by one court on the jurisdiction of another, the Act provides, that the Industrial Court has only that jurisdiction expressly given to it under the provisions of the Act and shall not entertain any action in tort. (IRA, s. 136). Therefore, if a person were to bring proceedings in the Industrial Court (or an industrial tribunal) for what he thought was an unfair industrial practice and the Court (or tribunal) decided that the matter was a tort, and not an unfair industrial practice, the Court (or tribunal) would simply dismiss the action, and the complainant would have to start again if he felt so inclined in the ordinary courts.

Similarly where proceedings in tort are commenced in an ordinary court, the court may stay the proceedings:

(a) where proceedings have already been brought before the Industrial Court or an industrial tribunal, on a matter in which they have jurisdiction, whether those proceedings have been disposed of or not, or

(b) where the matter brought before the ordinary court is one which under the provisions of the Act could be brought before the Industrial Court or an industrial tribunal, i.e., for an unfair industrial practice or breach of a duty imposed by the Act.

If the ordinary court stays the proceedings, then the action is dismissed and the complainant will be left with his remedy in the Industrial Court or industrial tribunal. (IRA, s. 131 (1), (2).)

Whilst not strictly within the context of our present discussion it is worth noting that a similar provision applies to proceedings brought under the Race Relations Act, 1968. Where a complaint has been made to the Secretary of State or to the Race Relations Board that there has been an unlawful act of discrimination, or where a matter is being investigated to decide whether such an act has occurred, it might appear to the Secretary of State or Race Relations Board that the act is really one of "ordinary" discrimination amounting to an unfair industrial practice, and has been, or could have been, brought before an industrial tribunal. If it does so appear then the Secretary of State or Race Relations Board must not proceed with the investigation under the Race Relations Act. But, if in fact a complaint of unfair industrial practice has been established before the Industrial Court or an industrial tribunal, and one of the factors was due to the complainant's colour, race or ethnic or national origins, then the proceedings may still continue under the Race Relations Act to secure a written assurance against a repetition of the act. (IRA, s. 149.)

Persons Acting on Behalf of Trade Unions and Employers' Associations

Where any person in contemplation or furtherance of an industrial dispute induces or threatens to induce any other person to break a contract, and is acting within the scope of his authority on behalf of a trade union or employers' association, he will be entitled to the same immunity as the organisation itself. The problem will be to establish not only the scope of authority, but also that the person was acting within it, i.e. on behalf of the trade union or employers' association. It has always been difficult to establish even in the commercial situation the scope of an agent's authority, because, frequently, of the lack of direct evidence as to actual appointment and authority. Three terms in this connection have become familiar, viz., *actual* authority, *implied* authority and *presumed* (or ostensible) authority, and it will be useful to consider the applicability of these terms in the connection of trade unions and employers' associations.

1. *Actual authority*. Here a person is appointed specifically to do what has been alleged to have been done. In this connection it does not matter what the person's status in general is (though here he will most certainly be an official) he will have been given direct authority by the trade union or employers' association to act as he did in inducing or threatening to induce. This type of authority will not only establish the scope of his authority, but also that he acted within it.

As IRA Sch. 4, para. 7 requires the rules of trade unions and employers' associations to specify the duties and powers of its governing body, officers and officials (see p. 114) it should *prima facie* be a simple matter to establish the scope of authority of any individual official, but it is suggested that the degree of precision in this respect will leave much to be desired, and that most cases will in fact have to be considered under the next heading.

2. *Implied authority*. It will often be difficult to be able to produce evidence of direct authorisation of a person by his trade union or employers' association for every specific act that a person takes. So that authority of an individual will frequently have to be established from the circumstances. One of these circumstances is to establish a pattern, and imply from a continuous course of conduct what the position is, and arrive at certain conclusions from the pattern. In other words, if a person frequently acts in a certain way and his acts are approved or adopted by his principal, there is a presumption that his present act will be approved.

3. *Presumed authority*. Where a person holds a certain status in an organisation, anything that he does which would normally be done by a person of that status in a similar organisation will be presumed to have been done in that capacity. Therefore, when it is established that a person is an official of a trade union or employers' association he will be presumed to have acted in that capacity.

Clearly in all these circumstances the person alleging that he acted within the scope of his authority will be happy to produce any direct authorisation that he might possess, and will be unlikely to deny such authority as may either be implied or presumed.

Where anyone, even a shop steward or other official wishes to engage in industrial action, he will be advised to first obtain approval and specific authority from his union or employers' association, and it may be that in some cases this approval may only be given in accordance with rules of this union (see p. 114).

CHAPTER 9

ADMINISTRATIVE PROVISIONS RELATING TO TRADE UNIONS AND EMPLOYERS' ASSOCIATIONS

EVERY trade union and every employers' association is required to keep a register of its members and to establish a satisfactory system of control giving a true and fair view of its financial position (IRA, s. 87).

Before the 1st June, each year (unless the Registrar otherwise directs in any particular case) such organisation must submit to the Registrar, a return of its affairs and a copy of its accounts audited by persons approved as auditors in accordance with IRA Sch. 5.

The annual return must contain:
  (a) revenue accounts, indicating the income and expenditure of the organisation for the period to which the return relates;
  (b) a balance sheet as at the end of that period; and
  (c) such other accounts (if any) as the Registrar may require.

Further, every trade union and employers' association must publish in every calendar year a report relating to its activities, either by supplying a copy free to every member or including it in a journal relating to its affairs which is available to all its members. The Registrar may on the application of an organisation exempt it from this last requirement if in his opinion it would be unduly onerous or because of the smallness of the numbers of members (possibly below 500). In the event of an exemption being granted the organisation shall nevertheless supply to each of its members free of charge a copy of its annual return for that year.

Any non-member may obtain from a trade union or employers' association a copy of its latest annual report on payment of such sum as may be prescribed (IRA, s. 88, Sch. 5), also a copy of its rules either free of charge or on payment of a reasonable fee (IRA, s. 88).

Any superannuation scheme established by either a trade union or employers' association established after the commencement of this Act must be maintained from a separate fund set aside for that purpose (IRA, s. 88, Sch. 5).

Both organisations must send to the Registrar within one month details of the following:

(a) all changes made in its rules (in this case only with a fee of £10 or such other sum as may be prescribed by statutory instrument);

(b) all changes of officers;

(c) change of address of its principal office. (IRA, s. 89.)

NOTE: The registers and other documents kept by the Registrar under the foregoing provisions are in effect public documents and the Secretary of State may by regulations make provision for their inspection by any person on payment of an approved fee (IRA, s. 95).

Offences

If a trade union or employers' association refuses or wilfully neglects to comply with the foregoing administrative requirements, it, and any officer responsible, may be fined up to £100. In the case of an officer, however, it will be a defence that he believed on reasonable grounds that some other person was responsible for that particular matter. If any person with intent to falsify, wilfully alters or causes to be altered any document required for the foregoing purposes in order to enable such organisation to evade those provisions, he may be fined up to £400 (IRA, s. 91).

If at any time it appears to the Chief Registrar that either of these organisations is insolvent he may appoint an inspector to investigate. The latter may examine on oath the officers, members or employees, and if found to be insolvent a petition may be presented by the Chief Registrar to the High Court for the organisation to be wound up (IRA, s. 90).

Political objects (limitation on use of funds)

As a result of the decision of the House of Lords in *A.S.R.S.* v. *Osborne* [1910] A.C. 87, which declared that trade unions could not use their funds for the furthering of political objects, the Trade Union Act, 1913, was passed for the express purpose of reforming the law and for providing that trade union funds could be used for such purposes, so long as two conditions are complied with:—

(a) A resolution must have been passed by a majority of the members approving the political objects as objects of the union. Voting to be by secret ballot in accordance with rules previously approved by the Registrar, who must be satisfied that every member has an equal right to vote (Trade Union Act, 1913, s. 4(1)).

(b) The rules of the union must by reason of the Trade Union Act, 1913, s. 3(1), provide that:—

    (i) all payments in favour of political objects must be made out of a separate fund, called the political fund,

    (ii) any member may, by giving notice in the form prescribed in the Schedule to the Trade Union Act, 1913, be exempt from subscribing thereto (i.e. contracting out),

    (iii) any member who exempts himself from subscribing to the political fund shall not be excluded from any benefits or placed under any disability or disadvantage compared with other members of the union except that he can be excluded from matters concerning the management of the political fund,

    (iv) contributions to the political fund shall not be a condition of admission to the union.

Political objectives are defined as follows:

(a) The payment of any expenses incurred directly or indirectly by a candidate or a prospective candidate for election to Parliament or to any public office, e.g. as a member of a local council, before, during or after election in connection with his candidature or election.

(b) The holding of any meeting or the distribution of any literature or documents in support of any such candidate or prospective candidate.

(c) The maintenance of any Member of Parliament or holder of a public office.

(d) Registration of electors or the selection of a candidate for Parliament or public office.

(e) The holding of political meetings of any kind, or the distribution of political literature or political documents of any kind, unless the main purpose of the meetings or of the distribution of the literature or documents is the furtherance of the statutory objects.

Any of these activities which do not involve expenditure are not within the provisions.

This Act has not been repealed by the Industrial Relations Act, but now that, in addition to trade unions, there are unregistered organisations of workers, unregistered organisations of employers and employers' associations, it was necessary to amend the Trade Union Act, 1913, in order to include these bodies. IRA Sch. 8 therefore replaces the term Trade Union in the Act with the terms "organisation of workers" and "organisation of employers", so that the provisions of the Trade Union Act will apply equally to organisations of workers or of employers, whether registered or not, who comply with the definition of those terms as used in the Industrial Relations Act.

CHAPTER 10

RESTRICTIONS ON THE RIGHT TO STRIKE — EMERGENCY PROCEDURES

As has been indicated (see p. 135), the general principle is that a worker's right to strike or to take other industrial action is inalienable, but there are circumstances where in the interests of the community at large, it has been thought necessary to place a restriction on the absolute freedom to embark on industrial action. The Act makes two specific provisions for dealing with industrial disputes which are of a grave and serious character, by establishing that the Secretary of State (a) in certain circumstances may apply to the Industrial Court for an order restraining persons from organising industrial action for up to 60 days, or (b) where he thinks that industrial action is being taken or contemplated and that the action is against the wishes of the workers concerned he may apply to the Industrial Court to order a ballot to be taken. These applications are not mutually exclusive in fact, but probably in practice they will be, because the reasons for applying for the first order are narrower than for the second.

Sixty-Day "Cooling-Off" Order

In any case where in contemplation or furtherance of an industrial dispute a strike, any irregular industrial action short of a strike, or a lock-out has begun or is likely to begin, and the Secretary of State is of the opinion that such action has caused (or would cause) an interruption in the supply of goods or the provision of services of such a nature, or on such a scale, as to be likely—

(a) to be gravely injurious to the national economy, to imperil national security or to create a serious risk of public disorder, or

(b) to endanger the lives of a substantial number of persons, or to expose a substantial number of persons to serious risk of disease or personal injury, he may make an application to the Industrial Court for an order to restrain the action for up to 60 days, if he considers that in all the circumstances the dispute could more readily be settled by negotiation, conciliation or arbitration if the industrial action were discontinued or deferred. (IRA, s. 138).

It is important to appreciate that this provision is only relevant to matters of national emergency or where there is a risk to *substantial* numbers of persons, and that all the factors which the Secretary of State has to be satisfied about are of grave and serious proportions. Further, before the application can be made the Secretary of State must be satisfied that not only is the action taken or contemplated a sufficiently grave and serious matter, but that a restraining order is going to be conducive to the settlement of the dispute by negotiation, conciliation or arbitration.

If the type of emergency envisaged in these provisions is constantly borne in mind it becomes easier to appreciate the limited application that they will have.

Two different kinds of emergency are envisaged, the first as set out in para. (a) is concerned with matters of national emergency, whilst the second as set out in para. (b) may be of a much more local character, but must involve danger to a *substantial* number of persons. One could perhaps give as an example of (a) a strike involving all the major docks, or national railway strike, but examples of (b) are rather more difficult for there is no way of estimating what will amount to *substantial* numbers, and it is probably foolhardy to seek to estimate in the abstract. But it is suggested that where the proposed strike, etc., would for example create a serious risk of a gas explosion of large enough proportions in a small town this would be included.

Having satisfied himself that the conditions are right the Secretary of State must now make his application specifying the action which he seeks to restrain and also naming the persons appearing to him to be responsible for calling, organising, procuring or financing the strike (or threatening to do so), or for instituting, carrying on, organising, procuring or financing the lock-out, or for threatening to do so.

The persons named by the Secretary of State shall, along with himself, be the parties to the proceedings (IRA, s. 138). Therefore, where an officer or official of a trade union is acting within the scope of his authority it will be the trade union who is named and not the officer or official personally. If such person, however, is not an official, or is acting outside his authority, then of course he will be personally named, and becomes a party as a consequence. In the case of an unregistered organisation it will be the persons who are leading the action who will be named because the organisation as such has no separate identity as has a trade union.

If the Industrial Court is satisfied on the evidence that the Secretary of State is correct in his assumptions, then it must make an order. The order must specify the following:

(a)   the area of employment to which the order applies, viz., one or more industries, one or more undertakings or parts thereof, and one or more descriptions of workers, or any combination of the three;

(b)   the persons who are to be bound by the order, viz., the persons named by the Secretary of State as being responsible referred to above as the "parties". But excluding those persons, even referred to as "parties", who have no responsibility for the strike or other action beyond that of being included among the persons taking part, or as an official of a Trade Union acting within the scope of his authority (IRA, s. 139(3));

(c)   the date upon which the order is to take effect, and the period not exceeding 60 days for which the order is to remain in force.

Once the Court is satisfied (and it must be satisfied) that the Secretary of State's fears are justified, the Court has no discretion but to issue an order. The practical effect of the order is that persons named as being responsible are directed not to call, organise, procure or finance a strike, or irregular industrial action, or threaten to do so, not to institute, carry on, authorise, organise or finance a lockout or threaten to do so, within the area of employment specified in the order, for the period of time specified, not in any case being longer than 60 days. The order might also require the party named as being responsible to take specified steps to have the action discontinued (or deferred) for the period that the order is operative (IRA, s. 139). I.e. the party responsible for the industrial action may be required to take steps to suspend the action, and if he makes a reasonable though unsuccessful attempt to implement the instructions he will have discharged his obligation.

It is vitally important to stress that where an order is made it is the parties who are named in it to whom it applies and not persons who have no responsibility for the strike, or other action complained of, other than being included among the persons taking part. There is, therefore, no restriction under this provision on the workers who are merely included in the persons taking part, so that where an order is made they incur no personal liability if they ignore a request to resume work. All the responsibility rests upon the party actually responsible for the action or proposed action.

Two questions immediately arise in connection with the Secretary of State's application. First, suppose it is discovered that he has named the wrong persons as parties, in his application, and second, what if the period of the order is too short?

The Act provides that so long as the order is in force, if it appears to the Industrial Court (on application by the Secretary of State) that other persons are responsible for the industrial action, then they may be substituted for, or added to, the originally named parties and any requirements of the order extended to them. And in the event of it being thought the length of time over which the order is to be operative is too short, the Secretary of State may apply to have the period extended, provided that the total period of the order does not exceed the maximum of 60 days (IRA, s. 140).

NOTE: It will not in any circumstances be possible for the period of suspension to exceed 60 days, for the Act provides that once the order has become effective, no application can be made to extend the period beyond 60 days (IRA, s. 140(2)) and that *no further application* can be made *in respect of the same industrial dispute*, or dispute falling within the scope, as seen by the Industrial Court, of the one for which the order was first issued (IRA, s. 140(7)).

Strike ballots

For a considerable period of time people have expressed the opinion that before any strike or industrial action of any kind can be undertaken there should be a requirement to take a ballot among the workers or other persons who are going to participate, this opinion is strenuously opposed as not being realistic or demo-cratic or in accordance with the principles of industrial freedom. There never was any serious consideration that such a provision would be included in the Act. The Act, however, does contain a provision requiring a ballot to be taken in strictly limited circum-stances similar to those discussed under the previous heading.

IRA, s. 141 provides that where it appears to the Secretary of State that in contemplation or furtherance of an industrial dispute a strike or any irregular industrial action short of a strike has begun or is likely to begin, and that the action has caused, or would cause, an interruption in the supply of goods or services of such a nature, or on such a scale, as to be likely—

(a) to be gravely injurious to the national economy, to imperil national security or to create a serious risk of public disorder, or

(b) to endanger the lives of a substantial number of persons, or expose a substantial number of persons to serious risk of disease or personal injury, or

(c) to affect a particular industry in such a way as to be seriously injurious to the livelihood of a substantial number of workers employed in that industry,

he may make application to the Industrial Court for an order requiring a ballot to be taken, among all workers falling within the area of employment specified in the order. Provided that before the Secretary of State makes application it appears to him that there are reasons for doubting that the action is in accordance with the workers' wishes, and that they have had an opportunity of expressing their wishes in this respect.

Before he makes the application the Secretary of State must, so far as it appears to him to be practicable in the circumstances, consult every employer, trade union or employers' association appearing to him to be a party to the industrial dispute in question.

Any application under this provision must specify the persons (whether they are organisations of workers, officials of such organisations or other persons) whom the Secretary of State considers to be responsible for organising, procuring or financing a strike or other action, or for threatening to do so. The persons specified together with the Secretary of State shall be the parties to any proceedings on that application.

On receipt of the application the Industrial Court, subject to its being satisfied on the evidence that there are sufficient grounds for believing that any of the conditions specified above are fulfilled, must order a ballot to be taken.

The order must specify—

(a) the industry or industries, the undertaking or undertakings affected, and the descriptions of workers among whom the ballot will be taken;

(b) the question on which the ballot is to be taken;

(c) the period within which the result of the ballot is to be reported to the Industrial Court (IRA, s. 142).

Included in the order made by the Court there must be a provision directing that during the period between the order becoming effective and the date on which the result for the ballot is reported to the court that no organisation of workers or persons specified in in the order may call, organise, procure or finance a strike of any of the workers eligible to vote in the ballot, or threaten to do so, or organise, procure or finance any irregular industrial action short of a strike, or threaten to do so. And that no employer, organisation of employers, or other persons may institute, carry on, organise, procure or finance a lock-out of any of those workers, or threaten to do so.

The order is addressed to the parties responsible for the action, and not to the individual workers, so that if the workers wish to strike or continue the action, they are free from liability if they do so. The order may, however, require organisations and any persons specified in it to take positive steps to ensure that for the period of time specified above any industrial action which has already commenced is discontinued, or where it is contemplated, then it should be deferred for that period (IRA, s. 143).

No maximum time is stated in the provisions within which a ballot must be taken, and it is therefore practically possible that in the case of an order requiring a ballot a period of longer than the 60 days limit fixed for "cooling off" could be allowed. The length of time will, of course, largely depend upon the industry, and in most cases it is suggested that the period will have to be short if it is going to be effective, but in a case like a seamen's dispute where the workers affected are widely dispersed, the period may have to be much longer.

When we considered the provisions relating to the 60 days cooling off period we saw that there were two sets of grounds upon which an application could be made, but that in relation to an application for a strike ballot there is an additional reason, i.e. that of possible serious injury to the livelihood of a substantial number of workers employed in a particular industry.

The extent of this last provision is not easy to establish, but it is probably safe to assume that it is intended to be invoked only in those cases of real emergency. The whole tenor of the provisions relating to the 60 day cooling off period and that of balloting is that of situations of a very grave nature, though it is suggested that on a strict interpretation it could be invoked even in the case of an industry of a purely local character employing a relatively small number of people in a small undertaking if the conditions described above were present. It is, however, more likely that in this last situation the services of the conciliation officials appointed under the Act would be more effective.

When the Industrial Court is deciding whether or not to make an order it may invite the assistance of the Commission in the formulation of the order (IRA, s. 142).

Conduct of the ballot

Once a ballot has been ordered the next question is who shall organise it? IRA, ss. 144 and 145 provide;

(a) it shall be conducted under the supervision of the Commission, who shall also be responsible for ensuring that the question on the ballot paper is in accordance with the order; and for reporting back the result to the Industrial Court;

(b) if all or some of the workers eligible to vote in the ballot are members of a trade union which is recognised by an employer who is a party to the dispute as having negotiating rights in relation to those workers, and provided also that its rules have been approved by the Registrar, such trade union may be requested by the Commission to conduct the ballot among those workers under the supervision of the Commission (and report back the result). The Commission will also pay the expenses of the union in this connection;

(c) where the trade union does not conduct the ballot the Commission has the responsibility for making alternative arrangements.

If any questions arise as to the way in which any order is to be interpreted, this will be determined by the Industrial Court on the application of either party to the dispute or the Commission. Where no such applications are made to the Industrial Court for a decision, then the Commission itself will determine the question.

Enforcement of Orders

As has previously been indicated the status of the Industrial Court is that of a superior court of record (Sch. 3(13)), and whilst its proceedings are to be conducted as informally as the Court considers it to be appropriate, any Orders issued by the Court have to be observed as if they had been issued by any other superior court of record. This means, therefore, that disobedience of the requirements of an order by any person named therein as a party will amount to contempt of court, and will be punishable accordingly (i.e. by fine or imprisonment). But in this event, only by, or with the consent of, a judge who is a member of the Court (Sch. 3 (27)(2)).

APPENDIX I

REMEDIES FOR UNFAIR INDUSTRIAL PRACTICES AND OTHER BREACHES OF THE PROVISIONS OF THE INDUSTRIAL RELATIONS ACT.

Industrial Court

Person or Body Commencing the Proceedings	Person Against Whom Proceedings Are Taken	Nature of Complaint	Remedies Available
1. Employer (not the worker, s. 105(1)).	Any person including trade union or other organisation of workers, or officials of either.	That the respondent brought pressure upon the employer: (a) knowingly to induce him to discriminate against a worker for exercising his rights in respect of trade union membership (ss. 5(2), 33(3)(a)); (b) knowingly to induce him to dismiss a worker unfairly (ss. 22(1), 33(3)(a)); (c) knowingly to induce him to enter into, or to comply with, a pre-entry closed shop agreement (ss. 7, 33(3)(b)(c)); (d) knowingly to induce him to make application to the Industrial Court for an approved closed shop	The Court may make; (a) an order determining the rights of the complainant and the respondent; (b) an award of compensation to be paid by the respondent to the complainant; (c) an order directing the respondent to refrain from continuing the action complained of, and to refrain from taking other similar action (s. 101(2)(3)). NOTE: where the conduct complained of is a *threat* to take industrial action the Court may in place of (c) make an order directing the respondent to cease the threat, and/or make an order directing the

| 2. Party to a collective agreement. | Another party to a collective agreement. | agreement (s. 33(3)(d)), (Sch. 1 (Pt. 1)).

That the respondent party failed to take all reasonably practicable steps for:

(a) preventing persons acting or purporting to act on that party's behalf from taking any action contrary to an undertaking given by that party and contained in the agreement (s. 36(2)(a));

(b) in the case of an organisation of workers or of employers such organisation preventing members of that organisation from taking such action as in (a) (s. 36(2)(b));

(c) where action has already been taken by a person as mentioned in (a) or a member as mentioned in (b) failing to secure that such action is not continued or repeated (s. 36(2)(c)). | respondent to refrain from taking action in accordance with the threat (s. 105(3)).

NOTE: where the respondent is a trade union official who acted within the scope of his authority he will not be liable but his union will. (s. 101(4)).

Remedies as in number 1.

NOTE: where the collective agreement is one made between an organisation of workers and an organisation of employers before s. 4 of the Trade Union Act, 1871, is repealed under the provisions of the Industrial Relations Act, the only remedy is that referred to in (c) above (s. 105(6)).
(S. 4 of the 1871 Act restricts the enforcement of certain contracts between trade unions and their members.) |

Industrial Court—*continued*

Person or Body Commencing the Proceedings	Person Against Whom Proceedings Are Taken	Nature of Complaint	Remedies Available
3. Trade union or employer.	The employer directly concerned or any person, including a trade union or other organisation of workers or officials of either.	Whilst a question was pending as to the recognition of a sole bargaining agent (s. 45) the *employer directly concerned* instituted, carried on, organised, procured or financed a lock-out in order to further the dispute, or threatened to do so (s. 54(4)(a)); or *some person* called, organised, procured or financed a strike, or threatened to do so, or organised, procured or financed irregular industrial action short of a strike, or threatened to do so in order to further the dispute (s. 54(4)(b)).	Remedies as in number 1.
4. Trade union or Joint Negotiating Panel.	Employer.	(i) That the employer instituted, carried on, organised, procured or financed a lock-out, or threatened to do so, knowingly to induce or attempt to induce any person to refrain from making an application for recognition of a sole bargaining agent (under s. 45), or for withdrawal of recognition of a sole bargaining agent (under s. 55(8)).	Remedies as in number 1, except in relation to (ii)(b), for where an employer has failed to take reasonable steps with a view to carrying on collective bargaining with a trade union or joint negotiating panel after having been ordered by the Industrial Court to do so, the only remedy where the Industrial Court thinks it just and equitable to do so is to make an order;

	(ii) Where an order of the Industrial Court was in force requiring the employer to recognise a trade union or joint negotiating panel as sole bargaining agent (s. 50) and the employer, (a) carried on collective bargaining in relation to that bargaining unit with another organisation of workers (s. 55(1)(a)), or (b) has failed to take reasonable steps with a view to carrying on collective bargaining with that trade union or joint negotiating panel (s. 55(1)(b)).	(a) authorising presentation of a claim to the Industrial Arbitration Board (under s. 125) (See 27 *post*), and (b) specifying the date on which, in accordance with the findings of the court the action constituting the unfair industrial practice first occurred (s. 105(5)).
5. Employer.	Any person, including a trade union or other organisation of workers, or officials of either.	Whilst an order of the Industrial Court was in force requiring the employer to recognise a trade union or joint negotiating panel as sole bargaining agent (under s. 50) the respondent: (a) called, organised, procured or financed a strike or threatened to do so, or (b) organised, procured or financed irregular industrial action short of a strike, or threatened to do so, in order knowingly to induce the employer,	Remedies as in number 1.

Industrial Court—*continued*

Person or Body Commencing the Proceedings	Person Against Whom Proceedings Are Taken	Nature of Complaint	Remedies Available
		(i) to carry on collective bargaining in relation to that bargaining unit with any other organisation of workers, or not to take reasonable steps with a view to carrying on collective bargaining with the trade union or joint negotiating panel named in the order (s. 55(3)), or (ii) within two years of the Commission submitting a report recommending, or otherwise, the recognition of a sole bargaining agent for a particular unit, to recognise some other bargaining agent for the same bargaining unit (s. 55(6)(a)), or to carry on collective bargaining with an organisation of workers or joint negotiating panel which was named in the report as not being recommended, in relation	

	Applicant	Grounds	Remedies
6. Employer.	Any person, including a trade union or other organisation of workers, or officials of either.	to employees of any description in the bargaining unit referred to in the report (s. 55(6)(b)). Within two years of the Industrial Court making an order after a ballot (s. 53) discontinuing a sole bargaining agent the respondent, (a) called, organised, procured or financed a strike or threatened to do so, or (b) organised, procured or financed irregular industrial action short of a strike, or threatened to do so, knowingly to induce the employer to continue recognising the sole bargaining agent (s. 55(7)).	Remedies as in number 1.
7. Trade Union.	Employer.	The respondent employer having failed after being required by representatives of the trade union to supply information, has failed to give the information, or to give (or confirm) it in writing at their request (s. 56).	If the Industrial Court considers it is just and equitable to do so it may make one or more of the following orders, (a) an order determining the rights of the trade union and the employer relating to the complaint, (b) an order directing the employer to fulfil his duty if it is within his power to do so (see 8, *post* for remedy if he fails to obey)

Industrial Court—*continued*

Person or Body Commencing the Proceedings	Person Against Whom Proceedings Are Taken	Nature of Complaint	Remedies Available
			(c) an order authorising the presentation of a claim to the Industrial Arbitration Board (under s. 126,) (s. 102(2)) (See 28, *post*).
8. Worker.	Employer.	That the respondent is a major employer (viz. employing more than 350 persons) and has failed to issue a statement in writing to every employee, as required by regulations made by the Secretary of State, after having been ordered to do so by an Industrial Tribunal (ss. 57 and 110(4)) (See 20, *post*).	If the Industrial Court finds the complaint well founded and considers it just and equitable to do so, it may make an order directing the employer, within a specified time, to issue to the complainant a statement that the Court considers appropriate (s. 110(5)). NOTE: failure on the part of the employer to comply with this order will amount to contempt of court, and as the Industrial Court has the same powers and authority as the High Court (Court of Session in Scotland) it can imprison or fine for contempt. No person can be punished for contempt of the Industrial Court, however, except by, or with the consent of a judge who is a member of the Court (Sch. 3, paras. 27, 28).

9. Worker.	Employer.	That the employer had entered into a closed shop agreement and had refused engagement to the complainant as a consequence (s. 7(2)).	If the Industrial Court is satisfied that the complaint is justified, and that the effect was to detract from the worker's rights in relation to trade union membership (under s. 5) the Court *shall* make an order declaring the agreement void (s. 7(3)). (The worker may also bring a complaint before an industrial tribunal, for an unfair industrial practice (IRA s. 5(2)(3)).)
10. Trade Union.	Employer.	After, either a majority of workers eligible to vote in a ballot, or not less than two-thirds of those who actually voted, had voted in favour of an agency shop, but the employer has failed either, (a) to take action to enter into an agency shop agreement, or (b) after entering into such an agreement has failed to carry out the agreement (s. 13(1)).	If the Industrial Court is satisfied that the complaint is well founded it may if it considers it just and equitable, (a) make an order determining the rights of the trade union and the employer in relation to the complaint, and/or (b) make an order directing the employer to fulfil his obligations (s. 102(2)). NOTE: failure to comply with (b) would amount to contempt of court (see 8, *supra*).
11. Employer.	Any person, including a trade union or other organisation of workers, or	After, either a majority of workers eligible to vote in a ballot, or not less than two-thirds of those who actually voted, had voted in	Remedies as for number 1.

Industrial Court—*continued*

Person or Body Commencing the Proceedings	Person Against Whom Proceedings Are Taken	Nature of Complaint	Remedies Available
	officials of same.	favour of an agency shop, and the respondent had called, organised, procured or financed a strike, or threatened to do so, or organised, procured or financed irregular industrial action short of a strike, or threatened to do so, knowingly to induce the employer not to comply with a duty imposed upon him by this decision (s. 13(2)).	
12. Trade union or Joint Negotiating Panel.	Employer.	In order knowingly to induce the trade union or joint negotiating panel not to make an application to the Industrial Court for the establishment of an agency shop agreement (under s. 11) the respondent instituted, carried on, organised, procured or financed a lock-out, or threatened to do so (s. 16(1)).	Remedies as in number 1.
13. Worker.	Employer.	The respondent has instituted, carried on, organised, procured or financed a lock-out, or threatened to do so, to knowingly induce a worker not to make an application to the Industrial Court for a ballot as to continuance of an agency shop	Remedies as in number 1.

		agreement (under s. 14(1)), (s. 16(1)).	
14. Employer.	Any person, including trade union or other organisation of workers, or officials of either.	Where an application has been made by workers to the Industrial Court for a ballot as to the continuance of an agency shop agreement (under s. 11) the respondent called, organised, procured or financed a strike or threatened to do so, or organised procured or financed any irregular industrial action short of a strike, or threatened to do so, to knowingly induce the employer to enter into an agency shop agreement in respect of those workers (Does not apply where ballot has shown a majority in favour of continuance) (s. 16(2)).	Remedies as in number 1.
15. Any person who may be regarded as being the other party to a contract that is broken or threatened. And against whom the action is taken.	Any person, other than a trade union or employers' association, or person acting within the scope of his authority on behalf of either. NOTE: trade unions and employers' associations are also included if the threat is to break a collective agreement, other than	In contemplation or furtherance of an industrial dispute the respondent knowingly induced or threatened to induce another person to break a contract to which the complainant was a party (s. 96).	Remedies as in number 1.

Industrial Court—*continued*

Person or Body Commencing the Proceedings	Person Against Whom Proceedings Are Taken	Nature of Complaint	Remedies Available
	any part which is incorporated into a contract of employment.		
16. Any person who may be regarded as being the other party to a contract that is broken or threatened. And against whom the action is taken.	Any person, including a trade union or employers' association, except where the trade union or employers' association is merely supporting an official who is guilty by virtue of s. 96 of an unfair industrial practice.	In contemplation or furtherance of an industrial dispute the respondent took, or threatened to take, any of the following actions, his principal purpose being to further any action which has already been taken, whether by him or by any other person; (a) called, organised, procured or financed a strike; (b) organised, procured or financed any irregular industrial action short of a strike; (c) instituted, carried on, organised, procured or financed a lock-out (s. 97).	Remedies as in number 1.
17. Both an extraneous party and a party to an industrial dispute.	Persons, including trade union or employers' association procuring or inducing the breach of contract.	That the respondent, in contemplation or furtherance of an industrial dispute, took or threatened to take any of the following steps,	Remedies as in number 1.

NOTE: either, or both simultaneously, may bring an action (s. 105(2)).

(a) called, organised, procured or financed a strike;

(b) organised, procured or financed any irregular industrial action short of a strike;

(c) instituted, carried on, organised, procured or financed a lock-out;

and in any case, knowing or having reasonable grounds for believing that another person had entered into a contract (other than a contract of employment) with a party to that industrial dispute, *provided* that his principal purpose in taking or threatening to take those steps is knowingly to induce that other person to break that contract or to prevent him from performing it, and *provided* that the other person was an extraneous party to that industrial dispute (s. 98(1)).

18. Registrar.

NOTE: the Registrar may present a complaint to an industrial tribunal as an alternative (s. 108). (See 24, *post.*)

Trade union or employers' association.

Registrar has failed to promote a settlement of a dispute as to discrimination by the trade union or employers' association against,

(a) a member of the organisation, or

(b) a person who was a member,

If the Industrial Court finds the complaint well founded and considers it would be just and equitable it may grant to the original applicant (i.e., the member, etc., not the Registrar) one or more of the following remedies;

Industrial Court—*continued*

Person or Body Commencing the Proceedings	Person Against Whom Proceedings Are Taken	Nature of Complaint	Remedies Available
		but who has ceased to be a member otherwise than by voluntary resignation, or (c) a person who has been refused or prevented, from membership (ss. 81 and 82). NOTE: this complaint can only be brought by the Registrar if the matter has not already been brought before an industrial tribunal, and it appears to him to be such a serious matter that it should be brought before the Industrial Court rather than such tribunal (s. 103(1)).	(a) an order determining the rights of the original applicant and of the trade union or employers' association; (b) an award of compensation, to be paid by the trade union or employers' association to the original applicant; (c) an order directing the trade union or employers' association to refrain from, and not to repeat the action complained of (s. 103(3)). (Maximum amount of compensation is: (i) an amount representing 104 weeks pay, or (ii) £4,160 (i.e., 104 × £40) whichever is the less (s. 118(1)).
19. Registrar.	Trade union or employers' association.	The Registrar having carried out an investigation on his own initiative and arrived at the conclusion that there has been a serious breach, or persistent	If the Industrial Court is satisfied that one or more breaches, etc., of the rules did occur, and that the respondent has not taken action required by the Registrar to

breaches of the rules of the organisation, or there have been serious breaches of the guiding principles relating to organisations of workers or of employers under ss. 65 and 69 as applied to the respondent trade union or employers' association. And having sought unsuccessfully by negotiating with the respondent to have the breach remedied, or its effect mitigated, or to obtain an undertaking that it would be remedied, etc. (s. 83) (s. 104(1)).

NOTE: any references to breaches of rules do not include breaches of rules made under the Trade Union Act, 1913 (ss. 3, 4(1) and 5(1) (relating to political funds)), or to taking a vote approving amalgamations or transfers under the Trade Union (Amalgamations, etc.) Act, 1964 (ss. 81(4), 83(2)).

remedy the defect, the Court may make an order directing the respondent to take such action as it thinks appropriate to remedy or mitigate the consequences of the breach, and to prevent its continuance or repetition (s. 104(2)).

NOTE: failure on the part of the trade union or employers' association to comply with the order of the Industrial Court would make it liable for contempt of court (See 8, *supra*).

Industrial Tribunal

Person or Body Commencing the Proceedings	Person Against Whom Proceedings Are Taken	Nature of Complaint	Remedies Available
20. Worker.	Employer.	That the respondent is a major employer (viz., employing more than 350 persons) and has failed to issue not later than six months after the end of the financial year, a statement in writing to every employee as required by regulations made by the Secretary of State (s. 57) (s. 110(1)).	If the Tribunal finds the complaint well founded, and considers it just and equitable to do so it may make an order determining the rights of the complainant and the employer (s. 110(2)), and may also give the employer an extended time within which to comply with the order (s. 110(3)). NOTE: if the employer does not comply with the order of the industrial tribunal within the time limit stated in the order, the worker may present a complaint to the Industrial Court (s. 110(4)). (See 8, *supra*).
21. Worker.	Employer.	The employer, or some person acting on behalf of the employer, (i) prevented, deterred, dismissed or otherwise discriminated against the complainant because he chose to belong to a trade union, or chose not to belong to a trade union or other organisation of workers, or for taking part at any	In all cases (*except* where the complaint relates to *dismissal*) the industrial tribunal may, if satisfied that the complaint is well founded and that it would be just and equitable to do so; (a) make an order determining the rights of the complainant and the employer, and/or

appropriate time in the activities of the trade union (s. 5(2)(a)(b)), or

(ii) refused to engage a worker on the grounds that at the time he applied for engagement he was a member of a trade union or particular trade union, or that he was not a member of a trade union or other organisation of workers or of a particular trade union or organisation of workers (s. 5(2)(c)), or

(iii) conferred any benefit on workers *other* than the complainant who agree to refrain from exercising their rights as to trade union membership (or membership of other organisations of workers) or withheld a benefit from the complainant because of his refusal to agree to refrain from exercising those rights (s. 5(4)).

(b) require that compensation be paid by the employer to the complainant (s. 106(1)(2)(3)).

Maximum amount of compensation is:

(i) an amount representing 104 weeks pay, or

(ii) £4,160 (i.e., 104 × £40) whichever is the less (s. 118(1)).

Where the *complaint relates to the dismissal* of the complainant the tribunal shall if it considers the complaint justified, and feels that it is practicable and in accordance with equity, recommend that the complainant be re-engaged or engaged, stating the terms on which it considers reasonable that the complainant should be re-engaged or engaged (s.106(4)).

Alternatively, or where such a recommendation has been made but not complied with, the tribunal *shall* require the employer to pay compensation to the complainant (s. 106(5)).

Maximum amount of compensation is:

(i) an amount representing 104 weeks pay, or

Industrial Tribunal—*continued*

Person or Body Commencing the Proceedings	Person Against Whom Proceedings Are Taken	Nature of Complaint	Remedies Available
			(ii) £4,160 (i.e., 104 × £40) whichever is the less (s. 118(1)).
			NOTE: that where the tribunal's recommendation of re-engagement is not complied with because of the worker's unreasonableness, the amount of compensation may be reduced, or increased if because of the employer's unreasonableness (s. 116(4)).
22. Worker.	Employer.	That the employee was unfairly dismissed (s. 22(1)).	The tribunal shall if it considers the complaint justified, and feels that it is practicable and in accordance with equity, recommend that the complainant be re-engaged or engaged, stating the terms on which it considers reasonable that the complainant should be re-engaged or engaged (s. 106(4)).
			Alternatively, or where such a recommendation has been made but not complied with, the tribunal shall require the employer to pay compensation to the complainant (s. 106(5)).

Maximum amount of compensation is:

(i) an amount representing 104 weeks pay, or

(ii) £4,160 (i.e. 104 × £40), whichever is the less (s. 118(1)).

NOTE: that where the tribunal's recommendation of re-engagement is not complied with because of the worker's unreasonableness the amount of compensation may be reduced, or increased if because of the employer's unreasonableness (s. 116(4)).

The tribunal may if it finds the complaint is well founded, and considers that it would be just and equitable to do so, grant either or both of the following remedies:

(a) an order determining the rights of the person presenting the complaint and the respondent organisation;

(b) require compensation to be paid by the organisation to the person who presented the complaint (s. 109(1)(2)).

NOTE: as compensation is not

That the organisation, or any official or person acting on its behalf, took or threatened to take action against a member, or person seeking to become a member of the organisation, which was in breach of the guiding principles (ss. 66 and 70) applicable to such an organisation, or that the action taken or threatened was a breach of its rules (s. 107(1)-(3)).

NOTE: this complaint may not be entertained by an industrial tribunal if an application on the same matter has been presented to the Registrar (under s. 81) and has not yet been given his

Organisation of workers or of employers, other than federations of either.

23. Any person other than a body corporate or incorporate.

NOTE: if the respondent is a trade union or an employers' association, only the person against whom the action was taken may present a complaint (s. 107(3)).

Industrial Tribunal—continued

Person or Body Commencing the Proceedings	Person Against Whom Proceedings Are Taken	Nature of Complaint	Remedies Available
		conclusions (s. 107 (4)) (See 29, *post*).	intended to be punitive it is suggested that it will only be awarded under this provision where the person presenting the complaint was the person against whom action was taken, and that where a complaint is presented by some person because there has been a general breach of rules a declaration of rights would be more appropriate. Maximum amount of compensation is: (i) an amount representing 104 weeks pay, or (ii) £4,160 (i.e. 104×£40), whichever is the less (s. 118(1)).
24. Registrar.	Trade union or employers' association, other than federations. (Not other organisations of workers or of employers.)	That an application has been made to the Registrar (under s. 81) by a person, that action has been taken against him, by or on behalf of the organisation, that was an unfair industrial practice in accordance with s. 66 or 70, or that it constituted a breach of the rules	If the industrial tribunal is satisfied that the complaint is well founded, it may if it considers it would be just and equitable to do so, grant one or more of the following remedies: (a) an order determining the rights of the original applicant

		of the organisation, and having been satisfied on investigation that the application was well founded (s. 108). NOTE: Registrar has an alternative under s. 103 to present this complaint to the Industrial Court (See 18, *supra*).	(i.e., the person making the complaint originally to the Registrar) and the respondent organisation; (b) require compensation to be paid by the organisation to the original applicant. Maximum amount of compensation is: (i) an amount representing 104 weeks pay, or, (ii) £4,160 (i.e., 104 × £40), whichever is the less (s. 118(1)).
25. Worker may require reference to be made to tribunal.	Declaratory judgment.	Where a worker claims that a contribution which the trade union requires him to pay as being an appropriate contribution payable in accordance with an agency shop agreement; (a) is not payable in accordance with the agreement, or (b) exceeds the limit permitted by s. 8 of the Act (s. 10(1)).	Industrial tribunal will determine amount payable, and this determination will have the same effect as if it had been an agreement between the worker and trade union (s. 10(1), (3)).
26. Dispute may be referred under industrial tribunal regulations.	Declaratory judgment.	A proposal having been made by a worker that he is allowed to make contributions to a charity instead of contributions to a trade union, and a dispute having arisen:	Industrial tribunal will determine amount payable, and this determination will have the same effect as if it had been an agreement between the worker and trade union (s. 10(2)(3)).

Industrial Tribunal—*continued*

Person or Body Commencing the Proceedings	Person Against Whom Proceedings Are Taken	Nature of Complaint	Remedies Available
		(a) whether his objections are genuinely on grounds of conscience; (b) as to which charity the contributions shall be payable; (c) what contributions would be equivalent to appropriate contributions to the trade union (s. 10(2)).	

Industrial Arbitration Board

Person or Body Commencing the Proceedings	Person Against Whom Proceedings Are Taken	Nature of Complaint	Remedies Available
27. Trade union.	Employer.	There being in force an order of the Industrial Court requiring the respondent employer to recognise the complainant trade union (or joint negotiating panel of which the trade union forms a part), and the employer having failed to take reasonable action with a view to carrying on collective bargaining with the complainant, and a complaint having been made to the Industrial Court (under s. 101) and the Court having authorised the presentation of a claim to the Industrial Arbitration Board under s. 105(5) (See 4, *supra*).	The Board may make an award requiring the employer to observe either the terms of the order, or other terms and conditions that the Board considers more appropriate in the circumstances. Such terms and conditions, unless expressly excluded in the contract of employment of any employee, *shall be implied in the contracts of employment* of the description of workers to whom the award relates until it is varied or superseded by agreement between the employer and employee, or by a subsequent award of the Board. The operative date of the terms and conditions will be that of the award, or if so stated may go back to the date on which the unfair industrial practice was first committed as found by the Industrial Court (s. 127). NOTE: any breach now by the employer will amount to a breach of each individual employee's contract of employment, giving such employee a right of action for

Industrial Arbitration Board—*continued*

Person or Body Commencing the Proceedings	Person Against Whom Proceedings Are Taken	Nature of Complaint	Remedies Available
			breach of contract. Subject to the Lord Chancellor making an order by statutory instrument a claim for such breach will be heard by an industrial tribunal (s. 113).
28. Trade union.	Employer.	The respondent employer having failed after being required by representatives of the trade union to supply information, or to give (or confirm) it in writing at their request (s. 56). On a complaint being made by the trade union to the Industrial Court, the Court granted an order authorising the presentation of a claim to the Industrial Arbitration Board (s. 102(2)) (See 7, *supra*).	Remedies as in 27, *supra*. Except that in this case the operative date will be the date on which the breach was committed as found by the Industrial Court (s. 127(b)).
		NOTE: the claim should be in respect of the employees represented in the collective bargaining by that trade union and should specify that in respect of one or more descriptions of employees the terms and conditions of employment to be observed by the employer should be those specified in the claim (s. 126(2)).	

Registrar

Person or Body Commencing the Proceedings	Person Against Whom Proceedings Are Taken	Nature of Complaint	Remedies Available
29. Any person who: (i) is a member of the organisation, or (ii) was a member but ceased otherwise than by voluntary resignation, or (iii) whose application to join has been rejected. Note: only the person against whom action is alleged to have been taken may be the complainant (s. 81(3)). Note: person has the alternative of presenting his complaint to an industrial tribunal (s. 107(1)) (See 23, *supra*).	Trade union or employers' association, but not federations of either (not other organisations of workers or of employers).	That action has been taken against him by or on behalf of the organisation that was an unfair industrial practice in accordance with the guiding principles of organisations s. 66 or 70, or that it constituted a breach of the rules of the organisation (s. 81(3)). Note: any reference to breaches of rules do not include breaches of rules made under the Trade Union Act, 1913, ss. 3, 4(1) and s. 5(1) (relating to political funds) or to taking a vote approving amalgamations or transfers under the Trade Union (Amalgamations, etc.) Act, 1964 (s. 84(1)).	If the Registrar is satisfied that the applicant has exhausted the procedure, if any, of the organisation for dealing with his complaint, and if he is satisfied that the complaint is well founded, he must endeavour to achieve a settlement of the dispute between the parties. If he cannot obtain a settlement, *and provided the same complaint has not been disposed of by an industrial tribunal*, the Registrar can present the complaint to the Industrial Court if he thinks it sufficiently serious (ss. 82 and 103) (which may grant the remedies in 18, *supra*), or he may present the complaint to an industrial tribunal (s. 108(2)) (See 24, *supra*).

Offences triable by Magistrates Court

Committed By	Offence	Penalty
1. Employer.	Being an employer who was specified in regulations made by the Secretary of State under s. 58, for the notification by the employer of procedure agreements;	
	(1) failed to supply the information to the Secretary of State as required by the regulations (s. 58(1)), or	Fine not exceeding £100 (s. 59(3)).
	(2) in supplying any information or particulars as required by the regulations made a statement knowing it to be false in a *material particular*, or recklessly making a statement which was false in a *material particular*, or	Fine not exceeding £400 (s. 59(3)).
	(3) where he is required by the regulations to furnish a copy of a procedure agreement, he produced as a copy of it a document which to his knowledge was not an accurate and complete copy (s. 59(1)(2)).	Fine not exceeding £400 (s. 59(3)).
2. Employer.	Being an employer who was required by the Commission on Industrial Relations for the purposes of a ballot to be taken under the Act, to supply the names and addresses so far as they are known to the employer, and the position held, of persons who were employed by him and were employees of one or more descriptions, as specified in the notice.	
	Did refuse or wilfully neglect to comply with the notice, or in furnishing the information made a statement which to his knowledge was false in a *material particular*, or recklessly made a statement which was false in a *material particular* (Sch. 3, para. 38).	Fine not exceeding £400 (Sch. 3, para. 38).

3. Any person including an organisation of workers or employers, or body corporate.	Being a person who for the purposes of an enquiry held by the Registrar (under s. 82 or 83) or by the Commission (under any provision in the Act) was required to attend to give evidence, produce documents or give other information, did: (a) refuse or wilfully neglect to attend as required, or (b) wilfully alter, suppress, conceal, destroy or refuse to produce any book or other document as was required to be produced, or (c) refused, or wilfully neglected to furnish any estimate, return or other information as was required, made any statement which he knew to be false in a *material particular*, or recklessly made a statement which was false in a *material particular* (Sch. 3, para. 42(1)(4)).	Fine not exceeding £100 (Sch. 3, para. 41(4)).
4. Any person.	Being a person who has unlawfully disclosed information supplied to the Commission in connection with the examination of any question under the Act (Sch. 3, para. 43) or to the Registrar on investigation of complaints under s. 82 or 83 (Sch. 3, para. 44).	Fine not exceeding £400 (Sch. 3, para. 45).
5. Any person.	Regulations having been made with respect to proceedings before industrial tribunals: (a) for requiring persons to attend to give evidence and produce documents, and for authorising the administration of oaths; (b) for granting to any person discovery or inspection of documents as may be granted by a County Court (or Sheriff in Scotland. Being a person who failed without reasonable excuse to comply with a requirement imposed upon him by such regulations (Sch. 6, para. 2(c)(d) 11).	Fine not exceeding £100 (Sch. 6, para. 11).

Time Limit for Commencing Proceedings

1. Any complaints made under ss. 101 and 102 to the Industrial Court must be made within SIX *months* from the earliest date on which the action to which complaint relates came to the knowledge of the complainant, or would have come to his knowledge if he had exercised due diligence. Subject to any extension of time which the Court might make because the parties have sought to settle the matter through conciliation procedures (Sch. 3, para. 25).

2. Any complaints made under s. 106 to an Industrial Tribunal must be made within FOUR *weeks:*

(a) in the case of a complaint relating to dismissal, from the effective date of dismissal, or

(b) in any other case, from the date of the action specified in the complaint (or, if the action occurred on two or more dates, the latest of those dates),

unless in either case the Tribunal is satisfied that in the circumstances it was not practicable to be presented before the end of that period (Sch. 6, para. 5).

3. Any complaints made under s. 107 to an Industrial Tribunal must be made within FOUR *weeks:*

(a) from the date of the action complained of (or, if that action occurred on two or more dates, the latest of those dates);

(b) the earliest date on which that action came to the knowledge of the complainant;

(c) where the complaint relates to a matter in respect of which an application has been made under s. 81 of the Act, the date on which the Registrar gave notice of his conclusions on investigating that matter or gave notice that he had determined not to proceed with the application (Sch. 6, para. 6).

Limit on Compensation awarded against a Trade Union

In any proceedings before the Industrial Court on a complaint under the Act where an award of compensation is made by the Court against a trade union (whether such an award is also made against any other party to the proceedings or not) the compensation awarded against the trade union in those proceedings shall not exceed the following limits:

(a) in the case of a trade union having a membership of less than 5,000—£5,000;
(b) in the case of a trade union having a membership of 5,000 but less than 25,000—£25,000;
(c) in the case of a trade union having a membership of 25,000 but less than 100,000—£50,000;
(d) in the case of a trade union having a membership of 100,000 or more—£100,000; (s. 117).

There are no limits on the amounts which an unregistered organisation of workers, employers' association or individual may be required to pay. In the case of the individual, however, he may escape personal liability if he can establish that he is a trade union official acting within the scope of his authority.

Enforcement of Orders

See page 172 for information about the enforcement of orders.

APPENDIX II

CASE SUMMARIES

List of Cases

1. Ford Motor Company Ltd. v. Amalgamated Union of Engineering and Foundry Workers and others [1969] 1 W.L.R. 339.
2. Bonsor v. Musicians' Union [1955] 3 All E.R. 518.
3. Baster v. London & County Printing Works [1899] 1 Q.B. 901.
4. Laws v. London Chronicle (Indicator Newspapers) Ltd. [1959] 2 All E.R. 285.
5. Rookes v. Barnard and others [1964] 1 All E.R. 367.
6. Pearson and another v. William Jones [1967] 2 All E.R. 1062.
7. Mogul Steamship Co. Ltd. v. McGregor, Gow & Co. [1892] A.C. 25.
8. Crofter Hand Woven Harris Tweed Company Ltd. v. Veitch and others [1942] 1 All E.R. 142.
9. Taff-Vale Railway Company v. Amalgamated Society of Railway Servants [1901] A.C. 426.
10. Torquay Hotel Company Ltd. v. Cousins and others [1969] 2 W.L.R. 289.
11. Morgan v. Fry and others [1968] 3 All E.R. 452.
12. Piddington v. Bates [1960] 3 All E.R. 660.
13. Tynan v. Balmer [1966) 2 All E.R. 133.

1. Ford Motor Company Limited v. Amalgamated Union of Engineering and Foundry Workers and others [1969] 1 W.L.R. 339

The Ford Motor Company had 23 plants employing some 46,000 workers of whom some 15,000 were members of the A.E.F. and 17,000 were members of the T. & G.W.U. There were some 19 unions whose members were employed by Ford, and some of them represented only a comparatively small number of workers.

Relations between the Ford Company and the unions were regulated by a document entitled "Agreements and Conditions of Employment. Hourly paid Employees." These agreements and conditions were incorporated into a publication called "The Blue Book." This Blue Book contained two main agreements, one of 1955 which was largely concerned with procedural matters and one of 1967, which was concerned with practical matters such as rates of pay and hours of work. Under the 1955 agreement there was set up a National Joint Negotiating Committee and under the 1967 agreement there was a proviso that any variations of that agreement should be negotiated by the parties thereto through the medium of the N.J.N.C. There was no reference in the agreement to legal enforceability. Each union regardless of the size of its membership at Ford was entitled to one vote on the N.J.N.C.

In January of 1969 the Ford Company submitted proposals for a variation of the 1967 agreement. In the following month these proposals were considered by the N.J.N.C., and after consideration the Trade Union side of the N.J.N.C. voted by seven to five to accept the proposals as submitted. As a consequence the Secretary of the Trade Union side wrote to Ford with that information. On the same day a notice was displayed signed by the Ford Labour Relations Director and the Chairman of the N.J.N.C. stating that following negotiations on the Company's proposals the Trade Union side and the Company had agreed to the changes in rates of pay and the conditions of employment.

It was assumed by Ford that this notice would constitute a valid and enforceable contract between themselves and each of the constituent unions which were members of the N.J.N.C. On 18 February the Ford Company presented to the Secretary of the Trade Union side a document setting out all the terms of the agreement and at the end of the document were 19 spaces for the signatures of the representatives of the various unions. The day following the presentation of this document the Trade Unions' Secretary wrote to the Ford Company indicating there was a disagreement among the union members and asked for the agreement to be reconsidered.

It appears that the unions who did not vote in favour of the agreement were particularly concerned about the way in which benefits could be lost by any man who took part in unconstitutional action. As a consequence of this disagreement an unofficial strike took place at the Halewood Factory on 21 February and was made official by the A.E.F. on 26 February, resulting ultimately in a large stoppage at the Ford plants.

The Ford Motor Company now applied to have the agreement enforced against the unions and for an injunction to prevent the unions from taking the strike action.

Held: that the Ford Motor Company failed in its claim as there was no clearly expressed intention that the collective agreement should be legally binding. The Court expressed the view that it is generally accepted that collective agreements are not intended to be legally enforceable and even if an agreement is so intended, it could only be enforced where the parties making the agreement were acting as agents on behalf of the persons they purported to represent.

---

2. Bonsor v. Musicians' Union [1955] 3 All E.R. 518

The plaintiff was a professional musician and had been a member of the respondent union all his professional life. In 1949 he was expelled from the union under a rule providing for expulsion for non-payment of union dues. Because the occupation of musicians was a "closed shop", he was unable to obtain work as such and was reduced to taking employment as a labourer. In an action against the union he was granted a declaration that his expulsion was null and void, on the grounds that his name had been struck off the register by his branch secretary without consulting the branch committee as was required by the rules of the union; although the act by the branch secretary had been later ratified by the union. He also claimed damages, but this claim was dismissed on the grounds that damages for tort could not be given against a trade union since the Trade Disputes Act, 1906, and therefore, because a registered union was not a corporation (in spite of the Taff Vale case), he could not recover for breach of contract either. On appeal to the House of Lords:

Held:

(a) that a registered trade union was capable of being sued for breach of contract as a legal entity, although it was not an incorporated body;

(b) the wrongful expulsion of Bonsor amounted to a breach of contract for which the union was liable in damages, because either:

    (i) there was a breach of contract between the union as a legal entity and Bonsor, under which the union by implication agreed that Bonsor should not be expelled otherwise than in accordance with the union rules, or,

    (ii) on the basis that the rules of the union constituted a contract between the members, Bonsor was entitled to recover damages for having been wrongfully expelled for breach of rules of the union.

(c) where a registered union is sued to judgment, the judgment creditor must look to the funds of the union and not to the assets of individual members in order to recover the amount of the judgment.

---

3. Baster v. London and County Printing Works [1899] 1 Q.B. 901

Baster was employed by the respondents and was responsible for the care and management of a printing press. As a consequence of the negligent operation of the equipment by Baster, damage was caused to the press, to the amount of £30. He was dismissed without notice from his employment. In holding that the dismissal was justified, Darling J. said: "in the case before us the machine was worth £800 and the appellant's forgetfulness caused damage amounting to £30. I think there was evidence of neglect to justify dismissal. It was said that complicated machinery had been introduced in modern times and that forgetfulness by workmen in charge of it ought to be leniently treated. It is easy to see how dangerous that argument is to the workmen themselves. The lives of hundreds of them might be sacrificed because of something done, or not done, in a moment of forgetfulness by a man in charge of some machinery. To anyone who knows about the working of mines and railways in this country, and remembers that a moment of forgetfulness may cost the lives of hundreds of men, it is impossible to give weight to the contentions put forward for the appellant—that forgetfulness is not neglect unless it is habitual, and that forgetfulness whilst in charge of complicated machinery should be treated with exceptional leniency".

---

4. Laws v. London Chronicle (Indicator Newspapers) Limited [1959] 2 All E.R. 285

The plaintiff was employed by the defendant company as an advertising representative. On the afternoon of 20 June, 1958, the Managing Director of the company had asked a Mr. Blakey to advise him and the company on matters of business efficiency. The Advertising Manager and two persons in his charge, one of whom was the plaintiff, were required to attend in the Managing Director's room to hear what Mr. Blakey had to say. An unpleasant argument developed between the Managing Director and the Advertising Manager, and at one stage the latter threatened to leave and take his staff with him, upon which the Managing Director ordered the plaintiff to stay where she was. She nevertheless left the room with her immediate superior, the Advertising Manager, and on the following Monday she was handed a letter by the secretary which stated "it is impossible for the Company to overlook your behaviour and actions in leaving the conference last Friday, in defiance of the Managing Director's request that you remain." Following an interview with the Secretary the same day the plaintiff left the service of the Company, and sued for damages for wrongful dismissal.

Held by the Court of Appeal; that the plaintiff succeeded, for ". . . one act of disobedience or misconduct can justify dismissal only if it is of a nature which goes to show (in effect) that the servant is repudiating the contract or one of its essential conditions." (Lord Evershed, M.R.).

---

5. Rookes v. Barnard and others [1964] 1 All E.R. 367

Under an agreement made in 1949 between B.O.A.C. and its employees it was provided that no lockout or strike should take place and that all disputes should be referred to arbitration. This agreement formed part of each individual's contract of employment, i.e., each contract contained a "no-strike" provision. Rookes, who was employed in the design office of B.O.A.C. resigned from membership of his trade union, and as this office was subject to a "closed-shop" agreement the defendants, who were officials of the union, served notice on B.O.A.C. that unless Rookes was dismissed they would withdraw the labour of their members, and would not go to arbitration. As a result of this threat B.O.A.C. lawfully terminated the employment of Rookes after giving him a much longer notice than he was legally entitled to. Rookes brought an action for damages against the defendants for using unlawful means to induce his employers to terminate his contract of employment and/or for conspiring to have him dismissed by threatening B.O.A.C. Rookes was awarded damages and the defendants appealed. The Court of Appeal reversed the decision and he then appealed to the House of Lords. The House of Lords allowed the appeal and in doing so enunciated the following principles:

(a) On the facts the defendants were guilty of unlawful intimidation because they had threatened to induce a breach of contract resulting in the interference with the employment of Rookes. And that they were not protected by s. 3 of the Trade Disputes Act, 1906, which provides:

An act done in contemplation or furtherance of a trade dispute shall not be actionable on the ground *only* that it induces some other person to break a contract of employment, or that there is interference with the trade, business or employment of some other person, or with the right of some other person to dispose of his capital or labour as he wills.

(b) That there is nothing to differentiate a threat of a breach of contract from a threat of physical violence or any other illegal threat. The nature of the threat is not material in an action for intimidation.

6. Pearson and another v. William Jones [1967] 2 All E.R. 1062

Pearson and another person who had formerly been employed by the respondent company, claimed that redundancy payments which had been made to them should have been computed on an average that would take into account overtime worked. A written statement of terms of employment under the Contracts of Employment Act, 1963, stated that their normal working hours were in accordance with the "Works Rules". These rules stated a 40-hour week, and any overtime as was required by the employer, to be in accordance with national agreements currently in force. The national agreements provided that in the event of overtime being necessary, no union workman should be required to work more than 30 hours overtime in any four weeks. Therefore, the employers had the right to decide when overtime was necessary, but, the Industrial Tribunal found, there was *no obligation* on the appellants to work overtime and that overtime working in this case should not be taken into account in assessing their redundancy payments.

Held: on appeal to the Queen's Bench Division; that the appellants had normal working hours of 40 hours per week and that overtime working was not obligatory on the appellants.

In arriving at this decision, Waller J. stated that counsel for the respondent company was correct when he contended that *in order that overtime should be compulsory there should be either an expressed term that an employee shall work overtime, or possibly an implied term to that effect*, and that in the instant case there was no such provision in the contract.

---

7. Mogul Steamship Company Ltd. v. McGregor, Gow and Co. [1892] A.C. 25

Certain shipowners who were engaged in carrying goods from ports in the China Sea, formed an association and agreed among themselves to regulate the number of ships to be used to visit the various ports, and to divide the cargoes and regulate the freight rates. They also offered a 5 per cent rebate to any shippers who would guarantee to ship only with members of the association. The plaintiffs were also shipowners engaged in carrying from the same ports, but were excluded from membership of the association. When the plaintiffs sent vessels to Hankow to pick up cargoes, the association sent ships and underbid the carrying rates of the plaintiffs. As a consequence the plaintiffs were obliged to carry at unremunerative rates.

The association also threatened to dismiss certain shipping agents from their agency if they used the plaintiffs' ships.

The plaintiffs brought an action, in conspiracy, for damages caused by loss of cargoes due to the action of the defendants.

Held: by the House of Lords—that since the action of the defendants was done to protect the genuine trade interests of the members of the association, and to extend their trade and increase their profits, and since they had not used any unlawful means, the plaintiffs had no cause of action. "*I am of opinion, therefore, that the whole matter comes round to the original proposition, whether a combination to trade, and to offer, in respect of prices, discounts, and other trade facilities, such terms as will win so large an amount of custom as to render it unprofitable for rival traders to pursue the same trade is unlawful, and I am clearly of the opinion that it is not*". (*per Lord Halsbury, L.C.*).

---

8. Crofter Hand Woven Harris Tweed Co. Ltd. v. Veitch and others [1942] 1 All E.R. 142

The defendants were officials of the Transport and General Workers' Union. The dockers at Stornoway, on the island of Lewis, were all members of the same union, as were most of the persons employed in the spinning mills on the island. Yarn was spun in the mills and then woven into tweed cloth by the crofters working at home. The woven cloth was finished in the mills and then sold by the owners of the mills as Harris Tweed.

The Crofter Company also produced tweed cloth, but from yarn which was spun more cheaply on the mainland. This cloth was also sold as Harris Tweed but did not bear the distinctive label bearing the trade mark. The mill owners making the genuine Harris Tweed were being pressed by the union to increase wages but were unable to do so because of the very serious competition of the Crofter Company. Aware of the reason why wages could not be increased the defendants placed an embargo on the yarn imported and the tweed exported by the Crofter Company, and instructed the dockers

at Stornoway to refuse to handle these goods. The dockers obeyed
these instructions but did not strike nor act in breach of contract.
The Crofter Company sued them for conspiracy and sought an
interdict (injunction) against the defendants to have the embargo
lifted.

Held: the union officials were not liable in conspiracy because
their purpose was to benefit the members and to improve their living
standards, and the means employed were not unlawful.

---

9. Taff Vale Railway Co. v. Amalgamated Society of Railway Servants [1901] A.C. 426

In August 1900, the Amalgamated Society of Railway Servants
called a strike of its members against the Taff Vale Railway Company. Members of the union picketed the Great Western Railway
Station at Cardiff, and the company brought an action against the
union for an injunction and for damages. The action was brought
against the union in its registered name and the union sought to
have its name struck out on the ground that it was not a corporate
body and could not therefore be sued in this way.

Held:

(a) that as a consequence of the Trade Union Act, 1871, once a
    union was registered it acquired sufficient corporate existence
    for it to be sued in its registered name; and,

(b) although trade union legislation gave immunity to trade
    unions from certain criminal liability, this immunity did not
    extend to immunity from civil liability, therefore, the railway
    company were entitled to recover by way of damages the
    amount they had lost (£23,000) as a result of the defendant
    union's action. The judgment being enforceable against the
    trade union's property and funds.

NOTE: the result of this case was clearly ruinous to the trade union
movement, for it meant that in future employers who suffered
damage through strikes induced by a trade union could recover
against the trade union itself. The Trade Disputes Act, 1906, was
enacted as a consequence to extend immunity from civil liability.

---

10. Torquay Hotel Company Ltd. v. Cousins and others [1969] 2 W.L.R. 289

The plaintiffs were the owners of the Imperial Hotel, Torquay, and the defendants were Mr. F. Cousins, the general secretary of the Transport and General Workers' Union, together with certain other officials of the union, and the union itself.

Hotel workers in Torquay who wished to become members of a union had generally become members of the National Union of General and Municipal Workers. In 1967, the Transport and General Workers' Union began an active recruiting campaign in the hotels in Torquay and by December 1967, it had recruited 400 members. A local branch of the T.G.W.U. was formed on 1 January, 1968. During the third week of January the district secretary of the T.G.W.U. sought to have that union recognised at the Torbay Hotel but the Managing Director refused because he said he was actively negotiating with the General and Municipal Union. A strike was called by the T.G.W.U. at the Torbay Hotel, which was picketed by members of that union. Because of the pickets, oil tanker drivers, most of whom were members of the defendant union, would not deliver fuel oil to the hotel. These events along with some remarks about the need to make a stand, made by the manager of the plaintiffs' hotel, the Imperial, were published in the press. None of the employees of the Imperial were members of the T.G.W.U.

Members of the T.G.W.U. then picketed the Imperial Hotel, and the officials of that union caused tanker drivers to refuse to deliver fuel oil to the hotel, furthermore, they warned Esso, the hotel's regular suppliers of oil, and Alternative Fuels Limited, who had made one delivery after dark in the absence of the pickets, that there would be trouble if any further deliveries were made. As a result of this threat, Esso did not fulfill their obligations to deliver in accordance with their contract, and Alternative Fuels Limited could not make any further deliveries, because their drivers refused to deliver.

The defendant union refused to withdraw the "blacking" of the Imperial Hotel, and so the plaintiffs issued a writ claiming injunctions against the defendant union, and damages and injunctions against individual union officials for conspiracy, intimidation, wrongful procurement of a breach of contract and for actionable interference with subsisting trade or contractual relations. The defendants relied *inter alia*, on ss. 3 and 4(1) of the Trade Disputes Act, 1906 (these sections provided immunity from liability for actions done in contemplation or furtherance of trade disputes by trade unions and other officials). Interlocutory injunctions were granted against the defendants. The defendants appealed to the Court of Appeal.

Held:

(a) the appeal would be allowed in respect of the injunction against the defendant union, since s. 4(1) of the Trade Disputes Act, 1906, provided an absolute immunity against actions for damages and injunctions in respect of any torts committed by a trade union.

(b) the appeal in respect of the officials would be dismissed on the following grounds:

(i) as the plaintiffs employed no members of the defendant union, and the defendants acts were directed against the manager of the Imperial, the acts were not in furtherance of a trade dispute within the meaning of the Trade Disputes Act, 1906. ". . . in my opinion, there was at the material times a trade dispute between the union and the Torbay Hotel; none between the union and the Imperial Hotel proprietor. Nor do I think that the 'blacking' of the Imperial is properly to be regarded as an act done in furtherance of the Torbay dispute. Any dispute between the union and Mr. Chapman (*sic*, Imperial Hotel manager) or his company was a personal dispute: the union may have a dispute with an individual whose view about the merits of a trade dispute or an issue in that dispute, the union wishes to controvert or cause to be disclaimed. Yet there may be in such a case between the same parties no trade dispute as defined in s. 3, which stresses primarily the characteristics of a dispute with an employer; neither Chapman nor the hotel employed T.G.W.U. members. In the present case I reserve my opinion upon the question whether there could ever be a trade dispute within the section with any person who is not an employer of a member or members of the union claimed to be in dispute with him: as at present advised I think not". (*per* Winn, L. J.).

(ii) The defendants were liable for their *direct interference* when they contacted the oil companies.

(iii) The defendants had directly interfered with the plaintiffs' rights under the contracts with the oil companies and it did not matter whether or not a breach of contract actually resulted. Interference causing a breach was to be equated with interference which did not. In both cases, *direct* interference was actionable *unless justified*, whilst *indirect* interference was *actionable only* if the *means used* were *unlawful*. The principle of liability at common law can according to Lord Denning, M. R., be sub-divided into three elements:

"First, there must be *interference* in the execution of a contract. The interference is not confined to the procurement of a *breach* of contract. It extends to a case where a third person *prevents* or *hinders* one party from performing his contract, even though it be not a breach.

"Second, the interference must be deliberate. The person must know of the contract or, at any rate, turn a blind eye to it and intend to interfere with it.

"Third, the interference must be *direct*. Indirect interference will not do. Thus, a man who 'corners the market' in a commodity may well know that it may prevent others from performing their contracts, but he is not liable to an action for so doing. A trade union official, who calls a strike on proper notice, may well know that it will prevent the employers from performing their contracts to deliver goods, but he is not liable for damages for calling it."

Lord Denning went on to say, "*indirect* interference is only unlawful if unlawful means are used . . . A trade union official is only in the wrong when he procures a contracting party *directly* to break his contract, or when he does it indirectly *by unlawful means* . . . This point about unlawful means is of particular importance when a place is declared 'black'. At common law it often involves the use of unlawful means. Take the Imperial Hotel. When it was declared 'black', it meant that the drivers of the tankers would not take oil to the hotel. The drivers would thus be induced to break their contracts of employment. That would be unlawful at common law. The only case in which 'blacking' of such a kind is lawful is when it is done 'in contemplation or furtherance of a trade dispute' . . . for, in that event, the act of inducing a breach of a contract of employment is a lawful act which is not actionable at the suit of any one; . . . Seeing that the act is lawful, it must, I think, be lawful for the trade union officials to tell the employers and their customers about it. And this is so, even though it does mean that those people are compelled to break their commercial contracts. The interference with the commercial contracts is only indirect, and not direct: . . . So, *if there had been a 'trade dispute'* in this case, I think it would have protected the trade union officials when they informed Esso that the dispute with Imperial was an 'official dispute' and said that the hotel was 'blacked'."

---

11. Morgan v. Fry and others [1968] 3 All E.R. 452

In 1962, in the Ports of London and Tilbury there were only 650 lockmen, but they held a key position, and without them the docks could be brought to a standstill. They were members of the transport union and made a claim for 5d. an hour shift allowance. After officials of the union entered into negotiations with the employers, the Port of London Authority, they were offered 3d. an hour, which they recommended the lockmen to accept. At a mass meeting of the Poplar Branch this recommendation was accepted by a majority of 84 votes to 43. A dissentient minority, however, of about 30, led by one Hammond, formed a breakaway union called the Union of Port Workers, four of them worked at a lock in the London Port called Black Wall Entrance. These four included Hammond and the plaintiff Morgan. Fry, the defendant, was an official of the transport union and sought to encourage the breakaway men to return to the union.

In January and February of 1963, Fry and other union officials met officers of the P.L.A. They instructed the employers that members of the transport union were pressing for action against the breakaway union.

On 14 March, Fry gave notice to the P.L.A. in the following terms: "I have to advise you that on and from Monday, 1 April, 1963, members of this organisation (the transport union) employed as lockmen at Blackwall and South West India Dock will be instructed not to work with the Union of Port Workers and other non-trade unionists." It was clearly implied in that notice and from what had been previously said that if the P.L.A. wanted the men of the transport union to work at the lock they would have to dismiss the others. On 25 March, Morgan was notified of this notice by the assistant staff relations officer, and warned that his services would be terminated unless he agreed to rejoin the transport union, and was instructed that he had until 29 March to make a decision.

As the plaintiff refused to rejoin the union, the P.L.A. gave notice to him on 29 March, that his employment would be terminated on 6 April. He was as a consequence out of work for six weeks and then became a gas board employee.

The plaintiff brought an action for damages for intimidation against Fry and the others.

Held: the notice given on 14 March, that on and after 1 April, transport union member employees would not work with members of the breakaway union, being a notice for a period longer than was requisite for termination of the contracts of employment, was not unlawful; accordingly the giving of notice did not amount to a use of unlawful means for the purpose of the tort of intimidation. The action for damages for intimidation therefore failed.

In considering whether the "strike notice" on 14 March, 1963, was an act of intimidation, giving as it did, two-and-a-half weeks notice—far longer than the week's notice necessary to terminate the employment altogether—or whether it was a notice of termination. Denning, L. J., said "every man was entitled to terminate his contract of employment by giving a week's notice. But the 'strike notice' in this case was not a notice to terminate their employment. It was a notice that they would not work with non-unionists. That looks very much like a threat of a breach of contracts; and therefore intimidation. In *J. T. Stratford & Son Limited* v. *Lindley*, [1964] 3 All E.R. 102, I stated the argument in this way:

"Suppose that a trade union officer gives a strike notice. He says
to an employer: 'We are going to call a strike on Monday
week . . . unless you dismiss yonder man who is not a member
of the union' . . . Such a notice is not to be construed as if it
were a week's notice . . . to terminate their employment; for
that is the last thing any of the men would desire. They do not
wish to lose their pension rights and so forth by giving up their
jobs. The strike notice is nothing more nor less than a notice
that the men will not come to work. In short, that they will break
their contracts . . . In these circumstances . . . the trade union
officer, by giving the strike notice, issues a threat to the employer.
He *threatens to induce the men to break* their contracts of employment
unless the employer complies with their demand. That is clear
intimidation . . ."

It is difficult to see the logical flaw in that argument; but there
must be something wrong with it; for if that argument were correct,
it would do away with the right to strike in this country. It has been
held for over 60 years that workmen have a right to strike (including
therein a right to say that they will not work with non-unionists)
provided that they give sufficient notice beforehand; and a notice
is sufficient if it is at least as long as the notice required to terminate
the contract."

---

12. Piddington v. Bates [1960] 3 All E.R. 660

During an industrial dispute at a factory pickets were placed at
various gates leading to the premises. Certain employees sought to
gain entry for the purposes of engaging in their lawful occupations:
this was prevented by the pickets and as a consequence the police
were called by the employers. A constable who visited the scene
considered that two men were enough at the rear of the factory for
the purpose of picketing. Another man, however, being desirous
of joining his colleagues at this back gate sought to push past the
constable and as he did so he was arrested. He was convicted of
obstructing the police constable in the execution of his duty and he
appealed to the Queen's Bench Division.

Held: that the conviction should stand and that the constable
had acted properly for he had reasonable grounds for believing that

there might be a breach of the peace. S. 2 of the Trade Disputes Act, 1906, was not argued in defence, but it is suggested that even if it had been the conviction would have remained because of the requirement that picketing should be peaceful, and once a breach of the peace was likely or threatened s. 2 ceased to give protection.

---

13. Tynan v. Balmer [1966] 2 All E.R. 133

During an official strike by draughtsmen at a factory in November 1964, the appellant Tynan and some 40 pickets who were under his direction began to walk in a circle in a service road which was part of the public highway near the main entrance to the factory. The object of this exercise was to cause an obstruction so that traffic could not reach or leave the factory. The traffic as a consequence came to a standstill. Tynan was requested by a police constable to remove the pickets from the service road as they were causing an obstruction in the highway. On Tynan refusing he was arrested and was convicted of obstructing the constable in the execution of his duty.

Held: on appeal by Tynan to the Divisional Court of the Queen's Bench that the circling manoeuvre was a clear obstruction of the highway and a nuisance and that it went beyond what was authorised by s. 2 of the Trade Disputes Act, 1906 (which allows peaceful picketing, i.e., for persuading others to work or not to work or to communicate information). The conviction consequently would be upheld.

INDEX

Note: all references in italics are to Appendix I (Remedies available under the Act).

SPECIFIC PERFORMANCE
Contract of employment; cannot be ordered, 136

STATEMENT IN WRITING RELATING TO
   TERMS OF EMPLOYMENT, 17

STRIKE
Action by Industrial Court, 168–169
Application to Industrial Court by Secretary of State
   for cooling off order, 166–167
Ballots, 169–172
Ballot, conduct of, 172
Ballot; application for; action by Industrial Court, 170
Ballot; application for; parties to be named, 170
Ballot; application for by Secretary of State, 170
Ballot; contents of order for, 170–171
Ballot; time within which to be taken, 171
Conciliation, 167, 172
"Cooling off" order—addition or substitution
   of parties, 169
"Cooling off" order—persons to be named in application, 167–169
Defined, 39
Due notice, 136
Effect of "cooling-off" order, 168–169
Employee may be dismissed for participating in, 41, 137
Employee participating in, 41
Endangering life, 132, 137
Endangering life or property, 137
Extraneous parties, 155
Financing, 93–94
Illegal in certain cases, 132, 137
Inducing or threatening to induce a strike not
   necessarily unfair industrial practice, 137
Industrial dispute, 144
Livelihood of persons threatened, 170
Lives or health of persons exposed to danger, 166
Maliciously breaking contract, 132, 137
National economy threatened, 166, 170
National emergency, 26
National emergency; application by Secretary of State
   to Industrial Court, 167–169
No person to be compelled by Court to strike, 136
No strike clause, 136
Notice of, 38
Notice of intention to strike not to be interpreted as
   termination of contract, 136–137
Offences, 133, 137
Picketing (new law), 139–140
Picketing (old law), 132–133
Position at common law, 131–132
Public disorder, risk of, 166
Restriction on right to: emergency procedures, 166, et seq.
Right to, 135–137

Workers' right not to belong, 42, 44
Workers' right to belong, 42, 43
Workers' right to participate in activity of, 42

TRADE UNION MEMBERSHIP
Infringement of worker's rights in respect of, 48
Pressure on employer to infringe rights of employee, 47

TRADE UNION REPRESENTATIVE, 97

UNFAIR DISMISSAL
Award of compensation for, 31
Complaint to Industrial Tribunal, 31
Employers refusing to join trade union, 29
Excluded cases, 28
Employer to establish dismissal was fair, 32
Fixed term contracts, 29
Irregular industrial action, 39–41
Inducing, 33–37
Lock outs, 38
National security, 29
Power of Secretary of State to vary provisions
    re excluded cases, 29
Remedies, 31
Strikes, 39–41

UNFAIR INDUSTRIAL PRACTICE (see also APPENDIX I)
Breach of collective agreement, 73
Collective bargaining, 90–94
Distinction between trade union (emp. assoc.) and
    unregistered organisations, 151
Employer failing to negotiate with sole bargaining agent
    after order of court, 94
Employer discriminating against employee for belonging
    to trade union, 43
Employer discriminating against employee for exercising
    trade union rights, 44
Employer discriminating against employee for refusing
    to pay appropriate contributions, 45
Extraneous parties, 155
Failure to ensure conformity with collective agreement, 69
Inducing breach of collective agreement, 152
Inducing dismissal of employee, 35
Inducing or threatening to induce breach of
    collective agreement, 73
Interfering with rights relating to trade union
    membership, 48
Newspaper or television broadcasts no liability for, 152
Person inducing employer not to comply with order of
    court re sole bargaining agent, 95

Person seeking to induce employer not to recognise
  agency shop, 57
Possible liability for, 150–157
Pressure on employer to apply for closed shop, 62
Relating to agency shop applications, 58
Sympathy action, 153
Tort and Unfair Industrial practices; summary of
  distinctions, 157–160

WAGES COUNCILS ACT, 1959
Creation of Wages Councils, 9

WHITLEY COUNCILS, 65

WINDING UP
Trade union or Employers' Association, 119, *et seq.*
Organisation on special register, 127

WORKER
Application to industrial tribunal *re* dismissal, 49
Definition, 123
Discrimination against by employer, 188(21)
Dismissed unfairly; application to industrial tribunal, 190(22)
Government employee, 22, 123
Position reasonably suitable, 38
Police officer, 22, 123
Redundancy, 26
Rights of, 17
Special constable, 123

WORKING TO RULE, 40
Threats, 41